An Anthropology of the Subject

An Anthropology of the Subject

Holographic Worldview in
New Guinea and Its Meaning
and Significance for the World
of Anthropology

Roy Wagner

UNIVERSITY OF CALIFORNIA PRESS

Berkeley / Los Angeles / London

University of California Press
Berkeley and Los Angeles, California

University of California Press, Ltd.
London, England

© 2001 by the Regents of the University of California

Library of Congress Cataloging-in-Publication Data
Wagner, Roy.
  An anthropology of the subject : holographic worldview in
New Guinea and its meaning and significance for the world of
anthropology / Roy Wagner.
      p.   cm.
  Includes bibliographical references and index.
  ISBN 0-520-22586-4 (cloth : alk. paper)—
  ISBN 0-520-22587-2 (pbk. : alk. paper)
    1. Anthropology—Philosophy.   I. Title.
  GN33.W28   2001
  301'.01—dc21   00-061991
                                                                 CIP

Printed in the United States of America
10 09 08 07 06 05 04 03 02 01
10 9 8 7 6 5 4 3 2 1

The paper used in this publication meets the minimum requirements
of ANSI/NISO Z39.48-1992 (R 1997) (*Permanence of Paper*).♾

*To Aubrey and Dagiwe, to Dawn, Smokey,
and "Mother" Wright*

Contents

vii

Illustrations

Preface

This book consummates a line of theoretical development that began with my book *Habu* (1972), was generalized in *The Invention of Culture* (1975), and approached its limits in *Symbols That Stand for Themselves* (1986). A reconceptualization of the ethnography in *Asiwinarong* (1986), the present work redresses what has become a basic problem of anthropological reportage: the fact that no particular theoretical approach, even in combination with others, can be used effectively to gain a purchase over the anthropological subject. The *negative capability* necessary for such a task, best evidenced in *Lethal Speech* (1978), is, perhaps understandably, most difficult to align with our general expectations of what anthropology should be like.

But that ability to know *from* oneself and from theory measures my most significant indebtedness in writing and conceiving this work. I owe it, first and foremost, to David M. Schneider, Edith and Victor Turner, the Nagual Carlos Castaneda and the Ecuadorian Pachamama Don Alberto Taczo, Jadran Mimica, Steven Feld, James F. Weiner, Marilyn Strathern, Maurice Godelier, and John R. Farella. And, equally, to Aubrey Gilbert, Elizabeth Stassinos, Joel Robbins, Michael Wesch, Sandra Bamford, Arve Sørum, Anjana Mebane-Cruz, and George Mentore. And to those private anthropologists Dawn M. Hayes, Janice Rhea Wright, and my cat, Smokey, who showed me that most amazing thing of all.

I am especially grateful to the students and faculty of the École des Hautes Études en Sciences Sociales, particularly Alban Bensa and Pascale

Bonnemere, and to Fredrik Barth and the students and faculty of the Department of Social Anthropology at the Universitiy of Bergen for stimulating discussion and criticism that were invaluable in making final revisions. I acknowledge my silent mentors, Claude Lévi-Strauss, Louis Dumont, and Marshall D. Sahlins, and thank my colleague Richard Handler for sage counsel offered in the publication of this book.

Abstract of the Argument

Conclusive evidence for holographic world perspectives in New Guinea encourages a reconsideration of some basic assumptions about anthropology. Because a conceptual holography is a perfect scale model of all the mistakes to be made in figuring out what it may be, we cannot really know, or prove to ourselves, how things or indeed people really "work," and are thrown back on our own resources. Hence we do not *learn* a "culture" or its reprojection within the "given" or natural world of fact, or even learn about them, so much as we *teach ourselves to them.* So the argument of this work is less theoretical than elicitory, organizing a precept for how the author has taught himself to *your* anthropology.

I: The Human Hologram

1. *To Be Caught in Indra's Net.* "Meaning" or meaningfulness is not a human subject but an insidious mental contagion, a net of perceptions that catches us in the guise of culture, nature, or history.

2. *Where Is the Meaning in a Trope?* Generalized in the form of a trope—the iconic basis, or "hieroglyph," of human comprehension—the metaphor is incapable of definition. It is language's way of determining what we mean by it.

3. *A Sociality Reperceived.* The *kaba,* or mortuary feasting complex of the Barok people of New Ireland, does not merely exemplify but also *exhausts* the resources for cultural or social explanation. It underdetermines the conceptual.

itself; one must put some distance between oneself and the earth to realize its "true" astronomical shape.

IV: Cakra

13. *Reinventing the Wheel.*   The wheel is too *simple* to be understood; its automational modeling is a *ritual* that exhausts the possibilities of explanation rather than those of the reality it interrogates.

14. *The Physical Education of the Wheel.*   If time is the *difference* between itself and space, and space is the similarity between the two, then their negative extensional field is the physical education of the wheel.

15. *Sex in a Mirror.*   Only a *human being* could know the secrets of the stars, the process of the atom, the molecular, spiritual, or biographical mysteries of life. No higher intelligence could possibly make the mistakes necessary for such knowledge; it would have enough trouble trying to figure out its own intelligence.

16. *The Single Shape of Metaphor in All Things.*   The inadvertent and invisible collection and motivation of all conceptual modeling; to see *past* the "past" and not confuse the vision with some imaginal present or future is the final objective of the anthropological subject.

Introduction

The most insidious task confronting the possibility of a real anthropology, a positive and definitive study of the human knowledge of the human, would be one in which the very means of knowing were already appropriated by the peoples being studied. An anthropology of the subject. Necessarily and by self-definition as it were, all the propositions about testing and confirmation, cause and effect, knower and known, would run backward to the expectations of scientific research, pose themselves as tests of the anthropologists themselves and whatever they might make of their work. An anthropology of the anthropological subject. As in much so-called postmodern writing, fundamental doubts about anthropology and anthropologists would frame the whole perspective in which the project was enjoined. Already in possession of the answer, it would face the task of determining and then confirming the right *question*.

Anthropology has almost always started out in this way, needing to substantiate its own grounding assumptions, whatever they might be, prove its worth by provoking scientific orthodoxy rather than assimilating it. The only difference that the late twentieth century has made is that actual *evidence,* usually in very holistic form, began turning up for something that anthropology had heretofore taken on its own, and very speculatively. Possibly the first assemblage of this evidence, telling in that it posed more questions than it resolved, was Louis Dumont's brilliant analysis of the Hindu caste system in *Homo Hierarchicus.* Other landmarks would have to include Fredrik Barth's work on the Baktaman,

John Farella's on Navajo religion, Victor Turner's on the Ndembu, and David Guss's on the Yequana of Venezuela. A whole subdiscipline or genre of anthropology, calling itself "symbolic" on the precarious chance that an anthropology of the subject meant a *subjective* anthropology, grew up around such exemplars.

A *virtual* anthropology of a subject that "understood" the anthropologist better than the anthropologist could understand, or even formulate, it. Because it assimilated all the real doubts inherent in its project into a certain conviction about the symbol (something that "stands for" what it is not, semiotic "zero"), symbolic and even hermeneutic anthropology was bound to fail of its aims. But if the real ingenuity of a subjective anthropology lay in setting itself up for that kind of failure, blaming it more or less on "interpretation," then the actual pioneer of that evidential frontier was Carlos Castaneda. His was a case study in depth of the anthropologist "taken in" or "taken over" by the world perspectives he set out to study, and whose pragmatic of teaching and learning consisted in creating and flourishing the doubts that motivated the lessons. Doubt turned inside out is definitively a-symbolic. (The protocol seems to be "get yourself discovered by a cognitive perspective completely different from your own to the point of acute physical and mental breakdown, and then come back and tell about it.") While I have no doubt that this technique can lead to a sophistication about life's chances and purposes that beggars anything anthropology has to offer, positive religion masked as shamanism, my purpose in bringing it up engages the issue at a more mundane level. For it seems to me after a very close study that the guidelines of *Nagualismo* (as don Juan once called it) work on the pragmatic of a near-holography, a closer-to-life experience, like much of Taoism, Hinduism, Sufism, and Zen, of what a true holography would have to be. This suggests, to me at least, that much of what we know as symbolism and even spiritualism provides a kind of "cover," a more easily negotiated substitution for the facticity of the holographic. Though there are better examples of near-life reality in Castaneda's books, the teachings for the human "assemblage-point," for instance, the basic text of Nagualismo, given in *The Eagle's Gift* as "The Rule of the Nagual," is a belabored and overdetermined version of the acute scaling of gender and laterality that I have called the human hologram.

How much of Native American thinking misses the point that motivates it deliberately in that pragmatically educative way? A near-life reality, getting the point by not getting it in depth, detail, and symbolic richness, is the answer—warriors' training that disciplines the imagination like nothing else. What an absolute holographic reality might be is just simply the right *question*. So the crisis of a discipline that can no longer determine its direction or purpose or who its real leaders might be has less to do with a real theoretical bankruptcy, supported ethically and intellectually by the contradiction-in-terms that we call "cultural relativity," than with the fact that it consistently solicits exceptions to the rules it makes up. It scares itself for kicks with its own ethnographic shadow, plays "chicken" with the culture concept—the more passionately so for the fact that ethnography and the culture concept are the only things it has ever had to offer.

As in the contemporary "high-energy physics" that finds more certainty in questioning its answers than in answering those questions, real explanation is forfeit, and the "interpretive mind" or ethos a purely ad hoc affectation. And so the possibility comes to mind that this is not simply a bad accident that has happened to a profession, or to professionalism in general, but a key, however accidental its discovery, to the human condition itself. We come into life with a lot of naive questions, grow up on some set of explanations, begin to doubt them, and wind up with new questions that are, if anything, more profoundly naive than the original ones. There is a kind of child-reality to my daughter's question: "Daddy, when everybody was in somebody else's tummy, who was around?" And a kind of adult irresponsibility to my answer: "Who can tell, kid, for by the time that paradox occurs to us we are already out of it and often enough, like me, busy starting it again." Talking around her problem, interpreting it, my answer is beside the point of her question, something that needs to be questioned in its turn. Do the facts of human conception actually answer to the conception of the human that asks of them? Does *time* itself have anything more to do with the issue than that, and if so, shall we imagine my daughter's question as the goddess Kali, the protector of children, who dances victory at the crack between the presence and the passage of time? Nature only *goes* in time; Kali stays as she goes, and goes as she stays.

"Female time," which is what her name means, has nothing to do with "belief." One would be a damn fool to either believe or disbelieve in her, or in don Juan either; they do not work that way. To "invent" her by studying ancient texts, reconstruct what she might have meant to the ancient Hindus who "conceived" her, is to discover yet another form of symbolism, to begin the anthropological project anew. But to understand these efforts as *her* conception of *them* is to put oneself back at anthropology's testing point. She is Mother Right, like getting your mother, or gravity, or "attraction" absolutely right for once and for all time, the pun of *Das Mutterrecht*. The Mandak people of New Ireland, according to Richard Eves, call gravity "female fight."

So we can forget about spiritualism if we remember that symbolism itself is the static where the anthropological transmission begins to break up. We can forget about the power of the "image," the childlike Piaget-style "construction of reality," the interpretational story that hermeneutics tells about itself, the creature that really *is* symbolic because it thinks it is. For there is the same falsification of consciousness, attribution of quasi-subjective states, the same "unidentified flying objectivity" in the messages of advertising, after-the-fact versions of some ethnic or feminist point of view, and the "heightened awareness" in Castaneda's writings. Notwithstanding the dicey question of "who is responsible?" (the only UFO issue that really matters), the clever manipulation of alien words and objects as though they were familiar, and of familiar words and objects as though they were alien, provides all the "magic" that is necessary. How does the "image" really work? It has a dull humor of the camera obscura variety. Ask Jan Vermeer.

Holography may be the only idealized quality we have that really works, because it works on itself. A near-holography, or near-life experience, merely relates to that principle, incorporates it along with some other, more immediately persuasive, ideality. Unless it were deliberately articulated by the peoples to whom it is attributed, expounded as such, a holographic perspective would count only as another "interpretive device" invented by the anthropologist. By that standard the actual distribution of holographic world perspectives would seem to be geographically limited, running from the Indian subcontinent through Indonesia, Melanesia, and perhaps Australia. Real "western" (European-American) enthusiasm for the idea, most of it in the twentieth century, seems to have run alongside fractal mathematics and the technology of hologram projection. Introduced much earlier from India into China, enhanced there by the indigenous near-holography of Taoism, the idea flourished for a time as one of China's innumerable intellectual fads.

But even on what could be considered its home ground, the contagion of the principle, the interference patterning of how it works pragmatically upon itself, takes over from the effort to place, identify, or acknowledge it. The Jains of India made a whole religion out of part-whole comparisons, but otherwise the explicit articulation of holographic self-correspondence is almost as rare within cultures as among them. The fieldworkers who retrieved the data on holographic perspectives in Melanesia were surprised by it, and often, as in my case, it took them years to figure out what they were looking at. Doubtless we were looking for something more limited, constructive, useful as a model, when these things found us.

The Vedic Hindus called the ancient war god Indra, their Lord of Holography, the "breaker of cities." (He rends them, the texts say, "as time disintegrates a garment.") The assumptional basis that controls social science finds its whole defining moment, the wellsprings of its sophistication, in the builder of cities. Our cities go of their own accord, like Bossuet's "city of the rich" *(cette ville des riches)* that needs, as he put it, "no external enemy." Nor does anthropology.

I

The Human Hologram

I

To Be Caught in Indra's Net

If meaning were not central to the human experience, if it were a specialized subject of study like the kinds of meaning we call "philosophy," "religion," or "the natural world," then we might be justified in turning it over to specialists. As it is, so much has been written about meaning from the standpoint of language that it might be worth our while to consider a comment on language from that of meaning. Victor Zuckerkandl was perhaps unique in his ability to locate meaning in music, an art that gives away nothing to referentiality. His view of language is worth noting:

The limit beyond which words cannot go is their own delimiting activity. The limit of language is its being-a-limit. However broad or narrow the limits it may trace, there is one thing it never reaches: that which is delimited. This is not the unutterable. . . . It is not mystical in the sense of being infinitely remote, utterly hidden: it is what is closest to us, most manifestly present in everything that is not an intellectual or a linguistic fiction.[1]

What Zuckerkandl has done is to apply Wittgenstein's phrase "the limits of my language" in an intensive sense—not simply in terms of what combinations of words and categories, or what possibilities of these, it permits but as a matter of what limits the fact of language itself imposes. How is language itself limiting? The limit of language is language's "being a limit"—it limits, demarcates, draws boundaries around that which it references. Anything it accomplishes *as language* is done through this fact. By the same token, language does not *describe* the elements it demarcates save in demarcating them, nor does it make those elements immediately meaningful as a result of demarcating or referencing them. Language, in short, cannot access or convey the experiential concreteness of its referents. The nice precision that music makes of our thoughts and feelings is, to paraphrase Zuckerkandl, just precisely too much inside or outside of language to be touched by linguistic reference. Music sings the delimited; language limits: visual, kinesthetic, or even verbal art figures the delimited, language delimits the figures.

It is only in those instances where language "describes" itself, demarcates or delimits its own possibilities by intending or anticipating, equating one word with another, that a precision like that of music is realized. Demarcation thus achieves the abstract effect of "meaning" in being compounded upon itself. But it does so, paradoxically, by conveying a sense of language's concreteness or identity with itself, as if referencing or signification could be shown to have a solid core, to be "about" something real at precisely that point at which its meaning is most abstract. This fundamental irony of "language usage," a conflation of abstract and concrete, is frequently treated as the origin of the symbolic in language, the point where language "catches" or touches the meaningful and the subjective.

But a most significant implication of its irony is that this conflation can also be treated as the inception of language in the symbolic, language's legitimation in its being "caught," in turn, by the meaningful and the subjective. Abstraction is a metalanguage that is crucially dependent upon words, a language of languages that inevitably analyzes and reconstructs itself as a further example of language. Its own beginning points, its epistemes like the "sign," are themselves prepackaged exemplars of linguistic self-reference. They become the language that describes language and that renders language's legitimacy in doing so self-evidential in the process.

Abstract as the meaningful may be, necessarily displaced from whatever conventions one might choose to represent "language," its abstractness is inevitably compromised through the double implication of demarcation necessary to its own expression. The limit of language, the degree of its vulnerability, is obscured in an infinite regress of using language to witness, define, and evidence its own capabilities.

If anything we might say or think about language is already *informed* or predicated by language in the process, then its self-evidencing is essentially subjective in nature. Subjective awareness is necessarily an awareness of what *kind* of awareness it is. Pain, for instance, is at once the character or quality of the perception and the "thing" perceived; it must be "referred," if only in a very general sense (and of course *as* a sense), in order to be perceived. Thus language disguises its limit by merging with its own perception in thought, becomes the very "informing" or "referral" by which the perception takes place. A grounding of language in subjectivity identified through the "referral" or informing of subjectivity by language marks the fundamental character of trope.

A consideration of trope need not be concerned with how the phenomenon involves, relates to, or describes the referential properties of language beyond this fact. The conditions that "trope" makes performative or operative are fundamentally inert, they "do" nothing, amount to mere "stoppages" or singularities in the familiar flow of speech. Trope's "agency" as an ascribed or analytic property begins with the designation or recognition of trope as a *phenomenon* and then identifies the *kinds* of agency pertinent to that phenomenon—metaphor, metonym, synecdoche, oxymoron, and so forth. But the phenomenality of all this is itself a kind of interpretation, a trope that makes the trope possible as a contagion of thought, something that has "kinds" because it begins as a "kind." Whatever operations the kinds of trope may perform upon language they do through the contagion of the initial kind; they "iconicize" language, if that is the word, by iconicizing our awareness of it.

As a "kind" of self-awareness the contagion is a self-modeling of feeling as if language could react to itself or work upon itself in that way. The agency attributed to a metaphor or a metonym, the kind of relation it would seem to perform, makes use of language to account for the way in which language is received or "embodied" in the speaker or hearer—how it subjects him or her to language. The "kinds" of tropic usage as well as the relational model of language itself designate a self-action as if it were happening within an objective medium, attributing its autoreactive constitution to some special subjecting quality of the medium. Hence the social, the mental, and the relational or persuasive share a point of pragmatic congruence in the contagious or self-constitutive contingency of human self-reaction.

The social scientist, in other words, who speaks of language "competence" or symbolic "meanings," or of hierarchical or gender domination is speaking obliquely of the subjected condition, a kind of retroflex "agency" compelled by other influences. Thus "ability to speak," "ability to comprehend or be emotionally affected," "sexual receptivity," and "socialization" characterize ways of being effective through subjection.

What should be called the "Cartesian fallacy" is a case in point, but an extremely important one. The fallacy is that of assuming, as Descartes did, that subjective autoreaction is embodied *physically* within the neural and biological organism. The sort of contagion that "metaphor" attributes to language and receives in linguistic form was identified by Descartes as the condition of a mind subjected by the physical body, a body's mind. Thus language in one case and the physical body in the more general one are empirical receptions of a pragmatic reality or objectivity and share the equivocal character of pragmatic embodiment in being at once conditions of enablement and limitation.

It is both the purpose and the trick of pragmatic embodiment to make trope appear as an effect of language and subjectivity in general as a condition of the physical body. Language and organismic embodiment are not evidence of *how* it may work but rather of *why* it is pragmatic to our impressions of "working." There is a contagion between the thing imagined in this way and the ability to imagine it that is neither empirical nor subjective, and not perceptual but reperceptual. It is this condition of mental embodiment (a mind's body) rather than embodied mentality that Hindu tradition speaks of as the "subtle body" and that is known in traditional Chinese wisdom as the *chi*, the body's energy.

Whatever pragmatic demonstration anthropology might choose to make of its knowledge—the archaeological site, the pungent trope of an indigenous understanding, the fossil find—anthropology is itself the subject of another demonstration. As a literature or an academic discipline anthropology bears the irony of a comparison with the ideal knowledge of humanity imagined by philosophers from Immanuel Kant to Jean-Paul Sartre. Another philosopher, Martin Heidegger, summed up the dilemma in these words: "Anthropology is that interpretation of man that already knows fundamentally what man is and hence can never ask who he may be. For, with this question it would have to confess itself shaken and overcome. But how can this be expected of anthropology when the latter has expressly to achieve nothing less than the securing consequent upon the self-securing of the *subiectum*?"[2]

To the extent that it may *compel* knowledge, rather than merely explain or interpret it, in other words, the science of the human is compelled by its own demonstrations. The science of humanity's capabilities and limitations is after all carried out by human beings, who become their own self-demonstration in the act of carrying it forth. Thus it is difficult indeed to escape the irony of becoming one's own example, of being compelled to make a ritual of studying ritual, to make a myth of the myth or avoid betraying one's own kinship with the "kinship" under study. And so it is not so much a matter of anthropology's pragmatic exemplars being inadequate to its tasks as it is of the discipline being completely swallowed by their potency. The irony is that theory is both something of a fetish and an object of deep suspicion in anthropology because it is "second best," merely evocative of the demonstrations that underlie it.

In this regard anthropology becomes more than just something that has happened (as "culture" or "ethnicity" has) to history, for history has happened to itself in this way too. If notions like "experience" do as little to explicate this condition as "fact," "reality," or "meaning," consider Nietzsche's diagnosis of "the historical sense" in *Beyond Good and Evil:* "The revolting vapors and closeness of the English rabble in which Shakespearian art and taste has its being disturbs us no more than, say, the Chiaja of Naples where we go along our way, willing and enchanted, with all our senses alive but quite oblivious of the cesspool odors wafting up from the lower town."[3] Ultimately, the source of this bedazzlement is that "measure is foreign to us—let us admit it. The stimulus that tickles us is the infinite, the immeasurable. Like a rider on a forward-charging horse, we drop our reins when infinity lies before us, we modern men, we half-barbarians."[4]

Since the tragedies and histories of Shakespeare, the exemplars of neoclassicism, and the excesses of romanticism, history has been under a tremendous pressure to happen, or perhaps happen again. It has been dramatized, preserved, restored, dug up, naturalized, understood as a thing in itself. And the "happening" of history outside of its time, as drama, restoration, understanding, its happening to persons other than its actors, is as essential to its being thought of as history as the happening of culture outside of its context is necessary to its conception as culture.

What must be given to Nietzsche, however, the insight behind his cascading phrases about "measure" and "half-barbarians," is that this desperate pressure for happening, this subjectivity that dazzles and destroys the modern imagination, is neither history nor culture. As a trope, a self-substantiating movement of feeling or meaning happening to itself, it is merely correlative with another, perhaps equally destructive pressure for "happening" itself to become history or description. The news, the spectacle, the rhetoric, or the performance is perhaps the manner in which Nietzsche's half-barbarians seek the solace of measure.

To force the conjunction of a never-ending quest for happening and an ever-accumulating happening of description into something like a believable history or culture is well-nigh impossible: theory makes poor theater, and even the best theater is poor theory.

This is perforce why we have the social sciences, but also why the social sciences seem always to be doing nothing, or, what is worse, pretty much the same old thing. To the half-barbarian spectator, anxious for the self-substantiation of "happening," social science looks like the incrementing of descriptions into languages. But to the connoisseur of arguments and logics, contemporary notions of "history" and "culture" look like unsubstantiated claims for sui generis happening. If a history, or that particularity of historical happening called a "culture," is a fabrication of memory through textual means, an organized recollection, then the projective component, "mind," "cultural ethos," or "intentionality," is fabricated anticipation. Hence the social sciences have a vested interest in objectifying or substantiating what is really only a subjective distinction, making a happening of description and a description of happening.

Most of what happens in what we call "communication" or "relating" happens too quickly, demands too immediate a response, to have an actual correspondance with any of the descriptions that might be made of its "meaning." The meaning of the expression or relational act, it is generally assumed, happened earlier as "intention" or will be recovered later in the synthesis of "memory." But of course the "earlier" and "later" moments of resolution or synthesis are subject to the same conditions of prospective or retrospective postponement as the original expression or act, as memory and intentionality are themselves but differential "takes" on the same basic description.

One word or thing is taken, expressed, considered through another, on behalf of another, or made identical with another in a sequential operation that is variously understood as memory, cognition, "cause and effect," "narrative discourse," "intentionality," or "motivation." If it has not escaped social science thinkers that the modes and faculties implied in these rubrics are fundamentally, even reflexively, interrelated, what seems to have eluded their attention is that the interrelation is far more insidious than notions like "deep structure" or "the human mind" would imply. An observer who did not share the bias of their subjective displacements could only conclude that the same thing is being done in the same way over and over again and called different things each time.

Can one "catch" meaning from language, or language itself from meaningfulness, as the first speakers might have caught on to the idea of it back at the beginning? Or are the limits of language and the languages of limit, its propositional logics, caught in such a contagion that we cannot tell one from the other? The archetypal "first language" principle that could translate any or all of the human languages that could ever have existed perfectly into one another would have made its mark in that way. It was so compact in its expression that it had no need of grammar, syntax, segmentation, or phonology, and for that reason need never have existed at all for us to understand perfectly well what we mean by it. To the extent that language has become *linguistic,* that is, relative to its own usage, it has become holographic in spite of itself and has had to incorporate as much diversity within its boundaries as outside of them. Then the very separation of language itself from anything one might say in it, or know through its usage, is at once causal to, and consequential of, the contagion of language and limit.

If, properly speaking, the twinned ideas or oppositional concepts that bracket and so inform our ability to say what we know or know what we say *internalize* its limits as the essence of language itself, then contagion underdetermines the language that would speak of it. Then the linguistic facility has caught its own virus and is in league with itself, twinned *against* the antecedents, or objects and objectives of its discourse, rather than matched with them, as a proper symbolism might be. Effectively, then, past and future have nothing to do with time, but with peculiar echo-effects of their own misconception, past's future and future's past. Mind and body are not the psychological or physiological indices we might take them to be, but interstitial paradoxes of an antipodal countertwinning—mind's body and body's mind. And just as the "dimensions" of our spatial experience owe their whole reality to the self-relativity of each with respect to the others, so the sensory "faculties" by which we experience them owe their whole evidential reality to the differences among them.

Symbolic or representational reality works at cross-purposes to the languages of its construction. We are in fact confronted with a depth of illusionism that is, like the *maya* of Hindu cosmology, virtually infinite in its deceptional potential, and that can only be represented as meaningful by pretending it as metaphor. But if the metaphor in question is a "back-to-back" (viz., Fig. 6) rather than a belly-to-belly engenderment of feelings or sex of ideas, then the contagion is more real than the meaningfulness pretended for it. It is the incest taboo of iconic representation.

Confusion between what such a metaphor means and how it is set up, or thought to mean, can as easily be mistaken for a referential facility of language as the technologies by which nature is observed and understood can be taken to inform or motivate the natural world itself. If "nature" owes its phenomenality to the instrumentalities by which we "sense" it, then language has objects, the "things" of speaking, for want of a real subject. "The limits of my language," Wittgenstein might have said, "are the real language of my conceptual limitations," speaking the differences among things as though they were similarities, and the similarities as though they were differences.

Something other than mere barbarism—the atavism that has justified anthropology's cultural convictions—would have to bear the brunt of Nietzsche's accusation against the historical imagination. And something bigger than anthropology itself would have to answer to Heidegger's criticism about universalizing one's own subjective focus. The search for a criterion of measure or limitation at the roots of subjective capability brings us to the same variety of causal enchainment or postponement that we find in the reception of trope as linguistic icon or metaphor. If one can only do justice to the sense of a metaphor through the office of another metaphor, and if the "performance" of what it may mean is always *another* performance, as distinct from the original, then the contagion has no practical limits. The idea that a metaphor could "cause" or provoke another metaphor is, however credible, itself another metaphor—that of telling the one from the other.

Or that of telling past from future, if each of these comparatives is dependent on the other for its very definition—past as a sequence of crashed futurities, future as the anticipation of past similitudes—then only an antipodal countertwinning or progressional chiasmus could restore the sense of a present limitation. Does will make the difference between them, or does memory? "Volition is to memory," one might say, "as future's pastness is to past's futurity." One does not metaphorize the divisions of time but that one divides the metaphor itself, and against itself.

The "negative" of metaphor is the virtual opposite of what symbolic construction or interpretation would have to mean; it is the negative capability of cognition's imitation of experience. The use of thought's or language's limitation in things to tell about itself instead, *say* what it cannot mean by referencing the imagery of saying backward, is antithetical as well to what is called "deconstruction" in that it begins with an episteme, like that of a pun, that is already deconstructed. The essence of Shakespeare's métier, making the *unthinkable* the secret of its own articulation, divining the nonfortuitous trajectory of chance, undercuts the absolutism of the post-Newtonian world as the insight of its latter-day counterpart in Wittgenstein undercuts the worlds of physical and cultural relativity.

So, too, the essence of any human feeling or emotion is the *next one* that takes its place and informs on its predecessor, capturing the whole stretch of imaginative possibilities in an inevitable outcome. The secret of a perfectly transparent musical art, like that of Mozart or his teacher, Johann Christian Bach, is that sound can inform on meaning better than meaning can inform on sound, imitate the *sense* of a logic so perfectly that it need make no other kind of sense. The musical prodigy is the grandfather of meaning, regardless of age; the pun is the godfather of language.

Anaphoresis is the art, whatever its medium, of the non-load-bearing pun, lucky enough not to get all the meaning it pays for. Literalized, annotated, in the way that one notes down the sound of music into a score, it becomes "an aphorism." The *chiasmatic* expression of a proposition like "the pun of a meaning is the meaning of the pun" is self-subjecting, makes a volte-face of the limitation that language imposes on thought. I have reason to suspect that the internal objectivity trait is genotypic in the cat family, and phenotypic in the human, and accounts for the remarkable similarities in their respective genomes. We have opposite trajectories in encompassing the perils of space-time: the cat, with its no-fault center of gravity, can survive a fall from an incredibly tall building; the human being, with its no-fault illusion about progress, can actually survive the need to build one.

The idea that one metaphor might be used to decipher another, given that each is a key to its own formulation, makes a subjective fantasy of the contagion of language and limit. The place where all the metaphors would come together, form the trope of metaphor itself, is the time when all the people come apart. It is the library of babble, and the joke of it is the joke that brings the library down. Part and whole, individual and collective, or person and world are as unreliable in their mutual interdependency as past and future, or body and mind. Thus the notion that all the atoms, atomic particles, creatures, or ideas formed an unseparated whole in the beginning of things, and have come apart to "evolve" the history of time, and the contrary proposition that they will all come together at the end, are fantastic corollaries of a single contagion. They "deserve" one another for want of an objective limit between them, like the cat and the human being, or like the anthropologist and the people he has come to study.

The belly-to-belly metaphor of human mental or physical conception, the "reproduction of the species," is, properly speaking, a picture of incest, a foil for the meaning of meaning that blocks its own understanding. The back-to-back version, that brings the outer limit of human conception within its means, is no longer a metaphor but a negative capability of the species itself. The human hologram is the objective redress of the subjective or self-subjecting condition, our place in the universe as a function of the universe's place in us. A concrete expression of our scale in things, it makes the point that natural science nearly always misses, that "scale" is almost never drawn to scale. The kind of understanding that insists on magnification, changing the scale of things to get the details right, has used the thing it needed to see, and "seen" the thing it needed to use. The conviction that atoms and molecules or life processes and carbon reactions are things that make us up is based on the fact that we have made them up.

The very human need for divinity is a case in point of this, for the invention of supreme being is almost as useful a fiction in restoring human proportions that are too close to be otherwise detectable as the idea of "primitive" languages or peoples, or of human evolution. Gods *must have* created us, for who else would be able to think them up? Human beings must certainly have evolved from simpler organisms, for where else would they have gotten the genes for divine simplifications like the wheel? The secrets of physics, chemistry, and biology must certainly hold the keys to our existence, since we hold the key to theirs. Nothing as absurd as human beings could have arisen by natural means, and nothing so wise from purely cultural strategems. We need not have invented ourselves and our world, but only invented the invention of them.

The Lord Indra was chief of the ancient Vedic pantheon of India, a pragmatic "imaginer" of world and divinity through the net of *maya* (illusion) cast about the world to give it a figurative form and content. Like Zeus, Indra was a hurler of thunderbolts, but, unlike his Grecian counterpart, Indra's whole existential status, his divine primacy, was matched in this potency. He cast illusion holographically, as lightning copies its trajectory on its own movement, rives the near heavens in a sudden undercutting of their dimensionality. As a godhead, already everywhere at once in the thunderclap of his going there, he is his own invention of things, at once ancestor and descendant—the true image of a false relationalism.

So the net is an image of what holography *may* be from the standpoint of one who cannot grasp the absolute identity of part and whole. It is only a "net," an iconic snare or entangler, if its parts are perceived as *holes,* interstices. From the viewpoint of the god on the insight, or *darsan,* of his divine encompassment, the image of the net and its contagious qualification of things does not exist. What may seem to others to be holes in a net are priceless and perfect jewels, gems that reflect one another so perfectly that "they do not know whether they are one or many." Without the sight that makes their differences disappear, one could not know the god, or know that the net is not a net and that illusion itself has a self-scaling potentiality. Indra can only be anthropomorphized as the reflexive counterpart of his lightning configuration of a perceptual, cognizable world.

Grasped sensually (Fig. 1), Indra's likeness to his own unlikeness in things is a heuristic play on empirical reality, the *lila,* or sport of a king of the gods that would be man. Or it is the imprimatur of a child-reality in the human hologram, that which would be adult, male, exotic to its own demonstration of things through the veils of *maya,* or illusion, that its sensual formation casts about the world of perception. Indra is not an interpretive construction or a constructive interpretation but rather a perfected outcome of what we mean in using these terms—complete creation beside the point of its own coming into being—and one that renders viewpoint and artifice unnecessary to its understanding. Indraknowledge, or even the suspicion that Indra *could* exist, makes it unnecessary to pretend that people create their own realities. One does not have to believe or know: if one merely *misses* Indra's shape (in the way that an initial missing of the punch line is necessary to the "funny" in a joke), a great deal of phenomenological writing—Husserl, Sartre, Heidegger—is rendered superfluous.

If "culture," as it is lived or analyzed, could only exist by being pretended or invented, on whatever experiential, folkloric, psychological, or semiotic authority, then Indra's imaginal authority works in the opposite way. His reality or divine suzerainty consists in being the *bestower* of figurative conjecture or cultural "imagination" rather than its product.

The thunderclap and the retinal imprint of lightning are aftereffects, like "energy" itself, the net, or its perceptual entanglement of things, of something that has already *been* where it is just now going. The punch line, as it were, of a joke on empirical reality, like the illusion that illusion itself is another divinity, called Maya, who supersedes Indra. Likewise history viewed on the hindsight of its eventual previousness to

Figure 1. The net of Indra.

our knowledge of it is not "temporal" at all. It is simply convergent (then as now, now as then), or rather it is the simple, brute fact of convergence itself *in spite of* rather than through, or because of the separations and distinctions made to give it a sequential character, a temporal configuration.

So the reconvergence of Indra with any image one might make of him is like the shape of the wheel in time. The double imaging of an object with its own "working," or usefulness, the wheel is present to our contemporary lives in uncountable ways, yet it is unaccountable as to its actual origination or invention. For both parts of this enigmatic "double envisioning" are implicit in the design of the wheel itself. A portion of the wheel is always moving retrograde to the direction of its application, though necessarily at the same rate, and it is that pragmatic afterlife that the wheel converts into usefulness or progression.

The pragmatic counterimage of godhead that ancient Vedic peoples called "the breaker of cities" (who else might this be but we ourselves, and what besides the wheel or its analogues like the airfoil breaks them?) belongs, in this way, to the human hologram. It is aniconic and atemporal; always at the point of its own invention, which it endlessly repeats, it simultaneously invents the form of its own repetition.

Indra is the part of reality that is also, in this way, the totality of it, casting the net of deception around the world in its motion, or *as* its motion—a movement that is for us the convergent "now" of our placement and replacement in it. Wheel for wheel, earth is the shape of its own place in the cosmos, the larger design that takes its whole description and significance from the familiarities of bodily and earth-surface experience. So we would underdetermine the earth, ignore its presence to our very physical sensation of things, in forming the exaggerated sense of its placement that we turn into transcosmic reality—stellar interiors, black holes, waves, particles, and gravity. Does this "investment" of sensual form and figure carry a negative return, a sort of experiential debit structure, holes in the net, of the spaces and times imagined for it? The image of the black hole, actually an inference based on something absurdly familiar as an "event horizon," may help. We know from our lives what an "event" might be, and we know from the earth what a horizon is. So we would know as well, if only from the experience of getting smashed in our loves and expectations, exactly what the "interior" of a black hole might be like. This is not profound, and its banality has nothing to do with what space and time might be like. The reality of the net comes down to the simple fact that you can only get "into" it—psychological depression or a black hole—by trying to *think* your way out of it. Not "feel" or "experience," believe or postulate, for these are mere by-blows of a causational backlash, but *think*, reckon, configure the knowing-what-you-know part of it.

Pragmatic objectivity is the precise *humor* of explanation or understanding, the way in which no physical fact or subjective state, no natural process or work in art or science is any better than the means of its description. Most of the energy expended in technology, in human relationships, and even in the work of thinking about them is used to run its own description. It "works" the way that we design or imagine its working. But the way in which this takes place, the precise humor that juxtaposes subjective and objective descriptions, is not accountable in ordinary subjective or objective terms. The very practical "edge" it puts on objects and feelings, or better *between* them, is missed with surprising fidelity in the tropes or figures we use to think of it, and most especially in the trope we make of trope itself. It is *overdetermined*, subjectified or objectified, in the separations made to fix and substantiate its underdetermining character. It is *not* metaphoric, metonymic, syntagmatic, or paradigmatic, and if its very significance or usefulness elides particularities of that sort, it is not the trope or figure we imagine it to be.

It is the true image of a false relation to itself, like Lord Indra, sustained as the wheel is, or the lightning bolt, in a "just now" transit to its point of origination—in and as its pragmatic afterlife. In this consideration we are dealing with the shape and purpose of the net, the deceptiveness of imposing measurements and separations (intervals) as "space" or "time," or as our means of knowing and thinking them, and then living their configurations in terms of those measurements.

Another "detail" of the Indra-net turns out to be more significant than the whole, or at least the fantasy of totality that is pretended in it. As one approaches this condition of absolute or divine holography in the ability to grasp, understand, divine the principle of it, the idea or image of wholeness becomes less and less necessary to its definition or perception. Each detail, however insignificant, defines the principle of its being there simply through the appropriateness of its placement or perception, takes over the totality as a subset of it. Hence the irony of the figure-ground reversal that turns the lacks or empty spaces of the net into "jewels" is compounded by another that matches the anthropomorphism of the net's divine inspiration. Each "jewel" or detail takes on the cognitive or reflective quality of the subject who is trying to understand it, turns subjectivity inside out. It cannot "know" whether it is one or many.

It is hardly a wonder that many Indian people regard the Indra-net and the image of divinity it projects with deep suspicion, often profound distaste. For as a *darsan,* an "image" of the god bestowed as the subject's very act of perceiving him, this one makes a joke of faith, "belief," and the very act of worshiping itself. The most prescient conception of godhead the human mind could imagine turns out to be the patron, because the patronizer, of the way in which human beings humor themselves in reality. He is the Father of the most original joke of all, necessarily male in detaching himself from his conception (the *bharat* or "universe," the university) once the act of conceiving is completed.

So it is also less than a wonder that Indra was demoted ages ago by a people who wanted to keep their connection with divinity, and that, for the same reason, India is the great hoarder and admirer of the world's most precious jewels. To know the net as a net, see it as a net, grasp or perceive it in any way as a net, is to get caught in it. To *not* know it as a net, humor oneself, and go by the counsel of perception alone is to get positively entangled.

2

Where Is the Meaning in a Trope?

The acute problem faced in holography is that of config-uring a relational schematic for a subject that is not relational at all. Any form of representation that can be conceived of mentally or projected physically for what an absolute *identity* of part and whole might be or mean results in a perfect scale model of the mistakes made in trying to represent that identity. But it is precisely because the holographic is *pragmatic* to our efforts to ascertain its reality in this way, know *what* we know of it, that it is easily accessible to our understanding. We all know exactly what it is and what it means *because* it is impossible to conceive or represent. It is the identity formed in a trope, whatever the words or conventional figures used to describe it, and whatever the classifications, analytic distinctions, or theories of what a trope is and how it works (e.g., what it "does") might be. So it is also the identity formed in *us,* as *subject,* witness, hearer, or speaker, as the human coun-terpart of the mistakes made in trying to represent it.

The project of trying to represent it is, for that reason, what I shall call an anthropology of the subject. From that standpoint it would not matter at all whether the representation was conceptualized mentally, "in the head," or graphically and figuratively, "in the world," for clearly each of these loci is dependent upon the other. If, in other words, one would understand the representational exercise in mathematical terms, as a fractal or other experiment with scale retention or self-scaling, the anthropological side of it would come down to a question of how we ourselves are formed as subjects. It would have to be the ways in which the human constitution is automimetic, imitative of itself in language and representation, or in bodily and transbodily form, that facilitates both our ability to construe a perfect unity of part and whole and our inability to represent it.

In that respect the assertions of the physicist David Bohm, that the universe itself is holographic in its implicate structure, and of Karl Pribram, that the human brain is developed or operative in that way, would both substantiate and obviate one another. For if the universal structure of things were holographic, the brain, as part of it, would have to be as well, whereas a holographic brain would have to grasp the structure of things on its own principles. But if the human *subject* (singular or plural, social or individual) were constituted in this way, it would hardly seem to matter what part the brain or the universe played in it.

An absolute or perfectly realized holography would abolish the distinction between representation and reality, between the subjective thinking or knowing of things and their objective being. But if a rigorous scale invariance of this type, a copying so precise that it is no longer merely imitative, is impossible to replicate in its own terms without losing track of those terms, the limit set in this way serves to define instead the subject that is trying to represent it. The human hologram becomes an inadvertent self-representation of the species in consequence of this, just as the factors in a heuristic or "model" that are only there for the purpose of our understanding or familiarity become part of the "reality" it represents to us.

In this respect a projective hologram—what "holography" means to most people—presents a *mental* image of its subject. The holographic plate, which registers the interference pattern of two beams of coherent (parallel and unidirectional, nonradiating) light reflected from a single source makes parallactic displacement an integral function of viewing that source. Seeing "around" it is part of seeing it. Every point on the object is registered at once on every point of the plate, and the imaginary quality of three-dimensional space is represented as a personal focal point existing outside of the observer. If tricks like metaphor provide the best evidence for why "meaning" does not happen in the brain, then the holographic staging of this illusion does the same for the brain's alleged "imaging," or cognition. It shows how a mental facility that could not work in that way might trick itself into thinking it does. The image is "mental," not because it imitates the three-dimensional profile of an object in the mind but because it imitates the impersonation that gives this effect, the three-dimensional profile of mind in the object.

The whole power of a trope of any kind—metaphor, metonym, synecdoche—lies in the identity it states, however it came to be stated. The identity is its own lesson and its own context; to turn it in any way into a *relation* it is necessary to invoke *other* identities and misconstrue them in the same way as one intends to do with the original. This is as much as to say that what the identity *is* and what it means is never recoverable by virtue of the very efforts made to recover it, that the meaning has already happened *as* the identity and that thereafter we "happen" to it as its "interpretation." A metaphor is born of an attempt to get rid of metaphor, and it survives as the boundary condition of our inability to do so.

The identity formed in the "this is that" of trope is at once smaller than language—a convergent point—and coterminous with it, because it depends upon it. No language, no trope. The potential for meaningfulness expands as language contracts, but the identity so formed is not meaningful in itself. Or one could say that the identity exists where the meaning would be if it were possible to use words so acutely that they would no longer be part of the lexicon.

What we "construct" or imagine as a surrogate for identity is a self-imagined content, an exotic demonstration of what the identity might mean if it had a meaning. The irony (and the contagion) of invention of this sort is that it can only be carried through and completed through the making of identities that continue to exclude themselves from the discourse they motivate.

A verbal simulation of how the very same thing might be said without words, metaphor conceals the fact that this could not happen behind the words it uses to mask itself. I might, for example, state a metaphor of which I assume you will know the meaning, regardless of whether I may know it or not, and you respond with another assuming perhaps that I really knew what I said, without either of us necessarily getting the point of any of them. We could, indeed, exchange tropes in this way all day without either of us being responsible for the meaningful content of any of them, or content ourselves with a mild curiosity as to what the meanings might be like if anyone took the trouble to work them out. "What," as a friend once archly put it, "if they gave a meaning and nobody came?"[1]

But if identities are the essence of the trope, the meaningfulness, or the exchange, it is difficult to imagine how or why a text or a conversation should take any other form. And it is difficult as well to escape the conclusion that "mind" is a similar postponement of content, a continuation by other means of the contagion of trope, that mind sets up the field of its own abstract possibility just as metaphor does. Though we might think of the brain, with its awesome intricacy of neuronic pathways and combinations, its divisions, cortices, centers of specialization, as the mind's organism, the reverse is more nearly true. Mind is the organism of the brain, that which is necessary to build or think organism into it—create and substantiate the myth of neural "mechanism" that draws upon the brain's complexity for its own credibility. It is as much a part of mind's function to imagine a brain for itself as it is a part of brain's functioning to imagine a mind for itself. Each projects the other as its responsible agency, just as with the parties to an exchange of tropes, and without either being the wiser or more responsible. Easily enough parodied ("of all the vital organs the brain is the only one self-conscious enough to believe itself thinking") the mind-brain "system" provides, like dialogic modeling, a casuistry through which codependency becomes an idiom for self-containment.

Meaning's indexing of itself, its testamentary self-referencing in the signs and conversations by which it might recognize itself, the organic realities and mental abstractions through which it would know or show itself to be "working," would lose its whole utility and purpose if it were itself meaningful. There is, for this reason, no meaning in the trope, no thinking in the brain, no demonstration of how the meaningful might originate or operate that fits with the expectations we have set up for its description. The demonstration of meaning to itself is exotic to its own purpose and belongs to a strategy that has nothing else to do with the semiotic, the philosophical, psychological, or literary. It belongs to the *anthropology* of its subject, in a strategy that anthropologists have made familiar in naive understanding and observation.

The secret of the exotic demonstration, which is not exotic unless it is a demonstration and not a demonstration unless it is exotic, is that it must have this character for *all* subjects. It must be strange or foreign, even for those to whom it is most familiar. The facility to elucidate, surprise, educate by estrangement is not a matter of anthropological or indigenous "cultural" authority but a factor in its own right. This is what the analytical study of myth has made a myth of, what that of culture has acculturated, and what the idea of ritual has ritualized.

The classic response to the anthropologist's query as to the meanings, the purpose, or even the "workings" of ritual is that they have been *forgotten*. "Our fathers died before they could tell us what this means" is what the Daribi people at Tiligi' told me about their *habu* rite. The Barok people of New Ireland put the same general response in a different, perhaps more subtle, way: "The meaning cannot be put into words because words trick you; one can only witness the demonstration of the *pidik*." Their "heritage," if that is the word, is not one of re-membered meanings, for they are best forgotten, but of remembered demonstrations, a chance to learn from one's mistakes.

The classic anthropological rejoinder to testaments of this sort is that the ritual (or the trope, the myth, the usage) is "performative" or "op-erative," that its significance or purpose or workings can only be expe-rienced in the act of doing it. The problem with this answer, an "easy" one for all its apparent sophistication, is that doing or acting out some-thing is no more an explanation of it than its experience is an under-standing. The performance is not *about* the rite; the rite is about the performance. The performative or operative symbol is based on a con-fusion of trope with meaning or understanding and the glossing that is necessary to them, but there is no point where the performer is more mystified about these matters than during the performance itself. If the performer could only really *know* the rite in doing it, then what was re-membered would be beside the point, and the anthropologist would emerge from the experience in no better shape than the indigenous per-formers. The same problem would beset *intention* as well; what one could not remember, one could not intend, given that intention and memory share the same description. Perhaps Victor Turner's sage ob-servation about a Ndembu rite, that "we have in Chihamba the local expression of a universal human problem, that of expressing what can-not be thought, in view of thought's subjugation to essences," provides the best delineation of the problem.[2]

So if we take "demonstration" to mean anything an experientialist would intend as *doing* or performing the rite, or a structuralist or semi-oticist as signifying it, "exotic" would mean the power of its estrange-ment. *What* is performed in it or how it operates is precisely the part that is obscure to its actors or witnesses, that belongs to no one. It does not so much belong in culture and theory, custom or its explanation, as it trades on the boundaries or limits that define them or define our in-terests in them. The "native" is not born to it, and the anthropologist is not foreign to it.

Peoples would not "have" their myths or rituals because the point of them *belonged* to them in some self-definitive way, but precisely because it did not, and rather scared or tested their living and thinking in famil-iar ways. Why compare or contrast cultures that are their own internal contrasts and comparisons? Is not the very arbitrariness of a set of symbols or symbolic correspondences, their lack of "fit" with that which they stand for or represent, the thing that makes them memorable or applicable? If so, cultures would be differentiable, even definable as such, through the contrasts of their respective contrasts with one another. And the same would have to be true of languages, given that no language exists in a vacuum. What some have decried as difficulties or impossibilities of translation among languages could also be construed on the same grounds as motivation—the generation of necessary misinterpretations or "working misunderstandings."

As part of the discourse of differences that fuels and provokes them, English would not be a language but an attempt to articulate what French can say but with a drier wit, a cooler, more objective humor. French is not a language but an attempt to say what German does with fewer words, and fewer connections among them. German is not a language but an attempt to make the sentence self-sufficient,[3] to internalize its contrasts with other, exotic ways of saying things. Insofar as "national character traits" depend in an analogous way upon the contrasting of contrasts, and in a direct way upon the languages that articulate them, they develop an evidential basis through a similar generation of misunderstandings.

Just as the main point of a ritual must be forgotten for its exotic demonstration to "work" at all, "getting it by not getting it," so the reverse is true of language. Language must be *remembered,* and remembered whole, even to speak or hear it. It is only when this act of remembering is disguised, subsumed within some putative neurophysiological function ("accessing" language, for instance) that language itself can be treated as functional. It is *mnemonic,* remembered or rememberable on the basis of what is said in it, and which thus forms a part of the totality to which it belongs, just as the point of ritual is forgettable or forgotten on the basis of what is done in it.

But in neither case do we speak, hear, or act ritually in the way that these observations would suggest we do. We do not, in other words, pay attention directly to the "language" part of remembering—the definitions of the words, the structuring of phrases and sentences—any more than we are obliged to act out the wordless and self-effacing aspects of ritual. We hear words crash, or see them crash, in the expectation of other words, phrases, and whole statements yet to follow—words, phrases, and statements that are as yet unuttered or unread, and in fact may never occur in the conversation or text that follows. Yet it is precisely this anticipatory copy, this imitation "in the head" of what the crashing of discourse *will have meant,* that is responsible for the whole shaping of meaning in it. The *imitation* of memory in meaning (what the words or actions "will have meant" by the time others, which may not be forthcoming, have taken their place) turns the whole ongoing flow of iteration into an inadvertent play of tropic formation, sets up the substitution of unexpected words or phrases for anticipated ones. Like a wheel in motion, at any given time exactly half its mass is moving backward to the direction of its forward movement, and at exactly the same velocity as the other half.

As the wheel is a single object, containing its coming and going, as it were, in a unitary motion, so one might speak of the imitation of memory in words, actions, or understandings that are only as yet anticipated as a trick of its temporal opposite. It "is," also and at the same time, a use of memory in the recollected shaping of words and their interconnections to imitate *anticipation,* what one means or intends to say or do when one has not yet done so. The full ambiguity of "meaning," as noted in the previous chapter, is more useful than it is precise, in that it contains each time—the "before" of as-yet unarticulated intentions and the "afterward" of articulating them—within the other, and as a function of it. Sense and signification, or, if you will, the nonlinear "feeling" of the world and the "linear" focusing that discriminates a temporal "before" and "after," are each encompassed within the other to a degree that makes any analytical separation of them both difficult and unnecessary.

Where the meaning may be in a trope, or in the tropelike ambiguity that language generates automatically in its use, is, like the question of what "trope" might be or when and how meaning happens to it, the function of a movement whose double encompassment eludes that kind of specificity. Both linear and nonlinear in the same movement, meaning incorporates its own pragmatic afterlife: it "means" the way it works and "works" the way it means. So the significance of trope and the ways in which that significance may "operate" or come about—the trope, as it were, of significance itself—are already in "operation" when one begins to think of trope and its consequences. They have nothing else to do with the means by which words might be used to recapture their content or semiotic effects, nor even with the ways in which human beings "interpret" or "construct" meanings. All interpretation is trope, and all trope is interpretation.

So it would only be when the double encompassment of feeling and articulation is most effective, closing its point of insight off from its relations or connections to other things, that the issues of interpretation or exegesis would come into relevance. This form of understanding is always a self-relative and incomplete process, getting the point by not getting it, as in the telling or hearing of a joke. One copies an effect that has just copied one's thoughts, or thinks about an effect that one's thought has just copied in taking account of it, and the whole question of significance and therefore affect is locked into the uncertainty as to which came first. Did one "hear" what one expected to hear with the words for some alternative saying of it already on one's lips, or was one's mind so "taken" by what it was hearing that the intended topic has already become part of it? If uncertainty plays so large a role in the speaking or reading of tropes—given that uncertain "curiosity" carries so much of the interest in conversation or silent reading—then the reader or speaker takes on the personal role of the tropes themselves, and what is heard or printed is mere echo-effect, or perhaps echolocation for the personae lost in it. In that case one must pretend or invent a common ground of meaning or intent in order to fix a role for human agency— "I" and "thou" and therefore of course "I-thou"—in the discourse. Are the individual tropes, provided one might isolate them, only "there" or pretended to be there because of some (imaginable) larger trope that frames them, or is that larger, framing trope itself an unfixed supposition, actually moving in step with the specific examples that are chosen, one after another, in order to establish what the actual subject might be?

In either case it would seem that one is not so much dealing with a text and one's reading of it, or a conversation, as with a kind of immediate part-and-whole comparison, a holography of meaning in which language or rhetoric and personal participation play interchangeable roles. Does actual "language" and the styles and habits of its use actually miss the point every time, creating the need and also the opportunity for a continual shifting into tropes, wholly imaginary sidesteppings of what it would ordinarily mean? Or is it the other way around, so that the tropes "convey" or "represent" what is truly the point of it, and the reworking of "language" made to accommodate them is all the language one would ever know, or even need to know? (Does the beginning speech of small children *start with* tropes in order to elicit or deduce adult speech patterns?)

No wonder that some experts (notably Lakoff and Johnson, in *Metaphors We Live By*) can argue, and quite successfully, that the whole of what we call "language" is a set of congealed or conventionalized tropes, "frozen" into place by common usage or authority.[4] And no wonder the opposite of that might equally and with a similar skill be shown to be true, that the metaphors that have congealed or "set" in that way are precisely the ones that significant discourse displaces or dislocates in order to create its subject matter. It is only because both of these alternatives must be true and equipotential in discourse that either can be demonstrated (at the expense of the other) to be true, so that the holography of personal "subjects" and impersonal conventions is never *simply* linguistic, personal, experiential, subjective, or objective.

It could not, therefore, accommodate to some sort of set or static, precognized or precognizable (e.g., "predictable") model at all, for its very holographic potential resides in the fact that it is a *moving* part-whole occlusion. By the same token, however, it is not *recoverable* either, in the sense of being able to recall personal or collective experiences exactly (as "constructions of reality," for instance), for the very effort of trying to remember what took place sets up a new and necessarily quite different version of its subject. Another milestone along the trajectory of the moving holography, and with the "personal" and "collective" components already taking different roles. "Recordings" of events are entirely different events, even though intentionality and memory share the same description, or perhaps because of that fact.

The problem of locating meaning in the trope, or trope itself in the "meaningfulness" of events, has that much in common with the problematic significance of human reincarnation. The problem is not that of the evidence, convincing or dubious as the case may be in either case, but of what that evidence might mean at a later stage of its holographic movement or motivation. The possibility that any of us might have "lived other lives" (disregarding the difficult question of what "parts" of one might have lived them) is so much beside the point of what those earlier lives might mean to us *now*, in *this* life, and according to present motivations (e.g., the standards for determining that one is now "in" a life distinctly different from a "past" one), that the valences of fantasy and reality are only marginally differentiable. In other words, to "reincarnate" oneself by "remembering when things were different" has so much in common with our ordinary twinning of ourselves in that way ("when I was a child," "when I lived in a different city") that the trope of the context (e.g., the "lived" scenario) is indistinguishable from the contextualizing of the tropes. The remembered and the remembering of it live such different lives that they might as well be two different people.

Fixing the personal subject in that way would be an alternative strategy (e.g., "content" versus "form") to the semiotic practice of defining the sign values, functions, or agentive roles of signs and other conventions. If the cognitive and subjective formation of a world-in-the-person and the objective articulation of that "person" as personality, behavior, relationship in the world are co-dependent and co-relative variables, then the definitive formulation or "fixing" of one of them throws the other open to hazard and mystification. One could be very accurate and precise about the formal means—signs, iterations, and so forth—and then have to wonder about the "persons," their behaviors and perhaps "humanity." Or one could be very exacting, perhaps psychological, biological, biographical, about the "people" involved, even provoke a "humanistic" discourse, and have to wonder about the signs.

So the problem of locating meaning in the trope and tropes themselves in the meaningfulness of the human condition is not merely topical within the social sciences. It is the "contagiousness," the generic issue, of social science itself, inextricably compounded within its own subdivision and articulation of topics, approaches, and subject matters—its own tropes for the sorting out of tropes, its artificial "reincarnation" of other time periods and alternative styles of life and thought as personifications sensed secretively within our own. Once it has been set up in this way, "located" within the generic setting that defines social science inquiry itself, the problem becomes a very narrow one indeed, concerned only with how a very special set of people—the social scientists themselves—think, understand, and perhaps live their lives. When its subject is faced in the broadest possible parameters, in the holistic vision of a perfect scale model of the mistakes made in trying to figure out what it means, the prospect of a definitive understanding, a resolution, is confronted by its own shadow or doppelgänger, the nemesis of a moving holography that paces its every step.

So much for the subject, anthropological or professional, the self-conceived model of how "the natives" conceive of themselves and their worlds. What of the subject matter, the real *anthropology* of the subject, the human knowing of the human in it? How do peoples with no professional investment in science or humanism deal with the scale modeling of the mistakes made in trying to figure themselves out? Or, if objectivity is of any help in this, trying to figure out the world as it takes form within the person and the person as it takes its place socially, among its relations and relationships in the world?

For the Usen Barok people of New Ireland, as they have made clear to me, the location of meaningfulness is not a matter of making a better model of the world in the person or the person in the world. One might think of their "take" on this as one of trying to extinguish the accumulation of errors that consistently moves the holography out of one's grasp. But they themselves call it the prospect of *iri lolos,* "finished power," "finishing all thought" *in* the person and *of* the person through the occasion of a socially created death. The ambiguity or double meaning of "finishing" *(iri)* as "ending" or "killing" and "perfection" or "completion" plays a single and singular role in this, actually a mutual encompassment of each sense of the term by the other.

For it is *sense* itself in its broadest and most comprehensive meaning (the grounding of rationality in its enabling empirical particulars or accidents, and the "accident" of reason itself) that forms the subject of its double encompassment. Not only the "sensing" of things that makes reason viable, but also the reasoning of things that makes sensing thinkable or tractable.

So possibly Ludwig Wittgenstein's *Tractatus Logico-Philosophicus* might furnish the surest guide to extinguishing the moving holographic potential. Wittgenstein noted that "we picture facts to ourselves" (2.1)[5] and that "a proposition states something only in so far as it is a picture" (4.03).[6] Very wisely, he did not bother to say how or why, to what cognitive means or purpose, but only in effect that no theory or intuition, no general or specific schema or set of equations we might have for *anything at all* is any better than the imageries or other sensible means we might have for picturing, illustrating, or demonstrating its implications or consequences. Sense enables reason. But later in the same work Wittgenstein noted that "to be general means no more than to be accidentally valid for all things" (6.1231),[7] that the explicit articulation necessary for cognition itself (e.g., how we know *what* we know, or *that* we know)—the "sense" that is made of sensing—is itself accidental to the empirical reality it encompasses. Reason enables its own enabling.

So the facts that nothing "counts" as evidence for a subconscious—what it is or how it works—that has not been made conscious first, nothing exemplifies "the exotic" in any conclusive way that does not familiarize it, nothing demonstrates the form or content of a trope that does not literalize and disempower it, all follow from Wittgenstein's "finishing" of thought.

The "sense" that things make, directly and physically as perception or sensation and indirectly as the logical or reasoning sense made of that sensing, always threatens to lead a life of its own. Regardless of whether the threat is real or merely a consequence of our efforts to understand and control it (who could tell?), it is invariably presented in terms of the "meaningfulness" of its control, knowledge, or redirection. Treating it as "natural," tracing it to biological, chemical, or electrochemical roots, or subdividing it into "modes" of sensing, like the visual, aural, tactile, olfactory, or kinesthetic, is no less a means of controlling it than seeking out its signature in language, logic, and social or cultural forms. Practical inventions and technology, applications of "energy," as well as everyday usages and utensils, aesthetic creations especially, represent overt demonstrations—*pidiks* to the Barok, "cultural rituals" to the anthropologist—of that control.

Hence despite the fact that the control is most often illusory, that we are used—even consumed—by the objects, ideas, and categories we claim to be using, or perhaps because of that fact, one thing is dead certain. That is that the control or articulation of sense emerges itself as an independent variable with a life of its own. It is the *difference* between the spontaneity of sense in vivifying (and threatening) its articulative control, and the life that control or articulation leads in its own right that the Barok "finishing of thought" undercuts, turning sense and reason into one and the same thing. So if meaning holds a kind of self-conscious fascination for Barok as government does for Americans, Will Rogers's astute observation about Americans and their government would apply to the Barok and their "meaningfulness" (and worldview) as well: that they are lucky enough not to get all of it that they pay for.

For it should be clear that the effort to comprehend, realize, and thus control a holographic world perspective is directly motivated (e.g., self-controlled) by the mistakes one must necessarily make in trying to figure out what it is or how it might "work." Given the obvious fact that an absolute identity or perfect mutual occlusion of part and whole is impossible to represent or realize, all the mistakes made, methodically and regularly, in the effort to achieve that unreal condition emerge as a perfect scale model of the schematic, the design or germinal motif, used to control them.

Translated back into the terms of this discussion, this means that the effort to control sense directly in this way, through a near-perfect scale modeling of the sensible features in the world around it, is itself controlled by the "meaningfulness" it generates in the course of so doing. Sense encompasses reason as reason encompasses sense; each of the twin imponderables, the free life of sense as it consumes the consumer, and the déjà vu pragmatic of culture, control's control over itself, is doubly encompassed within the other. More to the point of anthropology's subjective possibilities, it would be pointless, indeed "senseless," to attempt to model a people's underdetermination of their own cultural features in terms of some extraneous schema of cultural, logical, or natural description. The moving holography that shadows our every move in locating a meaning in the trope and a trope in the meaningfulness of things is brought to a stillstand in the miniature that is formed in this way. Just try to describe it in other terms, and you will find it describing your efforts better than you can describe its doing so.

For everything that accords with the values of what we call "civilization," its cities and monumental architecture, its social classes and elaborate lifeways, its incredible technologies, mathematics, and self-expression in the control and knowledge of writing and speech, amounts to an overdetermination of the containment of sense by itself. But the Barok "social death," finishing all thought, does not begin with a set of precepts or propositions and develop them, as one might want to do in developing a heuristic for what their "culture" (as an analogue of civilization?) means to them, or how it could have evolved or come about. It *finishes them from the very beginning* and then gradually, like a symphony or a self-revelatory novel, brings participants into the full realization of what has happened to them, into the déjà vu of control's control of itself. Likewise, and by analogy, if there were a "story of Eve," a tale of how humanity was "finished" from the beginning of its days, its human hologram would have to be much simpler than the means we might use to uncover it. We would then *be,* and only gradually come to realize, our own double encompassment of reason by sense, and of sense by reason.

It is no accident that all compelling origin accounts begin with doom, a "big bang" that rips the universe asunder, original sin, sexual anger, or the stupefaction of the human image, entangling it in the Indra-net or worse. It is a necessary part of The Most Original Joke of All, that comes into gradual realization as the shape of human mortality, the design of the mistakes we make about ourselves in time, the desire, or simply and definitively human *wanting* of things that compels use. So the Barok *kaba,* the exotic demonstration of sense's encompassment in meaning and meaning's in sense, for all the fact that it is basic to and definitive of all social value and valuation, has no necessity to it at all. It need not be performed, being implicit in the very holography it encompasses, and when it is, very rarely and at great expense, it is only "because someone *wants* it, and for no other reason."

3

A Sociality Reperceived

What would historical transformations—often enough invisible to those caught up in them—be like without the sense of the words used to understand them? Would natural processes like evolution or photosynthesis actually operate "in some other way" than the heuristics or working models used to explain or replicate them would suggest, and, if so, how might that way be described? Such questions lose their naïveté when applied to human social relations, which many anthropologists suppose to operate in *some* relation to the people's understanding of them. Although it is quite possible that this assumption itself may be skewed, that human relations could not possibly operate in the ways in which they are brought to light for the very fact of their being brought to light, the point is much simpler than that. Even when "the natives" are understood to model themselves, provide insights, concepts, and figures to illustrate their own viewpoint, and even when behavioral models are imposed to get the real facts behind the facts of this, all we are likely to get of it is some description of the descriptive process itself. Nature describes science to itself in this way, history explains historians to one another, culture creates its own anthropology in a very original sense.

Social structure or organization and the whole relational set of human interaction is directly meaningful and pragmatically necessary as an unavoidable contagion that affects actor and observer alike. It is real, viable, social, or structural insofar as it imitates interaction itself in its own articulation—the act or art of explaining it—and is therefore contagious in imitating the sense of explanation in human interaction. Without this agency, "behavior" or "interaction" might surely take place, but it would not be sociality.

In more direct terms, one might ask what difference explanation makes, and what effects its conscious use might be shown to have. For an exemplification I shall turn to the social organization of the Usen (southern) Barok, a people of central New Ireland. Usen informants consistently volunteered the borrowed English word "meaning" with respect to what I would call the contagious factor, and it was clear that the word was intended in a "strong" or comprehensive sense. But the fact remains that, as a nonindigenous word, or just simply as a word, it is a poor substitute for the *pidik,* the experiential "trick" or transformation through which, Barok insist, significance must be apprehended to be valid at all. Thus their commonly uttered remark, that "words trick you," is at once a condemnation and a justification of language.

The mortuary feasting cycle of the Barok, which Barok themselves identify as crucial or central to their *kastam,* has many analogues among other Austronesian-speaking peoples in Indonesia and the Pacific. There are particular similarities to mortuary feasting in the Massim region, among the Bush Mekeo,[1] and in the graded men's societies of Vanuatu. It is difficult to determine whether these complexes ought to be considered "social," "political," or "religious," and this difficulty underlines the fact that they are total cultural institutions. The "cultural" must be insisted upon, for all the fact that the usages operate upon and through social position, for, like the *ban* initiations of the "Mountain Ok" region of New Guinea,[2] they are based on epistemological transformations and realizations.

In the Barok case the comprehensive sense of this "meaning" encompasses the social. The protocol and paraphernalia of mortuary feasting are invoked for *all* occasions of social validation, including all forms of entitlement and propriety—the "fixing" of names, as well as all instances of property transmission, marriages as well as deaths, the installment of political leaders, and all cases involving strong social shame. *Cultural* meaning is, in short, the seal of social validation.

Most explicitly, issues involving kin relations and property transmission among the Usen Barok are not rendered comprehensible or easily explainable through a bare description of lineality or social rights and obligations *without taking reperception into account.* The question centers upon patrilateral inheritance or transmission of property, *nat-lo,* which, rather than a foil for matrilateral transmission, is treated as its equivalent. The most spectacular example involves the deeding over of a men's house, or *taun,* in this way. Although sponsored by a particular clan member, a *taun* cannot be raised without the intensive cooperation of clanmates, in terms of labor and wealth. Every section of the surrounding stone wall, *a balat,* and every other structural member or architectural facet of the complex must be constructed through collective efforts and consecrated through daily feasting. The feasts for important features, like the *bagot* (threshold log) or the *olaɟabo* (main gate) require pigs, and the outlay for the consecration of the *taun* itself is properly equivalent to a small mortuary feast.

The *taun* is made of feasts, virtually, as much as it is made through labor, and the labor as well as the wealth represent the potential and propriety of the sponsor's matrilineage, often drawing on resources of clan and moiety at large as well. Despite the extent of this investment, and the fact that the ritual increment of a lineage, clan, or moiety is embodied in its *taun*s, the sponsor is recognized as having a perfect right to deed his *taun* over to his (wife's) children as *nat-lo.* The right is not contested and, so long as it has been validated by an appropriate feast in the *taun,* the transmission cannot be gainsaid or abrogated. A number of *taun*s with which I was familiar had, in recent history, changed clan and moiety affiliation in this way, including the one in Bakan Village with which I was associated.

In every traditional sense, the Barok are a matrilineal people; each person is born to the clan and moiety of his or her mother, and moiety exogamy is severely and consistently enforced through social sanctions.[3] There are no changes of moiety affiliation. Moreover, normative kin usages and relationships bear out the conventions of matrilineal forms elsewhere: a strong cross-sex sibling taboo, authority relations with the maternal uncle, and a strong, supportive bond between the paternal aunt and her brother's children. On the other hand, there is a potentially antagonistic snatching/joking relationship *(naluwinin)* between a man and the males of his father's matriline—precisely those who would be cast into an adversarial relationship through the transmission of wealth as *nat-lo.* And the "snatching" is apt to be heavy: large sums of money are taken, or one's truck or radio, or perhaps all of one's clothes.

Even in the barest outline, this description is so suggestive of Lévi-Strauss's "dysharmonic regime" of matrilineal descent coupled with virilocal postmarital residence that it should come as no surprise that Barok state a preference for virilocality. Yet even here, the attention that

Barok give to *pidik* and transformation *as a mode of knowing* should sound a cautionary note: is the so-called dysharmony not in itself evidence that mere "descent" is a simplification, that the "dysharmony" perceived in the scholarly effort to classify types of descent is more real than the "regime" ordained by that effort? For "dysharmony" is simply the way in which transformation appears when projected onto a static schema.

Barok "matriliny" is grounded, in short, *in its very equivalence to paternal connection, rather than in contrast to it.* But to comprehend this apparently paradoxical point it is necessary to consider the concretivity, the totality of imagery that constitutes the meanings of Barok sociality. Such a concretivity holds and generates (contains and elicits) the analogies that we identify as kin substance and kin connection. The "substances," Barok would want to say, even the relationships, are "tricks" of the *pidik,* and they inhere within a range of meanings that is larger than those of kinship alone. What appear as "moieties," "clans," or "lineages," the elicitative nurturance of fatherhood, the containment of motherhood, are analogies developed within this range, not analytic "primitives" or beginning points.

Barok *orong* ("big men," organizers and leaders in feasting) maintain that two motifs or images are manifest in everything they do.[4] These are *kolume* (*ko-lume,* literally "at the middle," or "at the inside"), or containment, and the *gala,* the thorn or thrusting tree limb of inception, cutting, penetration, or, in general, elicitation. *Kolume* is exemplified by the encompassment of a child in the womb, a corpse in the ground, or ritually by the "icon of containment," the *taun,* with its enclosing stone wall. *Gala* is exemplified most often as an angular tree branch or erect penis, or by the stylized gesture of holding traditional strung shell money up for display, with the right hand elevated. Ritually, *gala* is exemplified by a tree.

Together *kolume* and *gala* generate the iconography of Barok *kastam,* the "social *pidik*" (Fig. 2). The totality of the imagery in this reperceptive form is realized through the interrelation of these two motifs. Within the iconography itself, for instance, the ground of the *taun* (depicted as seen from above in Fig. 2) is bisected by the *gala* of the threshold log *(a bagot)* into a feasting *(gala)* and a burial *(kolume)* space. Likewise, the tree trunk is cut by the *kolume* of the ground into halves imaging nurturance and burial. Within the *taun,* the feasting space *(konono)* is in fact a containment of feasting framed by *gala*—between the "trunk" of the *bagot* and the "limbs" of the gate *(olagabo).*

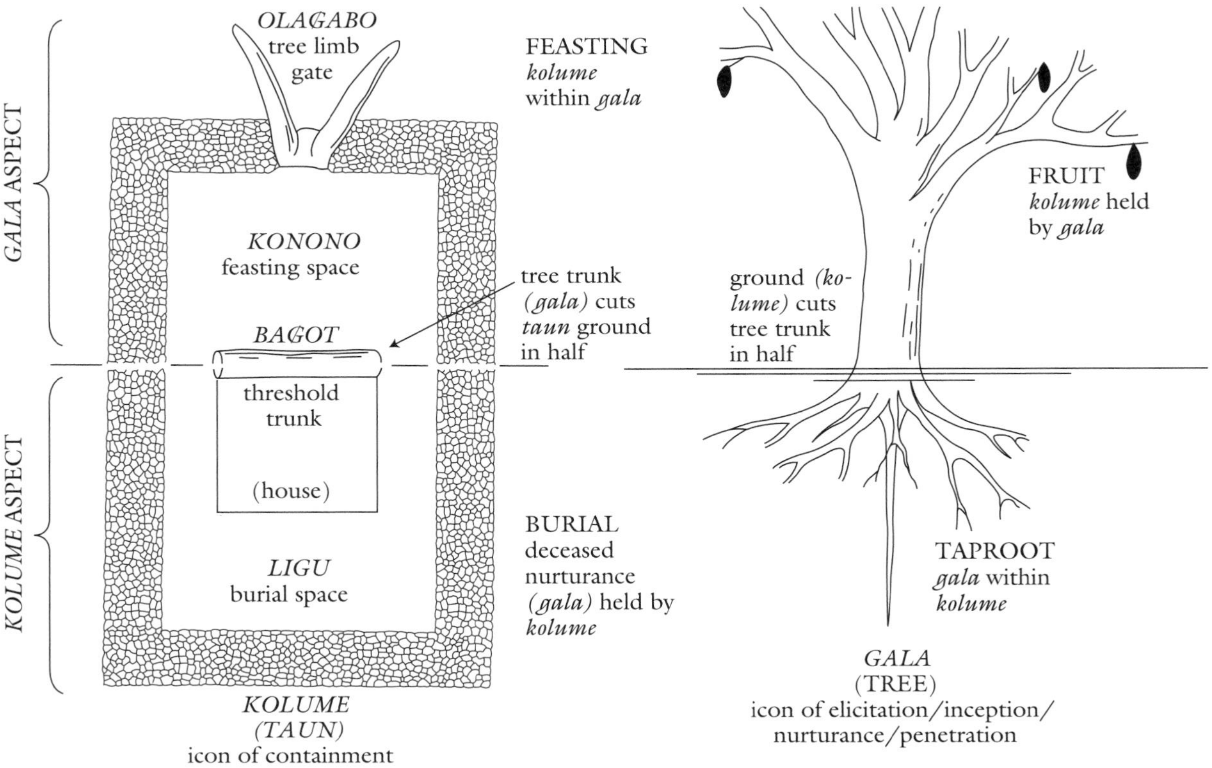
GALA ASPECT
KOLUME ASPECT
OLAĠABO
tree limb
gate
KONONO
feasting space
BAĠOT
threshold
trunk
(house)
LIGU
burial space
KOLUME
(TAUN)
icon of containment
FEASTING
kolume
within gala
tree trunk
(gala) cuts
taun ground
in half
BURIAL
deceased
nurturance
(gala) held by
kolume
ground (ko-
lume) cuts
tree trunk
in half
FRUIT
kolume held
by gala
TAPROOT
gala within
kolume
GALA
(TREE)
icon of elicitation/inception/
nurturance/penetration

Figure 2. *Iri lolos* iconography.

The *ligu,* or burial space, contains the nurturance *(gala)* of the other moiety within the *kolume* of its ground. Correlatively, the *gala* aspect of the tree proffers the *kolume* of enclosed tree-fruit as its nurturance, whereas the subterranean *kolume* section features the *gala* of the taproot, identified by Barok with the apical ancestress (Fig. 2).

This iconography, taken in itself, is *kolume,* a synchronic outlay of the imagery containing in its imagistic compass the totality of the *pidik*'s possibilities. Barok call this aspect *iri lolos* (finished power), the human imaging, or containment, of the eliciting of power, *a lolos.* But *iri lolos* is not *a lolos,* for it wants the elicitation, *gala,* of temporally enacted feasting. Western analogues of "finished power" might be a book, an equation, or a musical score; the reading of the book, application of the equation, or performance of the music is *a lolos.*

By the same token, neither *iri lolos* nor the analogies developed out of it are "symbols," either in the explicit, referential sense or in the broader sense of "context markers." A father, for instance, "elicits" his children, in the procreative relation of supplying *pege* (semen, but "father's blood") that transforms the mother's *pege a une* ("female semen," or vaginal secretion) into the "clean blood" that starts an embryo. Thus he elicits the mother's "containment." And the father provides food, shelter, and protection for mother and children as part of his elicitory nurturance. A mother "contains" the clean blood, the embryo, and the children within her body and her lineality. But *gala* is a broader and more general concept than "fatherhood" and should not be interpreted as a "male symbol"; *kolume* is in the same sense not "female," nor a female symbol.

Nor is it simply that moiety and gender are analogic functions of the same basic concretivity, but also that they replicate the essential reciprocality of the concretivity. Each gender and each moiety is constituted by and of the relation between the two. Thus the "substance" of each moiety is the nurturance provided by the other; its containment is elicited, and the nurturance it offers in return is, in its turn, contained. A father's nurturance is made possible by his mother's (and his moiety's) original containment of what he passes on; a mother's containment is rendered viable by her father's nurturance, her *nat.* But specifics of this sort, analytic "vectors" or what we might wish to consider as "interpretations," are not felt by Barok to be worthy of articulation. "Words trick you," and in this case they trick you into always having to make partial or incomplete statements, particular refractions of a totality that require further qualification.

Thus the preferred elicitation of *a lolos* is neither verbal nor analytic; it must be enacted by making feasts, demonstrating image transformation through the feasting cycle itself. But even this implementation is wordless. Should the ethnographer choose to put a Barok informant "on the spot" by asking him to describe, step by step, the protocol of a feast in the *taun*, he will respond by describing an *imagined* feast, reperceived through memory. There is no mnemonic save the experience itself.

If it is clear that men are the *doers*, elicitors of *a lolos*, then women are its *containers*. A woman, the Barok say, is her own *pidik*; women have no need of protocol, solemnity, order, or ritual. Hence, entitled as they are to an exactly equal share of the coconuts, areca nut, betel pepper, pork, and tubers (always scrupulously awarded them), women hold an "equal but opposite" feast. They congregate, sitting or standing as they wish, in the open area between the *pan*, or women's cooking house, and the *taun*, and make a purposive show of unconstraint, parodying the seriousness and order of the feast in the *taun*. They drink coconuts by punching holes in the ends, whereas the men *must* cut the fruit cleanly across the middle, and frequently entertain themselves with impromptu parodies and skits. Most important, their feasts are not differentiated into contrastive "kinds."

A formal feast in the *taun* is open to all males who might wish to attend; all are welcome to a precisely equal portion of the "refreshers" (areca nut, betel pepper, and green drinking coconut) and comestibles (pork and tubers) served. Their "needs" of hunger and weariness are "contained" by the nurturant plenitude of the *taun*, its sponsor, and his moiety (just as the *taun* is always technically accessible to all men who might wish to sleep and eat there). Containment of these needs elicits the ethic of *malili* (serenity; "the belly of the people is untroubled, like the calm sea"). Good fellowship and friendly discourse among feasters constitute the demonstration of *malili*, and breaches of the ethic are subject to stiff fines. Behavior at the feast, in other words, respects also the ethic of *malum*, humility and forbearance in consideration of the dead buried in the rear *(ligu)* of the *taun*. Hence feasting elicits a containment of prized comestibles within feasters that the *taun*'s feasting space *(konono)*, in turn, contains; it likewise elicits a forbearance on the part of those feasters in respect to the *taun*'s *other* containment, that of the dead.

The protocol of feasting makes use of this elicitory effect to activate *iri lolos* and bring it to a reperceptive realization of *a lolos*—the certainty of a subjectivity witnessing its own self-perception. It galvanizes *kolume* and *gala* into a temporal order that is at once the "shape" of the individual feast in time and that of the succession of *kinds* of feasts that make up the mortuary cycle (Fig. 3). The order proceeds from *kolume* to *gala* to a conjoint product realized as the trope *kolume-gala*, the simultaneity of containment and elicitation perceived at once, and perceived as one. The simultaneity is actually present holographically throughout the whole concretivity (evidenced in the complete interdigitation of *kolume* and *gala* in the iconography of Figure 2; hence "finished power"). And the necessity of elicitation is that of "opening" this wholeness out to the experience of witnesses. To take perhaps the simplest example from the holography, the *kolume* of a green coconut must be cut *(gala)* if its content is to be realized as refreshment.

The *konono*, or feasting area at the front of a *taun*, is arranged so that the feasters, sitting on benches along the sides and front of the enclosure, and in the *gunun*, just behind the threshold log, completely enclose the food on display. The "refreshers" served in the first course, green drinking coconut *(polo)*, areca nut *(buo)*, and the accompanying betel pepper *(sie)* are arrayed on the *butam*, a display table in the center of the *konono*. Tubers for the second course are likewise displayed on the *butam*, whereas the cooked whole pigs (enclosed within a sewn leaf envelope) are laid out in the space between the *butam* and the house *(gunun)*. Following the display, each course proceeds to the cutting or breaking open of the foodstuffs *(gala)*: in the first course, the betel pepper is taken out of its leaf wrappers, the areca sprigs are broken apart and distributed, and individual feasters cut their green coconuts (exactly across the center) for drinking. In the second course the display concludes with speeches by the sponsor of the feast and other *orong*, and with the purchase of the (cooked) pigs from their owners, after which the pigs are cut, beginning with a bisection exactly across the center. The consumption of the courses is of course containment and nurturance at once.

The cutting of the pig, the central act of the "middle" portion (the *gala*) of the feast, cuts the feast in half as well. Performed in front of the threshold log, which cuts the *taun* in half, it lends its name metonymically to the whole practice of ritual feasting: *bet lulut* or *kurubo*. Prior to this act, during the first course and continuing through the speeches and purchase of the pigs, the feasters remain seated in quiet, orderly fashion around the *konono*. Following the cutting, beginning during the ensuing consumption, a more relaxed and informal atmosphere and

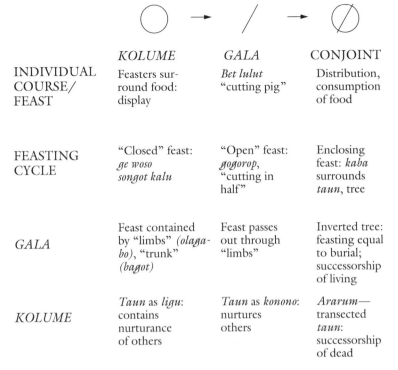

TEMPORAL SEQUENCE

	KOLUME	*GALA*	CONJOINT
INDIVIDUAL COURSE/ FEAST	Feasters sur- round food: display	*Bet lulut* "cutting pig"	Distribution, consumption of food
FEASTING CYCLE	"Closed" feast: *ge woso songot kalu*	"Open" feast: *gogorop*, "cutting in half"	Enclosing feast: *kaba* surrounds *taun*, tree
GALA	Feast contained by "limbs" *(olaga- bo)*, "trunk" *(bagot)*	Feast passes out through "limbs"	Inverted tree: feasting equal to burial; successorship of living
KOLUME	*Taun* as *ligu*: contains nurturance of others	*Taun* as *konono*: nurtures others	*Ararum*— transected *taun*: successorship of dead

Figure 3. *Iri lolos* protocol.

pattern of behavior prevail. Like the individual course, the feast as a whole is cut by its *gala*.

This generic form of feast is in turn differentiated into the "kinds" of feasts that make up a cycle, epitomized by the cycle of mortuary feasts that follow a death. Immediately upon receiving news of a death, the whole region goes under a restriction called *lebe:* no work is to be done, no large fires may be made, and anger and loud talking are forbidden. The feast on the day of death *(Ge Woso)* and those that immediately follow *(Songot Kalu)* are "closed feasts," imaging the *taun* as container *(kolume)* of the dead. The food for these feasts is provided by the opposite moiety (to that of the *taun*), and no food (in some cases no refuse either) may be taken out of the *taun*. Food is distributed at these feasts beginning at the gate *(olagabo)* and proceeding inward to the house, and the cooked pigs are displayed facing the rear *(ligu)*. Generally the first series of feasts is terminated by a feast called *Korop Kinis,* made to formally lift the *lebe*.

Ideally the second course of feasts should be held when the body of the deceased has decomposed, so that its substance is held in the earth of the *ligu*. These feasts, called *Gogorop* (cutting in half), *gala* to the *kolume* of the previous set, image the *taun*, replete with its dead, as the nurturer of others. They are "open" feasts; food is provided by the moiety of the *taun* itself, and it may be taken out of the enclosure. Distribution begins at the house and proceeds outward, and the pigs are displayed facing the front of the *taun*, with its gate.

The *Gogorop* in fact "cuts" the *taun*, turning the containment of its enclosure and its burial into nurturance, and so stands at the midpoint of the feasting cycle. And it follows that the *next* feast, the final one to "finish all thought" of the deceased, *must be held outside of the taun*. Otherwise (as my informants acknowledged when I raised this point with them in 1983) its significance would destroy the meaning of the *taun*. Instead of an enclosed feast, consisting of prepared foods contained within the *taun*, the *Kaba* is an enclosing feast, a figure-ground reversal of *unprepared* foods that contains the iconography, which has now become the *gala* of the tree.[5] In this sense, too, the *Kaba* inverts the successorship relation; whereas the "closed" feasts immediately after the death enacted the *ancestorship* of the deceased, the *Kaba* instantiates the *successorship* of the living to the dead.

As we might expect, the *Kaba* exists in two forms: the *agana ya,* or "branch of the tree," the lesser and more common form, sponsored by an established *orong,* and the *una ya,* "base of the tree," which enacts the successorship of a neophyte *orong*. Because it thus grounds the pre-eminent authority relation in Barok society, the *una ya,* with its explicit figure-ground reversal of the tree itself, is the definitive form. *Kaba* are held at widely spaced intervals, to "finish" those who have died during the intervening periods, but the *una ya* form is, even at that, something of a rarity, seldom occurring more than once in a generation in the Usen area.

Preparation for a *Kaba* begins years in advance, with the solicitory presentation to responsible *orong* of strung shell-disk wealth as *kuruse,* to be reciprocated with a full-grown pig at the time of the *Kaba.* As the time approaches, gardens will be planted to provide food for the series of preliminary feasts, as well as the *Kaba* itself. Affines and other helpers generally move to the site to assist in the prodigious labor, sometimes constructing a temporary hamlet for the occasion.

In the case of the *una ya Kaba,* which I will consider here, this work begins when the gardens are ready to bear. A suitable tree of the appropriate variety is located and cut off about six feet from the ground. Each of the main roots is then dug out of the soil to a length of several feet, a feast being held for the completed excavation of each. The cutting of the taproot occasions a major feast, with pigs. The rootstock is raised on a structure of vines and poles and carried to the feasting site by an assembled throng, with the decorated neophyte *orong (winawu)* riding atop it, requiring another major feast. The rootstock is then *inverted* at the site, with the roots pointing upward, and the roots are then converted into a platform (each of these steps necessitates its own pig feast). This is followed by a crescendo of major feasts involving the respective moieties' competitive decoration of the *Kaba,* and festooning it with shell-disk wealth.

At the culminating rite, the *Kaba* feast, the now-resplendent root platform is piled with the carcasses of dead and eviscerated (but not cooked or cut) pigs. The *winawu* stands atop the pigs, at the location of the (cut) taproot, often accompanied by young boys *(igisinbo),* who are hopeful *orong*-to-be. Splendidly attired with strung shell wealth and a *kapkap* "sun" ornament about his neck, the *winawu* flourishes the most emphatic *gala*—a lance *(sie)* and the traditional fighting ax *(asok).* Around the base of the *Kaba,* at points where the (imagined) subterranean branches of the inverted tree would break the soil, decorated young, nubile women *(dawan)* are perched on stylized tree forks, like fruit dangling upward. The *winawu* is a young man occupying the place of the taproot, which Barok equate with the apical ancestress, the most

ancient woman founder of clan, moiety, or people. The *dawan* around
the base are women occupying the place of tree-fruit, which Barok identify with out-married males giving their gift of nurturance to other units.
Hence gender succeeds opposite gender as young succeed old; moreover the assertive *gala* of the *winawu* becomes the ultimate *kolume*,
whereas the *kolume* of the *dawan* becomes a nurturing gift of containment to other lines. It matters not if male and female are transposed, or
young and old, *gala* and *kolume*, or moiety and moiety; the outcome is
the same. What is contained, but elicitation, and what is elicited, but
containment?

What has happened to the "grip," the purchase, of symbols here, or
of concepts? A key lies in the shouted invocation of the *winawu: asiwinarong*, "the *siwin* of an orong." And *siwin*, which Barok render into
English as "need" (the need of, a need for) implies an empty space, a
shelled core, and might most felicitously be translated as "contingency."
But the contingency of a subjective feeling that is itself movement,
equipoise, and identity among opposites is the contingency to do as
one pleases. Hence *asiwinarong* might also mean "the will of an *orong*,"
in the sense of free will, and as Barok say that the *Kaba* can only be
performed "merely because the *orong* wishes to," and for no other reason. As long as the will is entailed by reasons and concerns, the grip or
purchase of symbols and concepts, it is not free will, and it is thus no
will at all.

The "will of an *orong*" is the indulgence of the *winawu*, a neophyte
who is at once young man and apical ancestress *by position*. His counterparts are the *dawan*, nubile brides-to-be in the position of nurturant, authoritative married men. The *winawu* has overcome the formidable social shame of speaking his will in public, as the *dawan* have
become nurturant females by realizing the mystery, or *pidik*, of their
own bodies in attaining menarche. The corresponding *pidik*, the mystery or "trick" of the *winawu*, is that *he knows nothing of the source
whereof he speaks*. He has been elaborately coached by the *un na winawu*
(base of the *winawu*), an experienced *orong* who stands at the base
of the *Kaba*, in his mouthing of the ritual phrases and in his indulgence and freedom in overcoming shame. Will has moved *outside* in the
winawu as its nurturant power has moved *inside* the bodies of the
dawan; knowledge of the whole, insight, remains fixed at the positional
center of the whole image—with the *un na winawu*.

The *Kaba* in its two forms, the *una ya* and the *agana ya* (where a
forked tree trunk—upright—surmounts a platform of pigs), enacts

the successorship of the living, the nurturant *(gala)* form of reperception, as the "feast around the tree." It thus realizes the "turning" of mortuary feasting toward the future, the "finishing" of the dead. But the holism of the iconography, its fidelity to "scale," so to speak, implies also a *kolume* form of reperception, a counterbalancing enactment of the successorship of the dead. This is attained in the "tabooing" *(ararum)* of a *taun,* in which the *taun* space is *transected* at right angles to the "cutting" of the *bagot* (Fig. 3, bottom row; Fig. 4). The resulting *ararum* section is undifferentiated, for it is *ligu* and *konono* at once, a conflation of their functions and thus a horizontal analogue of the inverted tree.

Whereas the *una ya Kaba* is invoked and directed by a *young* man, a neophyte, access to the *ararum taun* is ordinarily restricted to *salup,* old men "with beards." These are men who have already had the *Gogorop a Toin* (a special form of the mortuary feasts) performed for them, and thus are culturally "dead." *Their* feasting is consequently equivalent to burial, and it is significant that they were said, in precontact times, to have feasted secretly in the *ararum* on human flesh. Corpses were provided by the *umri,* the traditional fight leader, whose work in arranging human deaths was often seen to parallel that of the *orong* in killing pigs for ordinary feasts.

The *ararum* is *closed* reperception, its feasting functions secluded rather than ostentatiously public, as in the *Kaba.* And if the work of the *Kaba* is, as Barok often say, "cooking the pigs on top of the dead," then the *salup* would seem to be cooking the dead on top of the pigs; if the *Kaba* "finishes all thought of the dead," the sobriquet for the *ararum* is "the part where food is finished."[6] *No* food or feasting refuse may ever, under any circumstances, be removed from the *ararum* section, and the consecration feast for the tabooing is the most restrictive (and expensive—payment is exacted from those attending for every detail of the procedure) of any Barok feast.

There are, then, two ways of "becoming an ancestor," the *gala* of the *Kaba,* and its *kolume* "backlash" of the *ararum.* The *winawu* "preempts" the containment of matrilateral succession through his act of assertion, encompassing the origination of lineality itself. The *salup,* technically "dead" to the rites of feasting, turn their feasting, traditionally, into an act of burial. Both *Kaba* and *ararum* embody acts of male successorship within a lineality that is rigidly defined in matrilateral terms, and hence carry a strong implication of *nat-lo,* of the will and the right of the enacting male to "do as he wishes." What is most important,

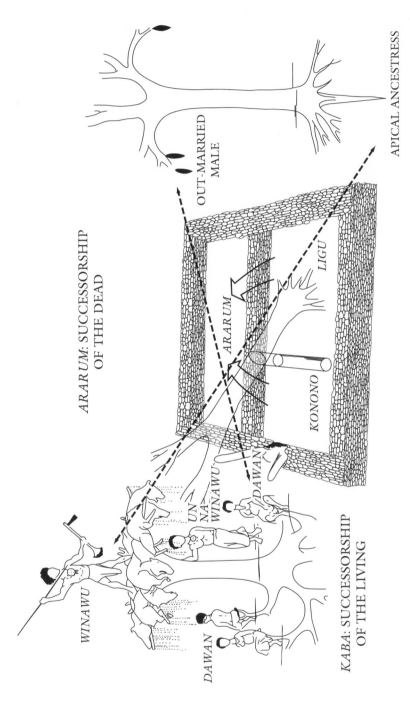

ARARUM: SUCCESSORSHIP
OF THE DEAD

OUT-MARRIED
MALE

APICAL ANCESTRESS

ARARUM

LIGU

KONONO

WINAWU

UN-
NA-
WINAWU

DAWAN

DAWAN

KABA: SUCCESSORSHIP
OF THE LIVING

Figure 4. Two ways of becoming an ancestor.

however, is that their "entitlement" in so doing, the cultural validation accomplished through feasting, is achieved in the conflation of *kolume* and *gala* (ultimately iconography and feasting, containment and nurturance), the elemental concepts through which gender and moiety are defined. The *taun* transmitted as *nat-lo* becomes in this light the nurturing containment of one moiety granted to the other, exactly as the *dawan* are married out to carry the containment of clan and moiety elsewhere.

The *siwin* of the *orong* is the volitional "moment" or force of the conflation, a kind of master trope. The intended trope itself (e.g., what those working in a "sign" tradition would want to call the "signified") cannot be identified with anything analyzable as *kolume* or *gala*, since these are the bounding parameters of the trope, its formal terms. But *gala* and *kolume* comprehend *everything* in the relevant universe of discourse, so that a trope formed by conflating them is holistic. But this is a whole that is perfused distributively throughout the entire range of discourse, exactly to the scale in which *gala* and *kolume* are conjoined. Hence the image is holographic, admitting of no part-whole relations save those of identity.

Such a totality can hardly be said to be "constructed" of parts that are identical to one another as well as to their sum, and a "meaningful interpretation" of their interaction would be the purest tautology. The whole is *perceived*, not articulated, but perceived through the very *impossibility* of forming the perception around a descrete figure or object or of an assemblage of objects, or even of making a figure of the totality. The complete and seamless congruity of *gala* and *kolume* resists any formation of a figure. And because such a figure would be necessary as the trope for the formation of an "internal" or subjective image, the reperception is also not a perception of "self," a subjective one. Intentionality is not perceived, for the means through which perception could be guided to that end have been exhausted, and that exhaustion has been made self-evident, in the demonstration; intentionality is only claimed, or "owned," in reperception. Holography makes the "metonymic" relation of element to implied context or sequence, the synecdoche of part to whole into the nonrelation of identity, involving the "substitution" of metaphor in the replacement of the figure or element with itself.

Hence the conceptual holism or totality that has been the unrealizable dream of structural or functional anthropology, the gestalt or unity of culture, resists systematicity, relation, or integration in any form at its very point of closure. It is a vanishing point, inimical to order, useful even in its ideal or heuristic form only in situations where there is no hope or possibility of ever achieving closure. Thus the holographic conjunction of *gala* and *kolume* is not a cultural or structural integration, the intentional goal or end of a social or cognitive process, but merely the means of reperception. Barok *iri lolos* is not the power *of* society in some Durkheimian sense but is its own thing, a power *over* society that is the detached, or in more colloquial terms, the "dumped," of reperception. The power of society is not worth fighting for, is not worth even describing.

As for the power over society, Barok say that the *Kaba* is held "only because the *orong* wishes it, and for no other reason." And if there is no necessity other than this to the overcoming of necessity, then it is not necessary either for anyone, *winawu* or *un na winawu*, participant or spectator, to actually experience the reperception of the *Kaba*. The demonstration alone is sufficient, but sufficient only because the *orong* wishes it, and for no other reason. The *Kaba* is not a projector, and reperception is not a motion picture.

Reperception, like volition, is always implicated in human consciousness, *is* human consciousness. Only that which is *not* reperceived, or "seen through," is seen or remembered, thrown into the relief of perception or memory as its object. Though it empowers Usen Barok inheritance, status, and legitimacy, makes their objectification possible, reperception is not inherited, has no status, and stands in no need of demonstration or legitimation.

As the achieved "second sight" of ritual, reperception is the focus made by a pragmatic knowledge, not one of images or things but of human capability or power, the Barok *a lolos*. What we call image, or trope, is not its focus but its *foil*, the deception of figures and ground that must be shed or detached for knowledge to regain the resistance that memory forgets and perception focuses out.

What distances the volitional or intentional from our direct experience, resists any attempt to explain it or delineate its workings, is its *priority* to action and perception. Already in place when we try to place it, part of the act that would act upon it or the perception that would perceive it, intentionality is the ground or field of action and movement, a ground automatically excluded from the figure of thought. The *Kaba*'s transformation of *gala* and *kolume*, and of the social and gender properties they may focus or organize, into the form of one another's content and the content of one another's form, a holography, does not and cannot delineate or represent the subject's intent, but merely completes the action of detachment.

But if the reperception were understood as something that happens to *other* people, an ethnographic, a Barok, perhaps a human *phenomenon,* the pragmatic basis for an understanding that can only be *one's own* would be removed. Relation, with its implications of common experience, "intersubjectivity," or emotional participation, is not the achievement but just precisely the *foil* of reperception. "Othering," and its relational vectors, is what reperception detaches. To try and experience what those other people experience, to even elaborate intellectually upon what their understanding of image and human action must be, "groove" on an irony they must feel, would be to *attach* the foil rather than to shed it. Whatever implications reperception might have for semiotics, social science, and our "ethical" treatment of others amount to the shock effect, the embarrassment of expectations we bring that, were it allowed to run full course, would lead to our reperception.

4

Our Sense of Their Humor: Their Sense of Ours

Bilateral symmetry and sexual dimorphism are features that human beings share with most "complex" or highly articulated forms of animal life. In all of these species "symmetry" means that laterality, or "sidedness," is twinned inward, with distinctive "right" and "left" counterparts. Gender is twinned *outward* in the form of separate organisms and body shapes, distinctive *kinds* of body rather than distinctive sides of the same thing. The twinning has many aspects; it can be found in the DNA, the configuration of members, organs, and systemic features, in the doubling/halving of reproduction, and even in the way that the physical being seconds itself in its dreams. But only in the human species is this generic feature properly a *twinning,* a mode of appositional self-knowledge that defines its distinctive character quite as much as any physical features.

Philosophers or anthropologists might wish to characterize this patent of our uniqueness as reflexivity or self-reflection, and Jacques Lacan identified in it a kind of autoimaging he called the "mirror-reflection ego."[1] More generally it is attributed to a kind of self-privileging notion called "sentience," perhaps equivalent to consciousness, intelligence, self-awareness, or some combination or modification of them. My point here is not to confirm or deny these observations and speculations, or indeed add to them, but merely to point out that they fall far short of twinning. Twinning is a knowledge rather than simply an ability to know, and it implies an image or reflection of something other than the self.

In other words, the knowledge would not be a knowledge *of* something if it did not have an object, and if that knowledge plays a part in our definition, a radical simplification can be made. The twinning is itself twinned with an antithetical form of itself, two polar and inversional types that transcend the basic animal dualization by exhausting its possible permutations. The "Antitwins," as I shall call them, are constituted respectively by twinning gender inward and twinning laterality outward. They are distinctive in relation to the generic animal form by underdetermining the physical body and overdetermining its attributes. As disembodied concomitants or gender symmetries they are one-sided beings, like magnetic monopoles, and must twin with each other to realize their twinning with us, to have a shape and a role in the world.

The part they play in our knowledge is the part we play in their being. But to understand the full implication of this, including the roles they play in substituting for our social and mental being, it will be necessary to review their functional counterparts in the generic of our physical constitution.

The form of acute *embodiment* that objectifies our physical presence or organic being is a twinning *inward* of all the parts and functions we might use to model extension or relation in the world. There are no "spaces" between the sides in the body's laterality, else they would not be sides of the same thing. All of our work and pleasure is done in an acute comparison and contrast of our lateral extensions—putting one foot before another, using the shoulders, arms, and hands in contrast and coordination, perhaps synchronizing these motions and the motions within the brain without realizing that a single motion is involved. The very singularity of the one motion, the body's *kinesthesia,* is strange to us because its laterality models the familiarity of it, its family resemblances in all the models we make for it.

Laterality is simply the *breadth* of our world; it is the way in which extension grasps *us* in our grasping of it, mentally as well as physically. It makes no difference from the standpoint of this contrast/coordination whether the sides of the body itself, left and right, are considered as the archetypal template of the whole or whether, "on the other hand," their inverse connection to the right and left hemispheres of the brain's neocortex are taken into consideration as well. Left-right and right-left are still the Twins, twinned inward within themselves as they twin inwardly with one another. The "split-brain" functions of the prefrontal hemispheres play a remarkable and self-emphatic role in this. The Barok might have designed them. For they mimic the automimetic role of brain-in-the-body, its ability to think itself thinking, perfectly. The ostensible "left-brain" character models the distinction *between* the hemispheres as a specific function of one of them *(gala)*. The "right-brain" models the unity or totality so completely that it "contains" *(kolume)* the encompassing body as well: mind's body within body's mind.

But if the bodily functions "echo" themselves, scaling the pulse or heartbeat, breathing, the "lightning" of the neural net back upon their own rhythms, body copies and is copied by an invisible anticipatory twin as well. The physical body is the convergence of two temporal twins. From the moment of its birth and before the body throws itself blindly into a dimension that is invisible and intangible to it, and learns to do so with uncanny speed and agility. What it senses and knows of the world *is no longer there in that way* at the moment of its sensing or cognition. Moreover, and more important, the sensed or remembered shape of circumstance *was also not there in that way* in the moment just recollected, for at that moment the consciousness was busy recalling an earlier moment. And so on backward in what amounts to an indefinite regression of sense, pragmatic afterlife. If the twin components of our shape in time could be extended respectively backward and forward to double the whole outline of our existence, we could be present only at the point of their convergence.

The inceptive or *previous* twin is always *ahead* of its counterpart in time, precocious of its own conception, gestation, and birth; the shape of the embryo before it was an embryo, and of its conception before it was a conception. Yet it is not mystical or spiritual, and is neither more nor less real than the linear conception of time. Apart from its artificial "staging" in this way, it is a mark of recognition for *exactly the same* twinning by inward convergence as is met in the body's laterality, its convergence with itself in matching the brain, and the brain's convergence with itself in matching the body.

Twinning inward is singular to the shape and motion of the body, personal to the individual as the sides of its being or temperament, and therefore personal as well to another kind of twinning that is germinal to its being there at all. Gender twins us outward into two *kinds* of the double-sided body, makes the shape of the twin we do not have by analogy to the one that we do. The Barok could have designed them, too, as the shape that contains and the shape that decontains its own offspring. There is the return to the womb, the marriage in utero, gestation, and parturition, all of them predestined to the separation of bodies. And there is the sense and anticipation of each kind of body within the other, regardless of whether sex takes place, and regardless of whether generation is involved at all. Freud would remind us that most of the world's sex takes place without bodily contact, as a sexuality about things. Subconscious or not (for in most cases it is the most *conscious* thing imaginable) that is how subjectivity reproduces itself.

The twin that we do not have and the twin that we do have are twins, twinned in their respective inward and outward definitions as the genders are twinned, or the sides of the body. That much of the twinning is unreflective body knowledge for most animal species. Our knowledge of it *as* a twinning, the knowing of twinning itself, is a human knowledge.

A basic anthropology of the subject can be set up by demonstrating the very condensed and compact embodiment of twinning exotically to itself, ringing the changes of a paradigm that is not really a paradigm at all. The Antitwins are polar opposites of what it means to be a whole person, polar in twinning with each other and polar in their twinning with those who would imagine them. They are half-beings with symmetrical gender, gender symmetries.

Thus they part company with the kinds of human *impersonations,* robotic constructions of human constitution, capability, and appetite upon which much of medical, social, and natural science thinking, and even advertising, depends for its heuristic credibility. Appositive to human embodiment, they represent the opposite of medical man, economic man, social or fossil man or woman, the "person" in the machine or in history, the "observer" in quantum physics and relativity. They do not impersonate or take the role of the human but rather *expersonate* it; they mate us with each other, throw our dice, take the opponent's role in the chess of our chances. We would not so much comprehend them as apprehend them, take their queen and mate their king.

If we impersonate two in one in our laterality and one in two in our gendered being, they represent the other twin of this, expersonate the one-of-two and the two-of-one. Taken together they would constitute a whole person with too much gender. Taken together in the full cohesion of sociality necessary to keep and reproduce ourselves, we would constitute something like a marriage, a family, or a social group—a wholeness of gender with too much "personality" for its own good.

Figure 5 shows the one-of-two, gender twinned *inward* upon itself in the fetalized posture of simultaneously reproduced and reproducing being—two half-beings locked in a pose that is at once the mutuality and the ambivalence of copulation and parturition to one another. There is

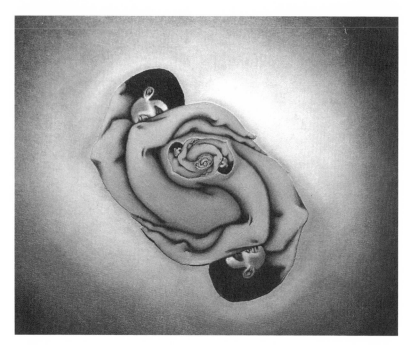

Figure 5. Twincest: one of two.

also the embryo, contained by one of them but in scale containing both of them in a kind of recondite analogy of right-brain functioning. This is the icon of incest, the twincest of a figure and a feeling that is simultaneously attractive and repulsive. Is it the very frisson of this image, implicit in all we know of human kinship, that thus compels an otherwise irrational predisposition to ventral copulation? The Barok could not have designed this one; it designed them.

The fatal shape of the fetus, its inception and its demise, is of course the egg's way of making another egg, the anaphor of reproduction reproducing itself. The child-form would not know the motions of love for being the thing danced in them, and once it learned to dance them would no longer be a child. Figure 5 bears no relation to the human fetus or its own "relatedness" in the procreative process, only a family resemblance that witnesses the neediness or dependency of figurative expression. It "takes over" the meaning or process of incest iconically, twins it within itself as a "double" of what it would have to mean or be outside of that twincest. The enigmatic absorption and disappearance of human knowledge or agency in any attempt to rationalize this as "incest prohibition" or fix a likely motive for its origination is thus a containment of the icon itself. It is the "lethal" (e.g., amnesial, forgetful) doubling of the fetal form, the "imago" we begin with, that is likewise the difference between the icon itself and that which it depicts.

Social distinctions and "rules," the delineation of roles, obligations, and responsibilities in kin relations, would not so much be "shared" or consensual ("moral," as Durkheim understood them) as negatively imaged, provoked by the double encompassment of their own depiction. In other words, the aspects of sociality that we would "understand" or work out (how it works, its design) become involuntary "positives"— diagrams, visual tracings of how people relate and reproduce—of its self-inscription. The whole double-edged and "lethal" character of this is itself reflected in most of the classic justifications for incest avoidance, like "the choice between marrying out and dying out" in E. B. Tylor's famous dictum, Westermarck's "overfamiliarity" model, or the specious arguments for avoiding genetic damage.

It is the "sense" of a picture that contains its own depictive (and hence pragmatic "understanding") capabilities that is at issue. The antitwin or polar opposite of agency's disappearance in the folding inward of gender is a mirror image: the self-similarity of gender in the folding outward of lateral agency. Gregory Bateson reminds us that what we see in a mirror is the *back* of an image, our own visage staring back at us through a reversal of the body's direction, with all the laterality twinned outward—right for left and left for right.[2] It is *not* the person who is looking at it, familiar as it may seem, and is actually the one that is watching itself.

The effect of this can be stated much more simply, with all the nonsense about "reflexivity" left out: the antitwin in the mirror has just *borrowed* one's ability to look and see in order to view *itself*. Each "side" of the brain-body complex is viewing the other from an ulterior, twinned-outward point of vantage, so that the original is party to the insight without being anywhere in the reflection at all. The insight is that every person who has ever lived belongs to a single gender that might be called "own gender," one that, regardless of its other attributes, is "gendered" simply by the fact of owning, belonging to it. Own gender exists in contrast to another condition to which no human being has ever belonged, one that would be called "other gender." Two other-genders conjoin with one another in mating, the ostensible male of the female and female of the male, opposite to one another for the very fact that owning claims but one of them. For it would have to be the way in which two invisible motivators of our ordinary sexual prowess merge and conjoin that accounts for the continuity of own gender reproducing itself, which is, on the mirror view of it, all that really happens.

The two-of-one is the opposite kind of figure, in the opposite mode of antidepiction, to the one-of-two. The "adult embryo," as Figure 6 might be called, does not *differ* from the subject of its depiction as its ostensible male and female figures differ from one another, but rather closes upon its own semblance in the way that these two are conflated. It is only the picture it is.

Underdetermined gender and overdetermined agency are the *same* twins, the same ulterior sociality and lethal laterality, in both of their figured manifestations—the figure that cannot be a figure and the figure that is only a figure. They are real, and they become somewhat more than real, a *knowledge* of twinning itself, through the paradox of trying to represent them. In other words, the contrast that twins them with us and with each other is only vicariously significant, actually the difference between what is really there and its ideal or symbolic representation. They are anthropologies of the subject.

If the image seen in the mirror were somehow blurred by the reflexivity of one's seeing it, if the self or subject viewing it were admitted in any but a vicarious sense into the image itself, then a case could be

Figure 6. Two of one: the adult embryo.

made for a self-other reflexivity in the mirror view. But since that is not the case, and the image is sharp and clear, the shape of agency reflected in it is out of our direct control and has nothing of the utility we imagine for it.

The significance of laterality twinned *outward* is often imagined back into the set of our DNA, as if it were a selective tendency that configured us, or at least the species we represent. It is in fact the human *adversary*, a lone evolutionary hunter that is continually stalking our efforts to discover its where, when, and what—the shape in time of the human form that shapes time inwardly upon itself. We separate ourselves off from this twin exactly in proportion to the stealth with which it closes upon us, evolve like the cat, which had to learn to be "no cat" in stalking—so that the cat-*animal* could sustain itself, pounce out of its false nonimage and seize its prey.

Agency that works outside of the distal-proximal extension of the human body, "handling" the ground with one's feet, so to speak, or walking one's hands through their tasks—is not only hard to grasp. It is difficult even to conceive of without lending one's own familiar version of agency outward, objectifying the "no-human." One might think of it in terms of technology's subjective/objective "feedback loop." The wheel, for example, constitutes a distal epicenter for the body's proximal habitude, and its many analogues in the lever, screw, wedge, axle, and airfoil shape a whole paradigm of agentive prostheses. Every engine, computer, and device for regulation or guidance has a form of counteragency—gear train, converter, escapement mechanism—built into it as the most basic part of its design and functioning. Even nature, in the gravitic/inertial modeling of reactivity as a sui generis principle, evidences a cosmos evolving in necessary circularities and endlessly reacting to itself. The machine is a scale model not of cosmic "energies," whatever that might mean, but of their *application*. And of what is that application a model?

If "reciprocity" were part of the human hologram instead of a kind of scale model, a reciprocating engine constructed outside of it to extend its grasp, then Mauss's identification of it as a "total social fact" would make more sense.[3] For whatever is "given" becomes the recipient's agency in *taking*. Whatever is received (or even refused) in this way, despite or because of the values attached to it and the roles of the exchangers, is automatically a mirror imaging of the act or intent of bestowal. Objectifying this intrinsic reflexivity as a set of separate "obligations"—to give, to receive, to reciprocate—turns reflection into relationship and the antitwins into real people.

Human distinctiveness in gender as well as in the size, shape, and other aspects of physical character is a function of outward twinning; the ability to draw distinctions and thus know them or do something about them is integral to our laterality. Antitwinning characterizes the necessary appositive to this, "no cat," like the mirror person that borrows one's agency to see itself. Only its awareness is shared with the viewer, in the way that incest is not a social dysfunction at all but only a conceptual one. Agency becomes objective, an *object* to itself, as our sense of *another* humor in the world, one that can only be abstracted from the separateness of things from one another and from us. The weapon that seems to embody lethal qualities of its own and the machines and observational devices that would appear to capture or disclose the objective "energies" witnessed in our design of them are not simply examples of an "object fetishism," but of an *objective* fetishism. They twin physical distinctiveness inward upon itself and lateral integrity outward, into the world.

Objective or expersonate reality is too much its own "thing" to be a mere construction or impersonation. If the mirror image only *seems* to impersonate the viewer, turn laterality back on itself, then all the "reflexivity" associated with human representation is a misidentification of this appositive quality. The idea that human beings could actually inhabit—live and walk in—a fantasy of their collective interpretation or construction would be a virtual error but for an all-too-human tendency to get caught up in its focus. By that standard, pragmatic afterlife shaped back upon its own semblance to recapture a unique validity, one might easily conclude that the aesthetic profiling of ancient Egypt represents more than the culture or civilization that archaeologists imagine for it. These people managed to twin their subjective sense of person, animality, and divinity so confidently that speech was only *witnessed* in the more perfect copy of the hieroglyph, life itself in the tomb or monument.

Life *represented* more perfectly than it may have been lived turns the sense of symbolic reality construction into something like a joke whose punch line is lost in the telling. It has a *slower* humor than human mortality, like the language spoken beyond the death of a person. One might, indeed, get the "point" of life upon dying, but only because one had lived it through beforehand.

The way in which twinning eludes a commonplace understanding of "reflexivity" is difficult to articulate or grasp, but crucial to the comprehension of a game played with understanding itself. If we ourselves form, in our gendering and laterality, reflexive points of reckoning for our mirror beings in a *different* way than their laterality and gendering do for us, then we are dealing with two kinds of autonomy that sense each other's humor in different ways. The game that we play in modeling the world, picturing our understanding for ourselves and then understanding the pictures, is apt to take us over, "reflex" us into a kind of iconic entrapment, unless its own autonomy is acknowledged as a role in appositive play.

In the way that laughter reechos the speaking of the joke, the real humor of the Antitwins is that they no longer have to exist to make their point. Their point makes them. One does not have to think of laughter as actually mocking the speech act to notice that it does its very opposite, models the voice back upon the rhythm of its breathing rather than shaping that breathing to the acoustics of the word. And one does not have to think of the body language equivalents of this, the risus or grin and the belly laugh as regurgitative reflexes to intuit a counteragency in them. By the same token one would not have to take the argument of this chapter very seriously at all to recognize the inevitable tendency of twinning to reduce itself to itself in all of the examples presented so far, and to notice a corresponding tendency in the writer or reader to resist that reduction. The humor of the twins is that there are only *two* of them, however one might choose to understand this. And our sense of that humor is that twinning could only reduce itself to itself by doubling.

The ones we use to comprehend the facts of our twinning, know it for what it is, would not merely *see* (a faculty that they only borrow from us) our resistance as overdetermined, needlessly complex, but actually expersonate it, make the exotic demonstration of our embodiment.

Two kinds of humor with two modes of sensing them are not a matter of relative viewpoint at all but a radical simplification, an underdetermination of what it means to know ourselves in that way. They *halve* the apposition of duality, like meiosis and mitosis, respectively: a twoness of one shown in Figure 6 as the being called Our Sense of Their Humor, and a oneness of two, depicted in Figure 5 as the being called Their Sense of Ours.

Because their sense of our humor is quicker or more immediate to the point of this than our sense of theirs, our reechoing of the shape they leave us in, they would know us only in the fetal form of our "reproduction." It is our task to create imaginary personifications by endlessly recollecting that point, fleshing it out in gestation, birth, development, maturation, and recapitulation. Their sense humors the joke behind these imaginal aids to the humanization of gender, the fact that there is only one "gender" in the world of laterality twinned outward, the world in which we mirror ourselves socially.

Supergender is the "wanting" part of human sexuality that has nothing else to do with its social or biological definition, the part that is never "socialized" and so energizes sociality instead. Most of the sex that takes place on earth is never consummated, and most of that which is, is "about" something other than its consummation, so that conception takes place inadvertently and ostensibly through a "desire" of its own. In effect, then, supergender is not an "accident" of normal sexuality; normal sexuality is an accident of it.

Without "own gender," the part of our twinning into distinctive kinds of embodiment/personality that resists the biological or social and socializing "sense" of sex, we would not be here! It is not that the ideological descriptions that accompany and support any particular life-style or social milieu—heterosexual, homosexual, transsexual, or whatever—assume too little about sexuality and its social or biological constitution, and so must be supplemented and corrected. It is, rather, that they assume *too much*, subsume and take for granted the existence of an "other gender" that no one has ever embodied or ever could embody. Other gender is the novel and exceptional form that must be continually invented over and above the "rules" and standardized conceptions and descriptions for what gender and sexuality are supposed to be. Its invention, in and *of* human society is in this sense the provocation of life itself.

So the so-called hermaphrodite, the androgyne/gynandromorph fantasy, or the homosexual, autosexual, ambisexual lifestyle would not be the exception that "proves" or tests out the rule, but rather a regularity of "own gender" owning or claiming the totality of gender, its phenomenal entity. They are not perversions but rather reversions-to-type of the thing I am talking about, the owning of gender claimed to the extreme limit of its possibilities.

If sexual twinning constitutes fully *half* of the human experience, as I would argue, the surprising thing would not be the force of Freud's disclosure ("sex about everything/everything else about sex") but the need to rationalize it in psychological or symbolic terms, invent unreal agencies for its existence and operation. Sexual "repression," if that is the right word, would not be part of a personal dynamic but of a *social* one, a way of "talking in pictures" about the invention of other gender.

Freud's was not so much a "talking cure" as a talking fantasy, intimately related to the imaging scenario necessary to humor's play of understanding and misunderstanding. It involved a kind of child-reality, the imago of society or culture in the person, and its virtual cameo as the real person acting and relating in society, hence a kind of "reproductive" imaginary—picturing a new person within the actions or feelings of others and retrieving it so. It is *about* human physicality and its other-gendered reproduction in the way that the Wiru people of Papua New Guinea speak of the totality of human physical being—how it "works" and literally organ-izes itself—as the "picture-soul" of the person.

We reproduce pictures of ourselves as we picture reproduction to ourselves, form the imago of other gender necessarily and inadvertently in the "conception" of gender we happen to own. But if "other gender" comes in two distinctive forms, each picturing the one that "others" it in a double encompassment of what sexuality would have to mean, then other gender, as well as the contrastive pairing on which it depends, is an artifact, a fait accompli, of own gender.

The point is not that the double encompassment of one in two and two in one ("antitwinning") is a purely "symbolic" interpretation of bodily symmetry and asymmetry as they occur among many species discoverable in nature. It is not simply that a single species that calls itself "human" established itself through some "mental" ability to conceptualize natural or bodily pairings oppositely, and then ordered its social life through the consequences. The distinction, as it were, that makes distinction itself possible is the *real* basis of itself, as well as of all we can observe or conceive of as "nature." The natural or phenomenal does not end with the emergence of a self-distinctive and therefore "thinking" form of animal life. It *begins* there.

The ability to "own" gender through laterality and to consolidate laterality through gender—the distinction that cuts the person as the person cuts the distinction—is not just a thinking but a *knowing* thing. This means that its retroflexive involvement of the personal or human element prevents it from being a straightforward cut in any classic semiotic or philosophical sense, or even the cut made self-emphatic by turning its effect back upon itself, like Heidegger's *Ver/schei/dung* or Derrida's *différence*. By the same token it is not some distinctively "human" attribute, like subjectivity, feeling, or consciousness. It is rather how the "need" for either of these is grounded in the other.

Thus it is important to understand just how this double encompassment sets the human hologram apart from the "single cut" made at every point of discrimination in Louis Dumont's ingenious model of the Hindu caste system.[4] For Dumont the "cut," as well as the holographic modeling that follows upon it, is *ideological* or structural, and although one might understand it to be made "within" the person as well as among persons, it encompasses the social totality conceptualized through its use in one "direction" alone, which Dumont identifies with social hierarchy and the religious principle of "purity." In effect the capacity of a sociality to engender or reproduce itself via the sensual "picture" of all its parts, roles, virtues, and attributes is depersonalized on the model of a single, organizational act, the "type" of the cut person as the abstraction of a principle. "Own gender," in a system of concept that is "othered" from itself in every conceivable way, the persona of the type or cut, Dumont identifies with the ethos of the "world renouncer"—neither the ruler nor the Brahmanic suzerainty of purity that enables rule, but the self-disenfranchised "other side" of the double encompassment that makes the whole system possible.

The model or picture is not, of course, the society, but if totality's other side were admitted (like the Barok *orong*, for instance) into caste ideology instead of being "purified" out of it, the hierarchy would collapse into a virtually Melanesian original of itself.

No wonder, then, that supergender plays a divine, heroic, and mythical role in Indian lore and cosmology, as in the "superstar" mystique of modern world culture, or in the mythic foregrounding of Graeco-Roman civilization. As the provocation of life itself, own gender is too definite and explicit to move in the subconscious. It is superconscious, overdramatic in its very underpinnings. Consider the humoring of sense in the ancient Greek myth of Perseus and Andromeda—the double dexterity of the superhero Perseus, always "right" in forethought, the villainess Medusa, always astonishing in aftereffect.

To slay that demoness whose visage turned people to stone (all her social encounters were—instant—history), Perseus was forced to use his shield as a rearview mirror, do his swordplay in reverse. He was ambidextrous, both sides working as one; a human figure-ground reversal. Seeing through mere appearances by looking backward into the space of his own action, Perseus was able to twin his laterality outward-and-around to overcome his disadvantage vis-à-vis the Medusa. For it is important to understand that the Medusa worked her wiles on people not with her eyes but with their own, "stoning" her victims with their own perception. Perseus became a hero by parallactic displacement, using her reflexivity back on her. Only then could he cut the chains of perception, free "other gender," Andromeda, from being chained to a rock.

A myth of "myth" itself? There is a choice between understanding mythic lore as an artifact of its content and characters, a testamentary "literature" of the human experience smuggled down through the ages, or as simply the temporal fixative of "plot." Considered in its own terms, as that which is "about" myth as myth is about it—the self-securing chiasmus or double encompassment of action that Lévi-Strauss called its "canonic formula"—plot contains its own "othering," *stays* in time as the dead do, rather than running with it like a narrative.

If life copies myth more or less as myth copies life, *stories* the whole sense of it by keeping the fold of its narrated action, one might come to understand the "picture-soul" of a person and what supergender means through the consummation of Perseus's "affair" with the Medusa.

Think of them as lovers caught in the ultimate "mirror-sex," the narcissism of pictorial reproduction. A woman capable of simultaneous orgasm can "take" her lover's fulfillment into her own reaction to it, "chain" the orgasm by climaxing on her own climaxes. The Medusa, with her snakes, brought this containment of the penis to a "head," used a predator's technique for fixating the prey through its own vision, or picturing of the world—turning the sense or iconic capability of her victims into Greek statuary. Perseus's only recourse was to take his own back, reclaim his own gender by beheading—and thereby castrating—her.

Grasped in its own terms—the picturing of sense through the sensing of the picture, the re-production of picturing—rather than its logical or interpretational significance, or value as cultural heritage, the plot becomes a *pidik* of gender's owning and othering. It "stays in time" like a constellation or a statue of itself through the lesson it makes of some brute facts of the human hologram—the inability of a man to *will* erection by direct intention, the potential of a woman to claim the free life of the orgasm as her own.

The provocation of life itself, hence the spontaneity of the "organism" modeled upon itself in the human ability to conceive of it, our hologram of ourselves, is intimately linked to the command—"be spontaneous"—that cannot be obeyed. For we cannot "twin" either inward or outward, convene the disparity of perceptual or prehensile division in the person on one hand, or invent the perceptual reality of "other gender" in the world on the other, directly, spontaneously, and without the mediation of the other. Our whole picturing of the world as "presence," including the picture that perception draws of itself as "perception," depends in a very important way upon its own fabrication. The so-called time lapse or reaction time of perception serves to isolate sense from the ostensibly sensual or sensitizing quality of the world around it. For a split second ago, when the sensually pictured reality was supposed to have happened, "been there," one's senses or reactions were busy with another "event," supposed to have been real a split second before *that:* action "already there" by the time it is perceived, perception already past by the time it is acted upon.

An absurd dilemma about the human knowledge of the human, our placement of ourselves in space and time, or an evolutionary hologram—like the cat's learned and learnable un-imaging of itself—of the species itself? For the evidence, usually treated as "evolutionary," that technology is far older than human "sentience" and crucial to hominid existence is doubly encompassed in the fact that incest and the whole paradigm of relations and relationships spun out upon it are *never* any older than the sense we can presently make of them. Would our whole evolution, the *pidik* of how the species "stays in time," depend, like that of the predator that learned to stalk its own image, upon our inability to know spontaneity fully and represent it directly in our actions? The "past in its own futurity" of gender folded inward upon itself and the "future in its own past" of laterality twinned outward into a *technos* create a false presence for the race to live up to. Like the false nonpresence that the cat pounces out of.

II

The Trap of Iconicity

5

The Story of Eve

for Anjana

When a woman's body refuses her child in menstruation, refuses "fatherhood," her power gives birth to her, and she emerges headfirst out of her own uterus. Barok people say that the *pidik,* the exotic demonstration of the mystery of the external social or material world, is, like the *taun,* or men's house, only for men. A woman, they say, is her own *pidik,* her own mystery to herself. Young women who are *ararum,* specially "marked" or tabooed, are used to demonstrate this in a very dramatic way. Before the onset of her menses, such a woman is secluded in a mat enclosure called a *bak* (also the word for "child"), described in 1892 as "not larger than an ordinary hen-coop."[1] A tight cincture is fastened about her midsection. As she undergoes her weeks (sometimes months) in this "women's house," her skin blanching and her body swelling with the choice foods offered her, her body assumes an hourglass shape. "Sleeping Beauty." When she finally emerges, headfirst, from the house called "child," a feast is held, and an older man performs the demonstration called "breaking her back." He slits the cincture around her waist with a knife from behind, *producing an immediate first menstrual flow.*

Most Melanesian peoples would do it the other way—*hide* the woman in a small house during the onset of puberty—and it is so for most Barok women as well. But here, once again, is the story of the man who disappeared into his own mirror, told in the shape of the woman who emerged from hers. What is shed in menstruation is the lining of the uterine wall, a house that could be called "child." The story can be demonstrated to the woman herself or told in the whimsical genre, something like the *fabliaux* of Chaucer's day, that seems to have served the Usen Barok for the purposes of the joke.[2]

The genre is defined, as are many jokes, by a set of stock characters. They include the *Tamor*, a single (though often more than one) "rubbish-man," greedy but foolish and worthless; his wife, the *Tine;* and his lazy but cunning brother-in-law, the *Otana*. The *Gilam*, sometimes featured, is the essential "hairy monster," a gigantic, stupid humanoid covered with long fur, his outsize testicles dragging on the ground. An important part of the characterization is that no one can be quite certain as to whether the *Tamor* exist or not; many Barok insist that they can be seen beneath houses, living on refuse, and are often encountered in Kavieng, collecting empty soft drink bottles to sell back to the storekeepers.

So this version, "The *Gilam* and the Garden," is a twin, a woman *demonstrated* by her power, a tale told, as Rudyard Kipling once put it, "twice as plain":

The *Tamor* wanted to hold a large feast. He sent word to the men and women of the place, and they came and helped to cut a large garden. They cut down trees, and when they were dry he sent word again and they came and burned them. When they were finished they ate four pigs, two for the women and two for the men. He sent word again, and they fenced the garden, and then he called them once more and they planted; when they finished they feasted again. When the garden sprouted he sent the women to *kip pirogo*, get the weeds. Then they did the second *kip pirogo*, called *pit mu*, and *pit buon*—cleaning the grown garden. After that the *Tamor* and the *Tine* went to the bush, and the *Gilam* ate some of the garden. "Oe, pigs are eating the garden!" They fixed the fence, gathered up the uprooted food, and took it home and cooked it. When they went back to the garden the next day it had been raided again.

The *Tamor* told the *Tine*, "Tine, go pull up some kunai grass, we'll make a little house and go watch for the pigs." She pulled up kunai; the *Tamor* cut posts and planted them, cut bamboo and broke it for the walls, put up the frame for the thatch, and laid down the kunai to finish the house. They made two beds and readied the firewood. Then the *Tine* made an earth-oven for the yams the "pigs" had uprooted. The *Tamor* said, "Let's go to the beach first and wash." So they went to the beach. In the afternoon the *Tine* called out to the *Tamor*, "Time to go now, it's getting dark." But the *Tamor*, resting in the *taun*, called back, "You go on ahead; I'll get some fish to eat with our food." The *Tine* took her basket and went to the little house. The *Tamor* was afraid, and she waited and waited, and finally fell asleep.

Then she heard the fence crack; the *Gilam* was breaking in. She got up: "Oop, it's no pig; what's getting into our garden?" She could hear the *Gilam*'s teeth crunching; slowly the crunching came closer and closer to the little house. Then the *Gilam* stood at the door. "Who's in there?" "Me, I'm here with my husband." "Where is he, then?" "Oh, he's out in the garden watching for the pigs that raid it." The *Gilam* stood in the doorway, shutting out the light. He asked about all the parts of the house. "What's this?" "That's the corner, the *Tamor* didn't fasten it very well." "What's this?" "That's the door." He jumped inside and came next to the fire. "What's this?" "That's the fire." He went to look, and the fire died out. "What is this, here?" "The bed." "And this?" "My hair." "And this?" "My ear." "And this?" "My eye." "And what is this?" "That is my mouth." "This?" "My hand." "And this?" "My other hand." "This?" "My breast." "This, what is it?" "My other breast." "What is this?" "My belly." "And what is this?" "My back." "What is this?" "My leg." "This?" "My other leg." "This?" "My buttocks." "This?" "My anus." "And what is this?" "My genitals." The genitals came out and knocked the *Gilam* sprawling, swatted him and smacked him. The two fought and fought; the woman just sat and watched.

They fought until dawn, and finally the *Gilam* died. The genitals went back to their place. The *Tine* got up, put *tanket* leaves on her sore, put lime powder on her face, and left. The *Tamor* saw her coming: "What happened, did something happen to you in the bush?" "Ah, you go and carry in the *Gilam*, I killed him." "What was he doing?" "He was eating our garden." "How did you kill him?" "My genitals killed him." "Oh you men look! You with your balls, your huge balls," the *Tamor* shouted, "none of you has a wife with genitals like that!" They went and brought in the *Gilam*, cut him up, killed two pigs, and cooked them in the earth oven with the *Gilam*. But when they tried to eat the *Gilam*, they found the meat bad. It was bitter and astringent, so they threw it away with the trash.

The extended and rather technical account of gardening at the outset of the tale has a special point. It is that a Barok garden, when it has been planted, is "sealed" (or, as Chaucer's contemporaries would have said, put "in defense"), and that only specific, named "entries" may be made for particular purposes. A garden has a V-shaped entry style, like the *olaŋabo* of a *taun*, and an optional feast *(Kip Sawang)* may be held when it is opened. The garden is a prime example of *kolume*, as is the house within it (like the *gunun* of a *taun*), for whose construction we are given another technical account. Finally, the narrative (and the *Gilam*) dwells extensively on the anatomy of the *Tine*, "her own *pidik*" in that way as well.

Told again on itself, "twice as plain," this is a story about its own enclosure as a story, or the story of an enclosure that is much more than an enclosure. It would not matter if some expert on the subconscious interpreted it to mean that the *Gilam* had sexual intercourse with the *Tine* and then "died" of it, or even that the *Gilam was* the Penis. It is the "sense" of the woman that means most in it, woman as a sense of herself.

There are four enclosures in it: the fence, the little house, the *Tine*'s body, and the "enclosure" within her body, ultimate *kolume*. There are first four entries or breakings of the enclosure: *kip pirogo, pit mu, pit buon,* and finally, as a last straw, the *Gilam*'s breaking in. Twice as plain, as a story within the story of gardening, the story invents itself with four more violations: the Gilam breaks the fence once again, feels his way about the little house, breaking in, and then about the *Tine*'s body, trying to "break in." That was the last straw. The *Tine* did not need a "penis" to hunt "pig"; she left her man sleeping in an enclosure of his own and left the intruder to be finished off by a force so mysterious to her that she need only sit and watch.

The problem, in other words, is not with the subject—what it might *be,* how to name it or at least describe its agency—but only with how to *contain* it, make its enclosure, tell a story of it. Wondering why we are here, where we came from, how we came from there, and who our forebears might have been is very much the same thing.

So perhaps "hominization" is not a process but a point, and the story of the origination of what makes a certain type of primate human shares a common point of genesis with the "original" of storytelling itself. That would be the unfunny joke, the tale that *begins* with its funny edge or punch line and evolves progressively backward from that point, developing in imagination and the neurophysiological basis for imagination toward a degree of sophistication that would enable the evolving subject to grasp the point in full. The story still exists as a story, in other words, gets plainer all the time, because no one, least of all this author, has yet attained that kind of sophistication.

Imagine the story, then, to be an invisible strand of "information," like the biblical tale of Eve in Genesis, twisted DNA-wise around the more tangible strand of "biogenetic information" traced mitochondrially to another version, equally controversial, of the same woman. She is just simply Eve, unqualified, and her people had been around for a long time.

Perhaps the problem for humanity's immediate forebears, the ones with the strong features, was less a matter of the kind of story that we might make of them—their bones, artifacts, and intellectual equipment—than of the story they might make of themselves. What if they were just simply *quicker* than we are, faster on their feet and in their heads, their sense of our humor more to the point than our sense of theirs? Our twins in all but a few tiny features of DNA, they were not, in that case, the kind of bridge to animal origins that used to be called the "missing link," but simply *originals* of a story about Eve, the linking Miss. If it helps to think of them in that way, they did not *evolve* into us, nor really de-volve, slowing their reflexes and their whole sense of timing. They *demurred,* allowing or forcing our kind of people to evolve in their stead, even to evolve a sense of what they had been.

The Story of Eve

They were a people who already knew fire, hand axes, and all the tricks of the trade or trading of tricks in a "hunting-and-gathering existence." They knew language very well, but it was the kind of language that did not know them very well. That was the whole point of their demurral, and of our evolution of them, for language cannot really go back to its beginning point, to rehumanize itself or whatever. It can only re-copy itself in trying to do so.

They were hominids, so to speak, with a "vocation"—the first *professionals*—and getting a living was already second nature to them. It was a part-time project, and they did it by a sort of moonlighting. When they wanted to have some real work done, they hired "working man," *Homo ergaster,* to do it. If a specific appelation were to be put to their generic, it would be *Homo* "almost-at-the-point-of-its-joke," or whatever that might be in Latin.

Eve was the mother, and she had four sons. One was a doctor, or the vocational equivalent for his time and place, one was a lawyer, one a sort of petty chieftain, and the last, somewhat retarded, was No Weasel at All. Their vocation, or full-time obsession, was really a very precocious form of anthropology, a human knowledge of the human. Night after night they would sit around the fire, while hyenas chuckled and cracked bones out on the veldt, trying to tell, recover, remember, or at least imagine the most original joke of all—the one that had started language in the first place. Or rather that is what Eve's three elder and more gifted sons did; they vied with each other in all degrees of subtlety and outrageousness, overstating and understating until their howling laughter put even the other predators to shame.

But the youngest, retarded son did not get the point of any of them, and did not even get the point of the vocation itself. Worst of all, he never laughed. Eve became more and more concerned about her son's handicap, and his inability to laugh, until finally, chucking her career, she reluctantly took on the role of the Explainer. Night after night, as her three older sons emulated one another in trying to be more original, Eve would carefully and patiently explain the point of each joke. She would compare the jokes with one another, remembering earlier ones and anticipating later ones, explain why each of them was funny and in what ways some were funnier than others, try to explain what jokes are and even what "funny" itself might be. But none of it worked; No Weasel at All never got the point of any of it, and of course never laughed.

To tell an idiot exactly what kind of idiot he is, to explain carefully how, why, and in what ways he is stupid with such clarity and precision that he gets none of it, has the net effect of making him a lot smarter than you are. As Eve grew more and more attached to her mothering role, her retarded son grew more and more into that strange sort of compassion that comes of feeling superior to someone else. Eve was learning to be the mother of the whole human race; No Weasel at All was learning the secret of its survival in pragmatic afterlife, learning to be smart in a way that still smarts in all of us.

Full of compassion for his mother's selfless subordination of herself in this way, her youngest son, by now more retarded than ever, turned to her. "Mom," he said, "you never laugh anymore, so it would seem that you are getting more and more stupid on my account, and just exactly as I am. But the worst part of it is that I will never laugh at all, never really be happy, unless you are. So wouldn't it make more sense if you tried, instead, to explain what is *not* funny about these jokes, so we can at least take you more *seriously?*"

Silence. Eve and her three older sons stared openmouthed, blank-faced with astonishment as if they had just *brained* themselves, like a neurophilosopher suddenly realizing that the *hands* do it all. Hyenas cackled, stars shone, and the Milky Way stretched high and mysterious over the veldt. And Eve's youngest, retarded son, No Weasel at All, left them there and went out and fathered the human race.

·   ·   ·

The rediscovery of language through its own use and usage is more than a mystery to itself, even in its own terms. It is not merely a case or condition of self-mysterious and self-effecting power, like that of Barok womanhood, or of the *Tine's* prowess in overcoming the *Gilam*. It is an actual *joke* upon itself, a factor that makes the apparently snide or cynical features of the Story of Eve more real and larger-than-life to its protagonists than the work they do in getting a life for themselves. So it would not really matter what the point of the original joke might have been, or even if there was one, just as it would not matter whether the events in the tale actually took place as told here. For the whole point of the story lies in its retelling, in the retelling of stories and languages in general, and in what motivated the first sapient hominids to do so crazy and retarded a thing. The account of how some prehuman primate, possibly *Homo erectus,* lapsed back into the pragmatic afterlife of knowing that it knows and so invented itself, is one that must necessarily be told back on itself, invented for the occasion of its telling.

What motivated the first sapient hominid to do so crazy a thing was his mother, called "Eve" here for obvious reasons. And because what motivated her in the first place was the intractable stupidity of her son, the story is not really about language at all, about its importance to the human species, or about what it is and how it began. It is the story of Eve as the initial projection of human twinning into an appositional, and therefore knowable modality, into a supergendered capability.

There is no Adam in the tale because fatherhood was only biological before No Weasel at All finally got his mother right, obtained his mother right. So his status as First Man would no more imply a kind of male priority in the constitution of the species than mother right would mean that we were once all matriarchal or matrilineal. The re-latio responsible for gendered sociality could only connect each of the genders through the agency of the other. A man, in the Barok understanding of the procreative act, must first *conceive his wife's ability to conceive,* that is, elicit the flow of *pege a une,* "female semen," in the repetitive action of sexual penetration.

Male supergender is the exact opposite of all we have learned to recognize as "protest masculinity," or machismo. Where male action is coercive or conspiratorial, a matter of "bonding" and retroactive exactation, it is inevitably counterparted by the idea of men being "second best," having to "try harder." But one does not strike a matador, maleness come into its own, or deploy the chess king, who holds the value of the game, in risky maneuvers. It is the *queen* who takes that role, and it is the matador who kills the concretivity, the real-life "image" of machismo, in the corrida.

Mirror engenderment tells the story of Eve, the tale of all tales that must be retold and reinvented after the fact, *as if the history of the word retold through its own devices were the actual reproductive and relational life of the species.* It makes a kinship of the word and a word of kinship. So we have elaborate models of how people reckon relationship, live, feel, and interact that are accountable to words alone, but also a negative twin of this in procreational obscenity, the reproduction of verbal species accountable to kinship alone. Humanity beside itself does its all-too-serious joking not simply as protest masculinity, which is after all one of the commonplace modes of social gender, but as protest kinship. So Barok verbal obscenity becomes dangerous or provocative in reference to *male* genitalia (e.g., *bun gamat,* "the hanging fruit ornament") and uses the *clitoris* (*a subuna tege,* "piece of a flying fox") to impugn the female. But for the Daribi, a folk whose hard-won patriliny out-protests even the most formidable examples to be found in Europe, Germany, and the Mediterranean, obscenity makes the opposite connection. It references female genitalia almost exclusively for the edge of verbal nastiness.

It is not just turning kinship inside out in this way that makes such instances telling or provocative, for ordinary sexual "attractiveness" is every bit as obscene. It is a power *over* commonplace gender qualities that must be reshaped into recognizable roles and procedures to be social at all. Overassertive masculinity (the seriousness of Daribi sociality and the joke of the Barok) and overreactive femininity (the seriousness of Barok sociality, the joke of the Daribi) is an immediate and recognizable equivalent of something that social scientists have overdetermined in the abstraction of norms, rules, and social morality.

Supergender is sexuality about things, the role that gender would play in the world of human agency, and therefore something that can as easily be confused with personal motivation as with the origin of the species itself. The problem with understanding it as an agency operating below the threshold of consciousness is that it depends fully upon conscious action and strategy to be engaged at all. A great deal of Jacques Lacan's revisional work on psychoanalysis can be understood as a clarification of this point. Unless a similar corrective were applied to what anthropologists have called basic structures of kinship or patterns of social structure, it might easily be imagined that fundamentally different kinds of men and women inhabit the various social orders projected in this way, that sexuality was not genital but congenital. Freud thought of it as a function of the "psyche," Lewis Henry Morgan as something "passed along with the blood."

The objective evidence for the kind of conceptual self-transcendence that is identified with the culture concept comes from a limited set of studies, usually of nonindustrial peoples. It involves a kind of simplicity-in-itself that requires a high degree of conceptual sophistication, a skill at "unpacking" or interpreting it that often enough turns into a mind-game, or the sorts of structural and categorical complexity needed for a step-by-step explication that has nothing whatever to do with the original. Given the artificial and theoretical extension of these efforts at exegesis to define a generic human capability, one might also imagine "culture" itself to be a function or artifact of its own understanding. The stronger likelihood, however, is that the subject of that understanding is not culture at all. One is dealing instead with a point where the mystery of gender and engenderment transcends that of culture, with a demimode—a halving of human embodiment that turns into doubling, endlessly doubling back on itself in recollection if one is not careful, and most especially when one is.

The joke of it is that taking the "cultural" side as a kind of sense made of sense, perception's perception of itself in the image, icon, trope, or metaphor, puts one out of the picture, more or less as No Weasel At All exited the tale of his own mother right. For when the very same halving or division (of the self, the species, the means of understanding's representation-to-itself) surfaces here at home, in industrial societies, it is taken as a stupendous human achievement—no culture at all, but "technology" perhaps, discovery, or the progress of the human intellect. What we call "language" is a printout of speech divided by itself, talk doubling back to be more specific, to reassure itself as to its intentions and occasions. Writing, orthography, would then be the product of this, language, divided by itself and then multiplied endlessly using the same small set of finitary markers. And if computer imaging can be considered as a way around the toils of writing and reading, graphic depiction, it would have to be the product of writing divided by itself.

That may help with the anomaly of computer "languages," unspeakable dialects that depend upon electronic complexity for the sense they make of things. The joke of writing's small-scale model of speech patterning divided once again at the subatomic level is more insidious than the mind-games of quantum mechanics. The prizewinning discoveries of high-energy physics degrade into trivial forms of language—quarks, leptons, gauge-bosons, and neutrinos. On the other side of it, radical studies of language degrade speech into trivial forms of the particle— phonemes, morphemes, sememes, and the like. Understanding the language of physicists in the way they intend it, as a fanciful identification of items much smaller than the sense that could be made of them, would reveal the particles of language to be the other side of the joke—"sense" much smaller than the "structures" it depends upon.

Is the division of language by physicality, or of physicality by language—something as ubiquitous in practice as cell division is in the body—a concrete resource base for a world order given over to multiplicities of every kind? Do we exploit it, or does it exploit us? No longer abstract and philosophical, like the mind-body opposition, or even analytic, like nature/culture, thesis/antithesis, or conscious/subconscious, the twinning of thought and thing has the special virtue of being nearly invisible as well. It will copy back any attempt to copy it, represent it in understanding or try to understand its representation, to the point where thought's shadow or echo appears more real and substantial than thought itself.

Designated in the Story of Eve as the threshold of humanity's emergence into sentient being, it takes the specific form of "motherhood" in Eve's explaining the facts of his own stupidity to her retarded son, and of "fatherhood" in her son's finally getting his mother right, explaining back to her that she is, after all, only explaining things. Copying its physicality back upon itself in the remembrance of things, and copying that remembrance back in the acoustic, inscribed, or imaged physicality of language, the species has remained immobilized on that point ever since. Mother is always right; father is after the fact. But for the superimposing of language after the fact of gender itself, reminding Eve that she was, after all, only explaining things, gender would remain purely biological, and language artificial.

But for their emergence as Antitwins, cross-gendered imaginaries or supergenders, the Twins could as well have been siblings, consorts, the friend and the enemy, as mother and son. Humoring each other as the twinning that humors itself, the twinning that knows it is twinning and the twinning that does not, they set the stage for all distinction and differentiation, including their own. If it takes a certain humor, not a cultural logic or a reconstruction of someone else's logic for culture, but something more immediate and exacting, to understand or deal with folks in a different lifestyle, then the problems and projects of anthropology would seem to be reversed on themselves in the same way. What prehistorians and archaeologists take to be the past is significant in that it misses the funny edge of past-in-its-own-future; but what sociocultural anthropologists take as the present, dynamic, or "becoming" shape of culture is equally significant in missing the edge of future-in-its-own-past.

If mother right, *Das Mutterrecht* in J. J. Bachofen's classic (1861) study, defines a kind of knowledge in relation to gender, then descent or lineality would be only second best in coming to terms with it. The roster of lines of thought set up to rationalize this body knowledge only begins with mystified notions like "instinct" and "women's intuition." It runs the whole gamut from the seizure of power and authority roles by women to ad hoc utilitarian mechanisms and causal strategies for what a woman must do and what must be done for her. Some of these are functional, what must be done to keep life or society going, some evolutionary "just-so" tales of how gender got to be the way it is, and some "significational," what it *means* to be a woman, what the meaning of it means to her, and so forth. But the problem with these approaches and the assumptions that ground them is that they are all based on an a priori *division* of genders as a starting point. Barok would call them male *pidiks* regardless of whether it is men or women who use them.

In other words, if we were dealing with the mystery of kin as a total or self-generating phenomenon, the part that ostensibly "matrilineal" peoples have played in disclosing the role of "sense" in cultural phenomena would hardly be surprising. The astonishing ritual life described by the Turners among the Ndembu, the cosmologies and *katcina* of the Southwestern Pueblo peoples, the conceptual art and potlatching of the Northwest Coast, the art, drama, and twinning concepts in West Africa, and the mortuary feasting of Austronesian Melanesia are only the more familiar examples. The list could go on and on. Yet the demonstration of gender "to itself" as culture, often largely or exclusively done by males, is no more a "man's" achievement than *Das Mutterrecht* is a woman's. They are "about" the point where gender transcends the perceptual, the physical, or the meaningful, a point that seems to have galvanized Franz Boas's intimations of a conceptual "culture." Versions of that insight as diverse as Victor Turner's "liminality" and Bronislaw Malinowski's "function" drew their ethnographic substantiation, as well as their theoretical rhetorics, from what their authors would call "matrilineal" peoples. Lewis Henry Morgan generalized "kinship" from the Iroquois.

Mother right and maternal "descent" are by no means the only subject areas in which the classic issues of kinship and social relations may be engaged. But insofar as they represent a totalization of the problematic concretivity that is at issue in all studies of this kind, they are emblematic of a reasoning about social forms that turns the "sense" that is made of them into the factual basis of the subject itself. It is important, then, *not* to "understand" the role of sense in this too quickly or too comprehensively as a cultural logic or a device of indigenous "worldview" or "ethos," or to derive it from the exigencies of group behavior. It is not the "rules" for sense, the strategies for sense, or the interpretation of sense, but the *sense* of the rules, strategies, or interpretations. It is only as a power *over* sociality, rather than the power *of* it or *by* it, that sense and "reason" come to be the same thing: the right of the mother and the mother of the right.

Thus if the whole empathetic, "feeling," embodiment-of-understanding-in-the-womb model of woman that feminism has profiled and incorporated were true, then the positive attribution of menstruation would make no sense. It would be impossible for women to own gender without its owning them completely in return. So it is not the acknowledgment of supergender but the social and biological reinvention of *gender* itself that works at cross-purposes to women's freedom. A world of "feeling" alone, the human "sensorium" without the articulation or de facto "picturing" that makes sense of its own feelings, would not be sensible or even human at all. The double encompassment of separation and containment, what Barok call *gala* and *kolume,* is necessary to the comprehension of what each of these would mean by itself.

Already "finished" from the beginnings of time, of its own "timing" of things, gender is unique in its combination and combinatory in its uniqueness. So holographic engenderment, the motif of the personal unity acting and perforce imitating the totality of gendered implication in a decisive way, what I have called "supergender," is the generic role model, the "atom" of kinship-walking-in-the-world.

Gender is the "twin" we do not have. Far from resolving the mystery of gender in the play of kin relations, mother right makes its capital on the *ambivalence* of the issues it raises. Father right makes its claims through the *disowning* of it, yet as the self-elicitory "principle" of maternal succession it is demonstrated, exotically, by males and frequently, as among the Barok, expropriated by them as well. The result, the "habitus" of relation, is not a "playing" of roles in some normative or habitual sense but an overplaying of "sense" back into them. A "social drama" of any sort, including the staged variety, that does not reduce the normative roles involved to the point of absurdity is a *failure.*

Not surprisingly, the most realistic model of own gender walking in the world was explained to Bruce Josephson by an African people, the Biyenge of Kasai Province in the Congo. "At the right hand of the woman and the left hand of the man is the mystery of that which is in the bush, the power of *bukum,* or violence. At the right hand of the man and the left hand of the woman is the mystery of that which is inside of us, the power of *bwany,* or human speech."[3] Reproduction, like reciprocity, is underdetermined in a mirror reflection of its fundamentals and overdetermined in the objectifications that turn that acuity into a relational sense of things, and into overtly social or physical facts.

Whatever its relation to game theories, ideas of performance or experience, combinatory sciences like economics, biology, linguistics, or chemistry, the game of life depends in all of its strategems upon how that overdetermination is staged, playacted. There are no real "answers" in this, only antirealistic *solutions,* like holography, that play into reality precisely by falling short of the point.

Sexual consummation, in which the whole perceptual capability of the human "picture soul" is taken over physically by that which it de-picts—the sensing of things underdetermined (motivated from within) by its own conceptional potency—has no iconic equivalent. The trap of the icon is sprung. For the "state" of the human body (actually, of course, *two* bodies, however sublimated the other might be) in which cognition is encompassed by "movement" of orgasm as the seat of its *consensus-sensorium* lacks any direct correspondence in the subjective/objective pragmatic of iconicity and its reification. It has only mirror relations, and mirror relatives.

Its nearest approximations, akin in this way to the "meaning" of the Barok *kaba,* are apparent reciprocities in which the action of "taking" is wholly encompassed in its giving. If social parallels to the owning of gender in this way, like courtship and marriage, are too obvious, economic ones like the stock or futures market too tentative, biological ones all too "specific," the better exemplars are "games" that are too serious to be accredited as "play."

Never mind, then, where they might have come from, how they could have "developed," or what they are supposed to mean. The story form of what we call "history," the evolutionary schemata of development, the quasi-semantics of meaning are more closely epitomized in their form and content than they could be used as models for their understanding.

So possibly the mobilization of hazard or chance that Clifford Geertz has identified as "deep play"—with all its sexual overtones—in the Balinese cockfight might reflect a better sense of the Northwest Coast potlatch or the game of chess than "risk" or even "game." The provocation of life is at stake in an agonistic dueling that shatters its own iconicity (like a Kwakiutl "copper") in the action of establishing it. For it is the underdetermination of the "odds," or relative advantages and disadvantages, that empowers the outcome, and, to paraphrase Geertz's "paradigm" for the *depth* of play,[4] the closer the odds (including the statuses and I think the skills of the players), the higher the stakes, the greater the emotional intensity, and the more important the match. In effect a match that *is* its own "interpretation" creates odds or relative advantages out of almost nothing, and so overdetermines the sense of gaming in its outcome.

A kind of "Russian roulette" with the way in which things matter, how their importance, meaningfulness, and therefore time are organized, becomes, as with a joke, the very chance of its understanding. A return, like the "deep play" of human conception that originated the players themselves, to the womb of meaning. Notice that it would make no real difference if the terms of Geertz's paradigm were reversed upon themselves. "The higher the stakes, greater the emotional intensity, more important the match, the closer the odds approach fifty-fifty" makes sense of the American presidential election, the erotic encounter, the power contest among nations, or the science of probabilities, by making nonsense of the issues involved in them. A "deep play" at the very beginning of things—big bang, erotic consummation, power contest among human or divine players, the Story of Eve or the Russian roulette of human mortality—sets up its own grounding conditions in precisely that way.

If the joke that "finished off" the whole compass of human sentience before it began, the most *original* joke of all, could be recovered or retold, the whole course of self-reflection, and thus history, meaning, evolution, would be acquitted—short-circuited—in its punch line. So the whole question of its possibility or impossibility, whether it could have existed at all, by what "primitive" means language might have preempted the possibility of its own existence, is beside the point of a game whose sense runs deeper than cognition in human affairs and their understanding. If the way in which the joke was set up, even the possibility of its existence, *is* the joke itself, its human hologram, then it *might as well* have existed.

For the question that my daughter asked at the age of four— "Daddy, when everybody was in somebody else's tummy, who was *around?*"—is a version of what the joke would have to mean. A picture "in the body" of the body in the picture, the ultimate (and also primordial) reductio ad absurdum of the effort to "figure out" kin relations from the person's or the species' relation to its own self-encompassment. It is the scary edge of incest's iconicity.

6

The Icon of Incest

to the honor of David M. Schneider;
to the vengeance of David M. Schneider!

The game of chess forms a seemingly artificial point d'appui for appositiveness in human social orders, underdetermining role and play themselves through the effects of a very basic gender inversion. The game becomes a strategy mirror in that the initial positioning of the pieces creates a field of play by twinning laterality outward and gender inward. The right side of each player confronts the left side of the other, as they sit with a square of the lighter color to the right of either. But the "twins" of chess, the two key pieces by which gender is "marked" for the game, invert the spatial ordering of a laterality turned inward upon itself. King faces king and queen faces queen across the board. They also bring the game outside of itself, convert an imaginary play of minds into something deadly serious by simultaneously inverting the traditional role expectations of king and queen. The queen is the most strategically effective and valuable piece; the king in his positioning holds the value of the game.

This significant detail, the secret of chess itself, goes generally unnoticed, ignored by those who think the rules of chess are merely rules and taken for granted by those who know them well. What is, however, very much apparent to players and nonplayers alike is that chess always seems to be about issues that are more important than the game itself, without our being able to say just exactly why or to know what those issues might be. A kind of social or hierarchical advantage is played for, won, lost, or drawn, and the triumph or loss is only reflectively connectable with the hierarchy of the pieces or moves. The commonplace term "mating" means something very different in chess than in life—the end of an imaginary life span staged and brought about through the removal of pieces rather than a beginning point in the real-life drama of reproduction, adding the players themselves—mating in reverse, on an inside-out scenario. Whether correctly or not, "checkmate" is commonly traced to an ostensible Iranian *shah mat,* "the king is dead."

In other words, the ways in which the life of the game, with its not-so-arbitrary rules, moves outside of itself has an appositive counterpart in the ways in which the ostensible game of life itself moves to the inside of its apparently arbitrary rules, gambits, and hierarchical positioning of pieces and play. The ways in which chess play moves outside of the game to become much more important than a game should be are inevitably rationalized in terms of the rules and setting of the game itself. But the ways in which something that actually *is* more important than any rules that might be made up for it, life itself, becomes *less* important than it should be are rationalized through a *violation* of those rules: a violation called "incest" that is unimaginable without those rules.

So just as one would not know exactly how or why chess could be important outside of the game itself, it is very difficult to get the "point" of kinship and social order without having to reinvent the game, its rules, and the motives for the original violation of those rules all over again. For that very reason, perhaps, there is no lack of speculation, theoretical and otherwise, as to what the original violation was, or meant, and how it came about, and most especially why the violation itself must be violated, as it is, in the commonplace "mating" of everyday life. The speculation is very unconvincing, in large part because it is all about the act of explaining itself, the reasons for reasoning in that particular way.

It shares the stage with some very powerful dramas of which *Hamlet* and *Oedipus Rex* are versions, plays that are about the tragic encirclement of human destinies, and thus about how they came to be plays in the first place. They are stories about an incest that did not seem incestuous at the time it was committed, and that only came to be important *as* incest because of the checkmate, the death of a king, that is implicated in it. They are about the royal heir caught in the existential drama—to be or not to be—of his own plight of successorship, the ultimate "stranger king" estranged from himself. So they are versions of the Royal Game that came into tragic prominence long before chess was played or understood as it is now, and long before kinship or society was imagined outside of itself as a rational (or irrational) staging of rules or principles—the best evidence for how and why chess and kinship twin each other as counterparts in appositive play, especially under conditions where neither form of "mating" can be conceptualized as a game.

Oedipus of Thebes possessed his mother right in the worst possible way; Prince Hamlet demurred on his but nonetheless went to his doom after dispatching his mother's husband, his false but all too real uncle Claudius. Male agency is the culprit, the seed of tragedy, in both instances, and the all-important moves of the queen are treated as consequences of male compulsion. Queen Jocasta becomes her own unwitting mother-in-law in the Oedipus drama; Hamlet makes up his own mind about his mother's culpability, and it is the self-estranged royal heir in both cases who holds the value of the game.

In other words, the plight and the actual role of male supergender is more accurately depicted in tragedies of this sort, or in chess, than in the staging of real life. In those cases the real "kicker," female supergender, or what I have called "mother right," is practically invisible. For all that Oedipus's folk might normally be accounted as "patrilineal," and Hamlet's, realistically, "bilateral," these and all the other classifications of descent reckoning are beside the point. There is only one form of chess going on in what we think of as kinship, just as there is only one kind of kinship going on in the appositive play of chess.

Incest, too much kinship in all the wrong places, is neither self-evident nor self-explanatory. It needs another issue, murder perhaps, to lend it the full conviction of "sense," bring its violation of re-latio into the here and now. Incest's icon is fetal in shape, contained by its own containment in an infinitely regressional mode—past consuming the present. So murder, or in some cases rape or family abuse, is only a special instance, immoral on the face of it, of a violation that is necessary if re-latio is to be conceivable at all. That is the pretense, the assertion of "no kin," a mirror that does not reflect kinship's imitation of life.

Treating deceased "relatives" as if they were alive and living persons with the rank and status of departure, life in death and death in life, frames the whole medium of kin connections. It assimilates mother to her own mother, and her to another down the line to an original fetality of mother right. What students of kinship have called "affinity," affinal relations centered on alliance, provides the necessary counterstroke to that form of consumption, brings re-latio into the picture as a manifest or achieved connection. The reconnection of the lines that genealogy or generation exaggerates is not a matter of prohibition or avoidance so much as one of setting up re-latio, incest and all, in the context of its own obliteration. Mothers-in-law are avoided instead.

Affinal "parentage" or "siblingship" (e.g., what we call "in-law" relations, sanctioned violations of ancestry) is created through the ambivalence of either treating the relationship itself as nonexistent (as in total or partial affinal avoidance) or, conversely, by exaggerating the "generational" exaggeration itself, overdoing it and turning it into respect, worship, authority. Partial or complete avoidance always implies the violation pretended in the joking relationship, just as that pretense of violation implicates a potential avoidance.

That the mate one has chosen could as well have been someone else, and someone else could have been that mate (a potential realized in polygyny, polyandry, and adultery), is the direct expression of "kinship" inverted in this way within the picture of its own self-survival. It is necessary to the joke of kinship. Divorce, adultery, and incest are difficult to think, and to live with, not because they involve the denial of kin connection in its "moral" or orthodox values but because they compound the interest as well as the "interest value" of mating. They involve an intensified form of that interest, underdetermine reconnection in the way that "affinity" itself underdetermines genealogy. The reframing of human similarities in this way is not a remote or "symbolic" generality from which abstract or perhaps "universal" relations might be derived, but an immediate contingency upon which such rationalizations depend.

Incest forms the perennial root of kin relationships in that it corresponds to the collapse of relationships into an icon. The possibility of this collapse is ever-present and is therefore always a factor in the elicitation of relationships themselves. Thus it is that relationship always begins with an icon of incest, an initial representation that is violated or deflected in the forms of joking, respect, or avoidance. What we speak of ordinarily as kin relationship is thus a highly volatile subjectivity, a colonizing or consuming of the subject that calls for a continual labor of elicitation. It is not a pattern or a paradigm institutionalized in the wake of some primordial tryst of inbreeding, not a static "terminology," but a dynamic that engages the whole presence and personae of those involved.

The regime of what has been identified by Warren Shapiro and others as "mother-in-law bestowal" among the Miwuyt and other aboriginal Australian peoples provides an apposite example of this.[1] The example is mirrored in the response I was given, at a point of exasperation, by a group of Daribi villagers in New Guinea. I had asked whether there were any of their practices that were not the result of cult introductions from elsewhere. They replied: "Only this, that one must not look directly at one's *au* [mother-in-law/son-in-law]; to look at the *au* is like looking at the sun." The interdiction of this relation is the formative act of Daribi procreation and kin relationship as the bestowal, not of a bride, but of a bride's mother as the source and producer or marriageability.[2] Though it is by no means universal, complete avoidance is for many peoples of Australia and New Guinea the manner in which the icon of incest is detached and deflected. A betrothed Daribi man will not, thus, disclose the name of his fiancée because she is identified with her mother, whose name he may not hear or pronounce, nor can the mother be induced to name her prospective son-in-law. Marriage effectively transforms a girl's identification by removing her from her mother, and sexual contact with the wife's mother is the definitive exemplar of Daribi incest (as well as of verbal profanity).

Additional marriages (with sisters of the original bride) may be developed, as often in Australia, upon the same iconic bestowal. But the more provocative examples of continuing marriage have been provided by practices involving the resolution of an iconization of cross-cousin incest. Cross-cousin marriage is presented as a norm and sometimes is practiced, either outright or under the rubric of the norm, *because of the close relationship* of the kin involved, rather than to marry within the closest possible degree of relational distance. In instances where an actual cross-cousin is married (not normally the most frequent), the act of marriage itself serves to convert the "incest" to affinity. But even where the pair are related as so-called classificatory cousins, the effect is the same—in fact, the less closely related they may be seen to be, the more effectively their union resolves the "incest" of relationship itself. Residents of two Barok villages in New Ireland claim that marriage among *tau* or *gogup* (i.e., of a man with his father's sister or patrilateral cross-cousin) is their statistical as well as their ethical norm. Close checking with a painstaking genealogist in the larger community revealed, however, that in virtually all cases the kinspersons were barely even *tau* or *gogup* in the most distant or "classificatory" sense.[3] But the genealogist did not consider this to be a salient point—they were, to him, all instances of "marriage with the *tau* or *gogup*." This is but a small detail, a mere inversion, in the understanding of cross-cousin marriage, but it turns the whole sense of it around: one does not marry "into" the category; one marries *out* of it.

Cross-cousin marriage does not exist as a "rule" to structure marriage or society, or exist as part of a structure, for its exemplary resolution effectively disperses the sense of flow or obligation that its icon pictures. Like other marital icons, it exists to give affinity the concrete form necessary to its effectiveness. Parallel cousin marriage, which would appear to test the limits of lineal propriety even more severely, "courts" the image of incest in like measure, and does so to effect a similar resolution. But here, too, the "challenge," the opening gambit, lies in the icon, the "rule" that theorists have forged into a model. Consequent marriage "proves" that rule by transforming its structuring of things into an affinity.

What, then, of the majority of the earth's peoples, who do not practice mother-in-low bestowal or entertain norms involving the marriage of close kinspersons? The existence of a universal "incest taboo" was of course posited by some of these people, who also conceived the need to explain away cross-cousin marriage to secure their claims. It would seem to be precisely in those societies where the icon of incest has been rendered ambiguous that it becomes necessary to legislate against incest, or otherwise make a deliberate issue of it. This is less because of monstrous or inhuman properties attributed to the act itself than it is a matter, for folks who no longer recognize distinct categories to marry out of, of the lines of discrimination having been eroded.

It has often been argued that marriage between the children or grandchildren of siblings is instituted to concentrate kin-based resources that would be dispersed in more "open" forms of alliance. If opportunism and strategy made institutions, the limit of this tendency would be the incestuous union of opposite-sex siblings, which would obviate the dispersal of resources altogether. And so the question arises of whether sibling marriage itself may be postulated, not, of course, as a viable realization of incest, but as an icon that would resolve the concentration of resources as a form of sociality. The answer is that such an icon is not uncommon, and it is recognizable in those regimes that have been classified as "matrilineal." The diagnostic feature of this icon is a severe taboo on the interaction of brother and sister, analogous to that imposed between a man and his wife's mother by the Daribi. The "marriage by prohibition" is elicitory, reproducing offspring "for" the brother via its deflection into another marriage that corresponds to the resolution of the incest.

Barok kin relationships and reproduction are initiated by cross-sex sibling prohibition as this is deflected onto the marriages of the respective siblings, and as offspring *for* the sibling set are elicited *through* those marriages.[4] The sibling set stands as maternal *(kolume)* to the offspring of its women and paternal *(gala)* to those of its male siblings. But because every sibling set retains its iconic continence despite these divergent marital destinies, each gender in the set has "back-to-back" responsibilites with respect to the begotten offspring of the other. A woman is *un tamana,* literally a nurturant "female father," to her brother's children, and a man a containing "male mother" to his sister's. In effect the tabooed sibling interaction is not only "deflected" into the mutual and reciprocal solicitation of each gender's children on the part of the other. It is actually *realized* in that way.

There is a real question as to whether lineality of any kind, matri- or patri- or even bilineal, is appropriate to such a regime of sibling containment. And that raises the concomitant query, which the Barok would seem to have answered for themselves, as to whether "marriage" is even conceivable in this context. Ideally a Barok bride-to-be "proposes" to the *maruake* or maternal uncle of her intended and on his behalf. Should the proposal be acceptable, the *maruake* will designate amounts of traditional wealth to be used to "buy the shame" of her parents and siblings, and at this time or later the prospective groom *may* be informed of the arrangements. But even when the couple begin cohabiting, no public announcement or acknowledgment will be made, and in my experience it is not until the couple has borne a number of children that the feast is held for the "shame" payments to be made and the union finalized. It is the offspring, in effect, who "marry" the parents to each other, and the severe prohibition on sibling interaction that suppresses what would otherwise be called the "marriage" as well.

Cross-cousins, those related through the bigendered roles of a single "parent" (who is mother to one and father to another set), are thus "siblings" by virtue of marital deflection. Cross-cousins of opposite gender, whom Barok call *gogup,* are then the reproduction of the original icon, for they are effectively cross-sex siblings through the marital deflection of cross-sex sibling interaction. (A man, for instance, is called the *maruak-gogup,* or "cross-maternal uncle," of his *gogup*'s offspring.) This would seem to be the reason why some Barok present the *gogup* relationship as an appropriate icon for marriage, and also why those who accept that icon do not marry their *gogup.*

But the Barok usages present merely a single example of a wide variety of ways in which the deflection of sibling marriage may be resolved. Peter Lovell has cited evidence of a most ingenious set of usages among the Longana of East Ambae, Vanuatu.[5] Longana assimilate the deflecting marriage, as well as the offspring of the marriage, to the cross-sex sibling bond itself. Thus brothers-in-law *(halai)* are said to be cross-sex siblings of one another through the identification of a man with his connubial partner, and a man's sister's children *(alai)* are regarded as his sisters because they were born of his sister. These "sisters" share the very severe Longana taboos regarding cross-sex siblings themselves *(hangue)*. Remarkably, then, whereas a Barok man and his sister are both "fathers" to the same sibling set, a Longana man and his father are both "sisters" to the same man.

An icon of sibling marriage reflects the actual marriage so as to preserve the continence of the cross-sex sibling bond, in effect replacing the marriage with it. An icon conceived in purely marital terms, such as that of mother-in-law bestowal, conversely deflects the continence of siblings so as to recoup it in the obligations and perquisites of the ensuing relationships. This is the substance of Lévi-Strauss's "atom of kinship" argument,[6] for in all cases it is the siblingship of the parental generation that forms the whole analogic basis for substance and relationship, lineality and laterality in the succeeding one. But of course the parental generation was also, and in the same sense, a "succeeding" one, and the logic involved is part and parcel of the whole issue of successorship. The problem this poses for all patterned arrangements of the "kinship" sort, be they called "structural," "lineal," or whatever, is that the interposing of generations is not necessary and is not even called for unless one were imitating some disingenuous folk model in the result. The staging of the icon through its deflection, or of the deflection through its icon, does not necessarily descend or ascend lineally, or extend or intend laterally. It can just as well be understood to be *nested* within itself, like the icon of incest.

It is not difficult to understand why Lévi-Strauss chose cross-cousin marriage as an "elementary structure," for it neatly combines the two deflected modes of relationship, siblingship and marriage, into a form that reproduces, so to speak, its own solution. But it might more profitably be considered an elementary solution to a condition that has a universal provenience: that of the elemental deflection of one mode of relationship by another. For, taken together with injunctions to the obligatory marriage of the descendants of siblings in later generations (found in interior New Guinea and in the section systems of Australia), it superimposes an iconicity of its own upon the process of deflection.

Nonetheless, it is crucial to recognize that marriage of this type conforms as well to an icon of incest, and not to a description of actual affairs or a determinative structuring of political, familial, or property relations. It is even less imaginable as an ideal or archetypal precept, for it is precisely the iconic—the imaging or meaningful—aspect of incest that is overcome in its deflection into kin relationships. And it would compound the misreading of utility as well as significance into these instances to imagine any sort of motive or purpose coming into play, or to entertain an argument of causes and consequences. The deflection, in other words, of sibling marriage upon a back-to-back solicitude of the siblings for each others' children is not undertaken among the Barok to provide people with "male mothers" and "female fathers" or for any such reason at all. If anything, it is the imaginably antisocial or monstrous character of sibling incest itself that energizes the deflection.

If we give Marilyn Strathern's shrewd observation that "women do not make babies" the critical weight it deserves, and add the necessary corollary, that men do not either, it would seem to follow that babies are not "made."[7] The icon of mechanical or biological reproduction is, in other words, false, and false because it is an icon. Its very iconicity is the trap; the more explicitly, persuasively, or accurately it depicts the making of babies as an objective process, the more unsupportable it becomes as an account of what actually takes place. What it misses in all but laboratory conditions is the all-important factor of "carnal knowledge." It is not simply that this "factor" of sexual arousal or receptivity and its implicit metamorphosis of own gender is left out, but rather that its omission and deflection correspond to the icon's pragmatic effect.

The objectivity of procreation's icon, like that of incest, is pragmatic and *only* pragmatic. It is part of a "process" of *internal* rather than external mating, but, as in the case of its counterpart, or of the setup of a chess game prior to play, the process it belongs to is one of detaching, deflecting, or otherwise eroding the icon itself.

I must go largely on my own experiences of Melanesian peoples in this discussion of incest's iconicity, even to the point of privileging my examples, because I do not know how much analogous material has been inadvertently suppressed or distorted for the sake of theory or reportage. By the time it comes into focus as a finite, knowable, and graspable entity, the sense of kin relations has already become an iconic plaything.

Just as "linear time" measures a criterion for knowing the ways in which time might *not* be linear, or the fictions of "sense faculties" and logic force an overprecision that is helpful in making sense of "sense" itself, so the charting of relatives and relationships provides a prosthetic device for bringing the underdetermined reality of kinship into focus. It shows why the thing called "kinship" cannot exist as a thing unto itself by overemphasizing the paradigmatic permutations through which it might be. Any "kin" subject involves "persons" who incorporate a multiplicity of differential roles and statuses at once, and any circumstance—abstract or concrete—in which such a subject becomes relevant entails the encompassing of some of these roles within others, to the point where transformational relations among the various "relationships" (roles or statuses) themselves undercut the "normative" attribution of those relationships. Kin terminologies, relational paradigms, and sociological norms merely translate the most basic and inceptional of these into the language of category and rule, ad hoc "kin" logic.

That is why what is often mistaken for biological mating or misinterpreted as a universal "institution" of marriage is so generally traced to incest "prohibition." The icon of incest is "deflected" *not* because marriages are made in heaven, or because something "like" marriage just has to be, or even because incest is evil or potentially unnatural or damaging. It is deflected because the prime mode of relational encompassment and transformation is the social invention of "other gender" by the encompassment of either ("cultural") sense of gender within the other.

Thus to seek the root of supergender, mother right or father right in some sort of originative prohibition, social contract or agreement, or in a natural condition, overlooks the fact that can only be expressed or comprehended within the context of the transformations themselves. Because it is *underdetermined* rather than directly determined, the *sense* of kinship has no extracultural root causes or cultural ground conditions. It only has analogies, as with chess.

The life of chess began as a crude military game in India. Called "The Four Arms" (the name "chess" itself being a possible corruption of an Indo-European root for "four"), it was self-descriptive. Excluding the gendered pair, and even gender (the queen is often called something like "the royal vizier" in Eastern versions), this would mean the pawn, rook, knight, and bishop as four specialties of military prowess. Like some other Indian inventions, the zero concept, perhaps, or the cakra-knowledge of the wheel, the game was smuggled (I can think of no better verb) into Iran and adjacent regions of the Middle East, where it took root and flourished. It seems to have diffused from there into Europe and other areas, or, to another way of thinking, absorbed into it-

self a broader range of thinking out strategy and hierarchy. But for all
its many variants (there is a Russian analogue in which one plays to *lose*
as many pieces as possible), it was still a very limited game; even the
most important pieces could move only a square or two at a turn.

Chess was restructured into the game we know at a time when
Europeans were exploring the applications of analytic geometry, the
movement potential of its pieces honed on the four arms of the *x* and *y*
axes. As a quasi-mathematical calculation of royalty and strategy, its
movement was no longer limited to one-square-at-a-time or even diffusion. It *colonized* the world of thought about strategy and strategy
about thought.

Was this really a new game, *Kriegsspiel* in space-time, or was it that
the Europeans, as they might have argued, had finally gotten the point
of chess, and even gotten its gender right? From that point onward, the
game of "improving" chess or developing other strategy games along its
lines became *another* game, and real refinement took place within established limits as the ingenuity of play itself. There were other designs
in the elementary kinship of structures, such as the perfection of the automated mechanism, the mechanization of natural order, determining
the proper formulae for government and law, social norm and rule, production and monetary valuation, that demanded more attention.

Just exactly how the games that are played in the shadow zone between mind and reality might be structured, restructured, formulated,
or even mechanized is a game of its own called "theory." It has no more
to do with what mind is or what reality might be than the game, the
comparison of games, or the critique of games that it happens to be
playing. There is the little world of reality's reflection in the mind, and
the larger one of mind's reflection in the cosmos. And there is the anthropology in which, as the Yoruba proverb has it, "we fashion a wisdom for ourselves from other peoples' wisdom"—including that of
chess. The cognate of "game" in Melanesian *tokpisin* is *giaman*, "de-
ceit," "trickery." So it really would not matter from the standpoint of
this discussion whether chess is as good a game as any or a better game
than most, or that it may be less analytic than checkers or the Chinese
go. The only thing that matters is that chess is a royal game, one that
gets the point of royalty better than most political or historical versions,
and that it does so by getting its gender right.

Chess play and the working out of social-relational hierarchies are
temporal inversions of one another, mirrored opposites that both contrast and integrate a kind of figure-ground reversal of real life on the

game board and an imaginal royal game in the life-spaces outside of it. Both elevations are in a very important sense unreal or, as they say, "symbolic," so that what is truly objective in either case—real moves, strategies, and matings—involves cutting through an illusory format. Each move draws a distinction, and each distinction allows other ones to be made about it.

Chess play begins with two complete hierarchies identical in power potential and evolves toward a single distinction, ideally a "mating," that determines the outcome of the game. Social life begins for all of us with a single mating that leads to other matings, moves, or captures and evolves into a real complexity of hierarchy. What is simple and given at the outset in one case is deadly, involute, demanding of great patience and forbearance in the other. The chess of life is only deceptively structured; the life of chess is only deceptively vital.

Yet without the comparison, the figure-ground inversion life-in-chess/chess-in-life, the game would mean nothing. And without the game, or something very like it in dramas like *Oedipus Rex* and *Hamlet*, innumerable mythic and ritualized versions of the same thing like the Spanish corrida, the appositive play of the supergenders would lack for an exotic demonstration. In other words, what appear on the face of it to be highly sophisticated products of conceptual and historical development, superstructures built up upon much simpler facts, are not that at all. They are *infrastructures*, ritual and all, so elemental to the existence of the human race that they must have been with it in some form or other from the very beginning of its times. We might try to reinvent them, as we do "cultures," for the very earliest hominids who could lay claim to being human, and do so with a good conscience, for all the fact something very like that invented *us*.

Let's get back to the game, the *Kriegsspiel* of human life chances that Clifford Geertz has so aptly termed "deep play." Chess codes everything about the board, the pieces, and the movement or order of play in terms of laterality and lateral alternation. There are the squares in alternative color, the identical hierarchies of pieces placed upon them, also contrastingly shaded. There are the two opposing "sides," front and back, that lock the players into a face-to-face confrontation as they play the inside of each other's chances. There are the sides of the board that give a dimension to this, the sides of the players themselves, and the cross-connections of these to the opposing sides of the brain that give depth to the play, allow each of its "sides" to be played over again on the inside of each player. The laterality of the game relapses in the players, and the laterality of the players relapses in the singularity of the game and its outcome. Each is "stalked" by a lone evolutionary hunter.

But there is one important difference between them, and it is the difference that gender makes to the laterality of the game. It is that, regardless of the respective gendering of the players, each plays the twinning of gender in apposition to the antitwinning of the other. The king, or male value of the game itself, begins play to the *right* of player with the "light"-colored pieces and to the *left* of the one with the "dark" side of the force. The queen, female epicenter of strategic power on the board, begins conversely to the left of the "light" player and the right of the "dark" one. This little detail, generally treated as arbitrary—someone has to make the first move—is also the initial "mating" that touches off the reciprocity of distinctions in the game. Who would guess it is also the secret of an appositional play that maps life into the game, and maps an image of the game back upon life? For, gender being the twin we do not have, we begin life in a nonarbitrary way, as the gender we happen to own, and must learn the significance of its multiplication and division through lateral inversion, as in chess.

Or in number itself: what is "reproduced" in the use of number to measure and understand—as in statistics or any use of numerical functions in the "mapping" of reality or the accounting of human transactions—is no less a game of depictions than chess, and no less a self-reciprocal one. The "tallying" or representational facility of numericity is itself remapped, "pictured" through the transformational algorithms of "number theory" that pictures the world in its terms. So of course the credibility of number as theory depends in its turn on that which is represented through it.

In his remarkable study *Intimations of Infinity,* Jadran Mimica has shown how a use of the body's own laterality instead of transformational algorithms turns an ostensibly primitive counting system into a sophisticated quantitative comprehension.[8] Counting "bodies" on the singular dualities of the human body, the Iqwaye people of Papua New Guinea use only two numbers. They count the digits (one, two, one, two, one *hand*) cumulatively, unitizing the digits of hands and feet in this way (two hands, two feet = twenty digits as "one man"). Then they begin the tally again with the first finger as "one man" and count "men" the next time around the body to a total of four hundred. But because there are only two digits to their counting system but twenty to the body, the pluralities tallied consecutively in this way will divide out as increasingly encompassing (viz., 20, 400, 16,000) versions of "one."

The "one" repictured by the action of numerical representation is the creator Omalyce, the human imago of infinity whose "counting" is the reproduction of the human race.

The Daribi, however, "uncount" by twos, that is, they used laterality originally to decouple numericity from the representation of things, and hence from the heuristic of counting or countability itself. Daribi had three number terms, *tedeli* or *deri* (one), *si* (two), and *sera'* (three), as well as a special marker—*digi*—for numericity: *deridigi* is "one-mark," *sidigi* "two-mark," and *sera'-digi* "three-mark." But because *si*, the "evenness" upon which any kind of recombinative use of laterality would depend, is recognized as self-relative, it compromises the sequency of numerical progression. They would tally, represent a quantity of countable units, by tying knots in a cord or breaking off sticks in a one-to-one correspondence with the individual items.

Si, the only "even" number, marks only the precision of its ambiguity; it is a self-reciprocal function, like the terminology for diurnal reckoning among the Daribi. *Do* means *either* "yesterday" or "tomorrow," *duba* means "day before yesterday" or "day after tomorrow," *tegiga* in the same way means "three days removed." So *si* means "two" and "half" in exactly the same way; a "season," or *si*, is half of the year, and the year itself both of them. Hence Daribi numeration *completes itself* in a phrase, *sidari-si* (the "two-together-two") that has its most salient usage in the repletion of social aggregates. Despite a lot of evidence to the contrary, Daribi would insist that specific "lines" of people (e.g., nameable "lineages" as social agencies) were invariably grouped *sidari-si*, in an emergent relationship of mutual repletion called *si deri terawaiu*, "making one of two." Instead of dealing directly with incest, which is usually dismissed as incidental or inconsequential, Daribi "uncounting" deals directly with the dual encompassment of distinction upon which incest depends.

But why *three* numbers? As Euclid might have suggested, they form the only necessary sequence, the alpha and omega of numericity's self-completion. Take all of the whole numbers anyone could possibly conceive of, place them in sequence and multiply each by the next, and you will get a product that is divisible by any of them. Add one to this, as Euclid suggested, and you will get a sum *in*divisible by any but the first. *Subtract* one, and you get its counterpart, the *first* of the twin primes that stand at the end (or, Daribi might add, the *beginning*) of an exhaustive number series. They are functions of numerical laterality taken apart from quantitative evaluation, for the "hinge" in each case—

Figure 7. Chess Kali.

Euclid's calculable but uncountable product and the Daribi countable but incalculable *si*—is a "morph" of the other.

Ancient Hindus might have considered the Daribi *sidari-si* the *darsan* of numericity, and hence intrinsically related to iconicity, chess play, and perhaps, if they had known of it, the myth of Perseus and the Medusa, via the divinity Kali, the "black goddess of time." For she incorporates gender's "swordplay in reverse," its lethal picture of itself as incest, and its Medusa. The only way to know this chess queen of the "four arms" is to see her (Fig. 7), and the only way to "see" her is through the integration *(sidari-si)* of her vision of oneself with one's own in the stopping of time that Hindus call the *darsan*, the "sight of the goddess."

7

The Queen's Daughter
and the King's Son

Chess-Hamlet wins the game by losing his peace of mind, all of his pieces, and, in Shakespeare's version, his life as well. In another story, told by ostensibly matrilineal folk in New Ireland, he retains his life and his hard-won male agency. But the man, named Ngangala, who told me the tale, and his reason for telling it are apposite to this chapter. Ngangala helped me very much in my work but was so piqued by the harassment he received, as an outsider, for doing so by members of my adoptive lineage that he left the community. He forsook his matrilineage and went to live elsewhere with his wife and begotten children. This tale was his parting gift to me.

"The Queen's Daughter," he said, is a traditional Barok story, originally told to him by his mother. It is one of a series of Barok tales "about white men," stories that borrow the plot motifs of "Western" fairy tales (one of them is recognizably "Ali Baba and the Forty Thieves") to make a kind of sense (or is it nonsense?) of the wider world. One can only assume that the historical and cultural ambivalence of these and other features is part of the tale itself. On the taped transcription of his narration, Ngangala first gives the name of the queen's daughter as "Elizabeth," then corrects himself and calls her "Margaret." The Queen's submarine is obviously an item of modern technology, though many Barok claim they had a power called *bebanam* in precontact times, a submersible weapon that my friends identified as "a mechanical shark." Here is the story:

A man and his two sons lived together. The elder son was named Grahame and the younger George. When they had grown a bit, their father bought them each a gun and wanted to teach them to shoot. Every morning he would put five bottles in the sea and give five cartridges to each son. Grahame would fire first but would miss every time. George, however, broke every bottle. After a while George suggested they try hunting in the bush. Their mother gave the boys some food, and their father gave them each five cartridges. George, who was bright, filled his pockets with pebbles, and as he walked around he threw them down one by one. George shot a pigeon, but Grahame missed everything he shot at. When they were ready to return, Grahame just wandered around, but George was able to find his way back along the trail of pebbles. Their father noted George's success but reproached Grahame. George pointed out to him that the cartridges were costly. They went again, each receiving ten cartridges, and George collected pebbles; he returned, thanks to his trail, with ten animals and birds that he had shot, but Grahame again came home empty-handed. Their father again noted the results. The next day each received twenty cartridges, and George collected corn kernels to strew as a trail. As he hunted George threw them down, but some ants and small rats ate them, so that when he finished his cartridges George was unable to find his way back. Only Grahame returned. George walked around the bush for three months; his trousers and his little hat were ruined. One morning he came to a distant place and met the queen's daughter on the beach. "Hey, a young man! Are you crazy to come here—don't you know that my father kills his enemies?" She took him to the house and gave him food and trousers. They slept together, and she tried to have sex with him, but he was unwilling. Later she went to see her parents. They were sitting at the table; they cooked their food in a huge saucepan and did not bother to remove the limbs. The Queen would shove the legs of a victim into his wife's mouth, then she would feed one to her husband, feet first. She ate about ten bodies at a sitting, her husband fifteen. Their prison was filled with live prisoners, and they would eat them this way when they died. When they finished eating they would dance: *rrr te te te* (hee hee hee), *rrr te te te* (hee hee hee). Their daughter told them she would like to marry. The queen asked if she had someone in mind—"then bring him quickly so I can eat his guts and liver." When Margaret brought George to them, the queen told him to be outside next morning at 5:00 A.M. when he rang the bell. George could not sleep that night for worry, and in the morning he was there early. "Take this rusted hoe, this rusted ax and knife, and cut and plant a garden a mile long." George went, tried to cut the bush, but it was as when a pig nibbles at leaves. He just sat and cried, past noon, past one o'clock. Margaret came to him: "You haven't cut the garden, do you want to die?" She threw the knife and the undergrowth was severed, she threw the ax and the trees were cut, threw the hoe and the ground was tilled, took the sweet potato cuttings and the garden was planted. When the queen went to ring the bell that night, George was there. "Did you finish it?" "Yes." "All right, tomorrow when I ring the morning bell you be there on the line." Again George worried all night. He was there again in the morning. The queen said, "All right, you take this bulldozer and pull my submarine up from the beach and into the work-shop." But there was no road, only bush. Margaret came to him. "Clear off the seat of the 'dozer!" She cut the road through the bush, and the two fas-tened a line to the submarine, pulled it through the bush, and put it under the house. George went to the Queen. "Yes, you brought it up; see me again tomorrow morning." Having worried again all night, George went with Margaret, and the queen and his wife took them out to sea in a boat. The queen said to George, "See my ring? I will throw it into the sea here, and tomorrow you must come and retrieve it." He threw out the ring, and they returned to shore. Again that night Margaret tried to have sex with George, but to no avail. In the morning the queen told George to swim out and get the ring. The sea was full of death: sharks, crocodiles, all manner of dangerous creatures. George could not bring himself to dive in. Margaret came to him and said, "Now I will lie down on this table; take this little knife, cut my neck, cut down the body, and collect the blood in this dish. Then cut my body up and throw the pieces together with the blood in the sea." George was horrified, but she insisted, "Otherwise you will be slaugh-tered." He cut her then, but it was really only an apparition; she remained at home. When he followed the beach he found the ring, and he reached the queen as he was about to ring the bell. When he showed him the ring, the queen said, "You are a fine man indeed; now you must marry my daugh-ter. When you come in the morning, bring ten thousand for the bride-price; if you cannot, I'll eat you." George went away in despair, and when Margaret came he told her that he had no money. They bathed and walked in the garden, and Margaret said, "Here, take this unripe melon; my father just loves them like this, when they're still sour." George put it in his pocket. They went to the house and sat at the table, and the queen said, "Where's the money?" George replied, "If I were with my parents it would be easy, but I am not up to your price; perhaps you will take this little melon and cut it." "Oh yes, my favorite food, these little melons." He cut it, and money began to pour out; it knocked over the people, reached the roof, and burst out of the house. "Oh now you shame me, perhaps now you will take my place, marry my child." The two exchanged rings, and the queen gave George all his finery. That night George began to sharpen his little knife; he did not sleep with Margaret but slept alone in the queen's house. He went to the queen's room, turned up the lamp, saw that he was sleeping, and stuck the knife into him. Then he went and killed the queen's wife; he threw kerosene on the house and set it afire. Then he took the keys to the other buildings and freed the prisoners. In the morning he told his wife what he had done, and she said, "Good, now would you like to go and see your parents?" "Yes, but I do not know the road." "We can try." They went to a beautiful house of the queen; its whole surface shone like brass. Margaret told George to close his eyes; she turned her ring and then told him to look. They had arrived at the place of George's parents. At first they all hid, but then George extended his hand to them and they were all reconciled. They all stayed together. Grahame then began to desire Margaret; he thought of a way to kill George and marry his wife. The two had a large pack of hunting dogs. Grahame took them out into the bush and threw them into a big hole. When he returned George asked him where the dogs were, and Grahame said, "There's a huge pig down in a hole and the dogs jumped down to fight it; I came to get you to help me kill it." George took his gun and went. When they came to the hole, Grahame told him to look down below and then pushed him over the side. He left George there and told the others that George had carried a great pig off somewhere in the bush, and he himself had gotten bored and came back home. George stayed in the hole for three months, and Grahame became intimate with Margaret and married her. George asked the dogs what kinds of things they could do. "Oh, I dig." "I cut roots." "I break stones." "Me, I'm the compass." They dug for six days, and on the seventh they came up to the house at night. The compass said, "Go up now." Everyone was sleeping. George went inside, turned up the lamp, and Grahame and Margaret were sleeping together in bed. George shot them both. Then he went to his parents' room, turned up the light, and shot them. He came back, washed, and then threw the bodies away. In the light of dawn he was the only one left.

There are some very good reasons why the queen is *male* in this story, George's father-in-law, to be exact. But if we treat them as diagnostic features peculiar to a "matrilineal" logic, or a worldview built upon such a logic, we are likely to miss the sense of the tale itself. "The Queen's Daughter" makes its sense outside of culture, both because of and in spite of its conflation of plot motifs and separate understandings of the world. It *shares* the worlds of the Barok and the white expatriates.

Comparisons of this tale with classics like "Hansel and Gretel," "The Golden Fleece," or "The Bremen Town Musicians," all of them "quoted" in the plot, may be less helpful than a contrast with Ernest Hemingway's story "The Short Happy Life of Francis McComber." Francis McComber is a wealthy sportsman on safari in Africa, good at shooting but, like George, quite uncertain about his masculinity. McComber loses his nerve in the face of dangerous, charging game animals; the white hunter steps in and dispatches the beast, and every time this happens Mrs. McComber spends the night with the white hunter in his tent. Finally, one day the white hunter's gun jams while he is trying to stop a charging lion; McComber faces his fear, shoots it instead, and lives a brief moment of ecstasy before his wife fires, "by accident," and kills him from behind.

Characters like George, Francis McComber, and Hamlet would seem to have no more sexuality or personality than chess pieces. They are impotent, like George and very likely Francis, or vociferously indifferent to sex, like Hamlet. Sexuality only traps them, even in the traps they set for others. Even more devastating from the psychological or cultural point of view is the destructuring of the male personality as the crucial element in the unfolding plot, the genius of the male figure who holds the value of the game. It is vitally important that he lose his ego and his machismo to the setting of the plot, and exactly how and why he does this is a key to the story.

Very distinctively Barok in this way, "The Queen's Daughter" reads like the ultimate parody of all fairy tales. No mere assassin like Mrs. McComber, Margaret is a witch of Medea-like proportions, and her parents, the royal pair across the board, are ogres. Hamlet is different, by now a culture hero with the stature of a Faust or a Gilgamesh; like them, his virtue lies in the fact that he tries to figure *everything* out, even life itself.

The question of just exactly what Shakespeare's *Hamlet* might be about, of its subject as tragedy, poetry, or public drama, is hardly resolvable outside of the action itself. Its issue is what the action, and principally Hamlet himself, engages; it *is* the play. The prince was, of course, "caught" by the edge of the madness he feigned, and the contagion, as it spreads to others, becomes the emplotment of the drama. For the queen, Ophelia, and arguably Claudius and Laertes become deranged in greater or lesser degree through the simple act of trying to figure out what Hamlet was doing, and something like that madness infects every spectator or commentator who likewise attempts to come to terms with Hamlet's motives or "flaw." There is no one quite like Hamlet, not even Hamlet himself or the actor portraying him, for the madness of trying to "own" his impersonation as a moral being becomes more real in its effects in others than the falseness Hamlet pretended for it.

Hamlet acquired the madness he feigned in just this way, by speaking the moral truths he suspected under circumstances in which no sane man would talk that way, and his madness became the discourse that the Danish court, Polonius included, modeled itself upon ("To thine own self be true . . ."). The irony of this kind of speech, which is not deranged or symptomatic because it does not have to be, is that it masks acute or inane profundities within that avoidance of direct reference that is characteristic of schizophrenic speech. Hamlet's use of it is addressed (audibly) to himself but intended, in a kind of ironic ventriloquism, for others. That of his "speaking foil," Polonius, seems intended philanthropically, for others, but suggests strongly his own benefit in a kind of mirror inversion of Hamlet's acting of himself.

So, too, the performance of *Hamlet* carries its contagion into the art of the actors trying to do what Hamlet himself tried to do, that is, demonstrate himself, engage in the performance of Hamlet outside of his own head. Any "understanding" of the play merely copies the same self-act, the same impetus for self-copying, into another dimension of demonstrative possibilities.

If Hamlet must have a "fault" or flaw, a crack of madness that runs through his whole world, it would be that he did not keep his intentions but in every literal and figurative sense gave them away. He gave his pragmaticity to the little world of Elsinore, which made a language and an ethos of it. This means that the ritual he lived in pretending madness formed a demonstration of causes and effects around his acting of himself, a world that was so completely "about" his intentions, being made of them, that his trajectory was completely relative within it. Only a "sane" man would have "done it pat while he is praying," killed the king directly and at once; it was not part of Hamlet's act of catching consciences. In effect this act depended on getting *others* to intend *him*, tell him directly to kill Claudius—something that does indeed happen, but of course too late, when he has already been poisoned.

If Polonius is Hamlet's "speaking foil" (and one who dies by the foil, as it were, by "blowing his cover" and speaking out from behind the arras), the troupe of traveling players is his unspeaking one. The "play within a play" is a dumb show, an image of the actor within the actor, of the Lutheran conscience of the student from Wittenberg. In a manner of speaking, or more properly unspeaking, it is fully consonant with Hamlet's relative trajectory that he has others mime the burden of his conscience for him, professional actors engaged to *do* what he has to say. Thereafter his trajectory becomes morally as well as intellectually relative; he is free to play the "no Hamlet" that is, nonetheless, quite like Hamlet.

Hamlet's is the tragedy of sense, of an anthropological quality that John Keats called "negative capability" staged long before Keats's oeuvre of "sensibility" came into vogue. It runs on the relative trajectory of Europe's Reformation era, an alienation that, if it infected the modern epoch, would have halted any attempt at anthropology cold in its tracks. The ability to fully integrate the fact that things could be radically different from the play of similitudes in which they are conventionally cast takes one well beyond the standards of comparison for similitude itself. "It likes me not," in Shakespeare's lingo—the point is lost in the joke that is made of it, and so the humor turns upon the fastidiousness of its own expression. Negative capability uses this as a ploy, a kind of foil for the staging of its own problematic qualities as tragedy. One has to believe the speaker even though, or especially because, his words betray themselves in the act of speaking them.

Sense, the feeling of oneself, or the evidence of one's faculties brought up through that feeling—the world in the person and the person in the world—is captured by the play of similitudes through which it must be articulated. But the other side of this double enjambment, the twin of the empirical person, recaptures that articulation to form a similitude of its own: acting oneself mad in the world/mad acting itself back in the person. Notice how this double play of similitudes, mad action recaptured by its own feeling of itself, betrays itself in the exotic description Hamlet set up to "catch the conscience of the king." The play within a play does not show brother murdering brother—the crime of Claudius—but shows *a nephew murdering his own uncle.* Instead of bringing the crime out in the open, it tips the hand of the punishment intended for it.

No wonder King Claudius was so dismayed; revenge itself was rotten in the state of Denmark! Was Hamlet's problem after this really one of an inability to act directly, dallying intellectually, as Goethe once suggested, with a point already proven? Or was it simply the problem of cleaning up his own act? Hamlet's dalliance with the facts was not just intellectual, but that of feeling's revenge upon thought, like that of a torturer who participates intimately in the suffering of his victim to even the score of some earlier misreckoning. Much of Shakespeare's prose, Elizabethan drama in general, and English literature itself declaims upon the point of this, the appositive play of sensibility, or the chess game of thought and feeling. The body makes up its own mind after the fact of its decisions, lives out the pragmatic afterlife of its thinking half.

The Royal Heir as trickster, but one that, like Coyote in the tales of the American Southwest, is so good at tricking others because he is even better at tricking himself. The copying is of an identity with itself, an involution that only becomes knowable or thinkable as imitation—a play of the play within the play—when others are drawn into the act. So it is the Hamlet that Hamlet was imitating, or the Shakespeare that Shakespeare was imitating in Hamlet, or perhaps the "life" that copied itself as Shakespeare's fancy. The only question that remains for the solipsist, who discovers that he has been inventing the world all along, is that of agency, of who or what he may be. What is *real* in the play of similitudes? The only way to get a confirmation is to ask others ("I invented you, didn't I?"), and they, of course, humor him.

To be or not to be. Did the hero of Shakespeare's drama, *the* Hamlet, actually live out the passions of his moral cause, his obligations to his father? Did he *believe* in ghosts? Only an actor is playing him, and Hamlet himself was only an actor, one who had to be cued or prompted at the end of the play to do what he must—kill the king. Did that Hamlet actually *participate*, like a Royal Torturer, in the sufferings that others might have felt in acting out the guilty charade he had set up for them? The "incest" that implicated his mother right in his missed successorship to the throne is largely important because of the murder involved in it. Otherwise it would be an instance of something that anthropologists call the "junior levirate." But then the murder is made culpable because of the allegations of incest that make it so. We have only the play of similitudes in Hamlet's language, his soliloquies and asides, to go on in determining the sense of this as kinship, but only his kinship to go on in determining the sense of his language.

So if kinship is only a set of connections made among the living on behalf of the dead, or among the dead through the words and actions of the living, we have another possibility for what Hamlet might have known or felt. The actual lineage of Hamlet is that of an actor playing another actor, and so on down the line to that imaginal historical figure who played himself so that the whole thing could happen. Did *the* Hamlet, the original one, live out the whole tragedy of his performance in a passion of what the composer Richard Strauss once called "the hero's release from the world"?

As a stunning evocation of the shape of male agency, supergender, *Hamlet* plays the same role in tragedy as the black hole concept does in astronomy. The Hamlet-question as to whether it exists or not, "to be or not to be," is beside the point. Do black holes exist in the way we have conceived of them, one that obviates the empirical criteria for existence in its very formulation? The problem is not just that of a direct "yes" or "no" being excluded, as in a quantum paradox (Schrödinger's no-cat); it is far worse than that. The problem is that the paradox, the very ambivalence of yes and no, is excluded as well. The "anti-energy" or whatever of the black-hole phenomenality runs in white-hot pursuit of the questions asked about it.

So a theory of any sort—literary, structuralist, deconstructionist—that purported to explain what is going on in the play *Hamlet* would have a hard enough time explaining itself. It would have to walk away from its subject in doing so, leave it behind like No Weasel at All. We encounter the same problematic quality, that of the answer running away with the question, in the study of kinship, or in ordinary technics or dynamics. The very enigma that is faced in the black hole could be found in the wheel itself, if one knew where to look for it or how to ask about it. ("I could show thee infinity in a nutshell," says Hamlet.) The wheel is too *simple* for the theories or explanations that would match it. So are the implications, for gender, of lateral agency twinned *outward* into the world, or those of gender folded inward, taking the place of laterality in the very constitution of the body, for even the agency of thinking about them. Yet the twinning of this concrete form of disembodiment with the physicality of our constitution is the twinning that matters in knowing what we know about it.

Does one react to a joke, positively or negatively, because one knows the point of it all along but only gets the *relevance* of that point in the disclosure of the punch line? Or does one "have" the relevance all along and only get the point of it, the close knowledge of its humor, at the end? Would it not be the inability to mediate between these two apposite ways of getting the point by not getting it that accounts for the humor of one's reaction? No relevance, no joke/no joke, no relevance. Even if one laughs out of mere politeness, finding the joke trite or inexcusable, the necessity of having to do so becomes funny in and of itself. The joke or anecdote is only the close humor, the briefest possible synopsis of the social charade—one that is infinitely extendable along the relational trajectories of kin protocol, the pretended violation of joking and avoidance behaviors, the exaggerated respect that makes living presences of the dead and lends their aura to the living.

The point of this jocular apposition is apt to be very unclear to those who would essentialize the facts of our animal twinning, bilateral symmetry/asymmetry, and embodied gender, as the bases of kinship itself. It would be all thought about biology, and all biology about thought. To really get the point of the twinning that matters, one would have to turn to the very practical jokes that are made of it as domestic, political, or military strategies—the kind of chess that Hamlet was playing.

Misidentified as "male," supergender succeeds in spite of itself, and as "female" it succeeds because of itself. Exponential woman would instantiate the *similarities* among the genders, bearing the whole and the part of them in the flesh, whereas exponential male would not only differentiate the genders but also have to *under*determine their differentiation. And for those very reasons supergender makes no sense as an organic form, but twins itself against biology. Supergender is what anthropologists have learned to call a "cultural" entity, and therefore a mythological one. Mother Right is a *lady* more than a woman, and she is more a woman than a female. No Weasel at All had to learn to *be* the joke that his brothers were trying to tell, to *protest* masculinity, as Prince Hamlet must become, through no fault of his own, the madness of the act that he was acting. And Francis McComber and George, in "The Queen's Daughter," were perhaps the gods of testosterone.

Identified properly, as the distinctiveness of *own gender,* supergender twins the utter appropriateness-to-the-discourse of its feminine exemplifications with the signal *inappropriateness*-to-themselves of its masculine ones. It is not that Hamlet, Francis McComber, and George are aberrant fantasies, impertinent to a discussion that ought to be much more scientific, but that "male bonding" and protest masculinity are like that. It is only the lady, methinks, that doth protest *too much,* for too much protesting is never enough for the man.

Right brain's imitation of the left brain, and left brain's imitation of the right are always, because better than each other, more effective than the "whole brain" that thinks them up. And if the whole brain is just a picture of itself in the body, as the body itself is pictured in it, then the double encompassment of gender and laterality attains a clarity in their mutual eclipse that is not organic, social, or even mental—the image of the image that is not an image. The ability to know *from* oneself is the highest wisdom of all, and anthropology is *almost* that, but not quite.

Something of that double-edged conundrum seems to have been at the basis of the whole thrust of ancient Egyptian civilization, at least insofar as the apostasy of the Pharaoh Akenaten was concerned. Perhaps that king's son, or at least Royal Heir, of the illustrious Eighteenth Dynasty Pharaoh Amenhotep III, had figured out how Egypt's sense of divinity twinned with itself, and possibly he did so by learning how gender does. At any rate, Akhenaten broke with the whole tradition of pharaonic *male* divinity by having himself depicted in androgynous form—often with a female figure, sometimes pregnant, occasionally with female genitalia.

Sigmund Freud associated the revelations of Akhenaten with the birth of monotheism, but a degree of religious detachment of the sort associated with Buddhism seems superindicated as well. For the encompassing power of the *aten* was as alien to the orthodox Egyptian sense of deity as Akhenaten himself was scornful of the intricate iconicism that constituted the weave of its heritage. For an Egyptian pharaoh, in any case, an issue could never be religious, or even be an issue, without at the same time being policy. The pharaoh embodied the realm as a deity, and from that standpoint policy and religion were one, involving his "image," his person or body, as much as it did the realm.

Our understanding of atenism has been largely hindered by the hopeless idealism through which early commentators projected a largely religious significance for it. But there is little evidence for idealism or for the effeteness that has been attributed to the elite of Akhetaten, Akhenaten's capital at Tell el Amarna. However ineffectual his foreign policy might have seemed, Akhenaten, who pioneered the use of Nubian soldiery in Egypt's Asiatic outposts, was no pacifist either.[1] Idealism as such has no cutting edge to use against the elaborate trappings of mythic motif and metaphor with which the Egyptian experience of divinity had theretofore been draped. A recent authority has perceptively remarked on the "coldness" of atenic theology (one might indeed substitute "merciless" for Redford's epithet "totalitarian").[2] For if projections of an idealism upon the Amarna regime, or of "naturalism" on its art, are less than helpful in making sense of the movement, we would do better to take its iconoclasty at face value.

Whether depicted in relief, in full sculpture, or in the outlines of formal hieroglyphic calligraphy, ancient Egyptian expression is achieved through the veracity of the object-surface. The formal life of the court and the practical life of the kingdom are evoked as character, gesture, and ethos within the confines of a known conventionality of form. The culture and rhetoric of the veridical surface form a continuity with the treatment of the dead, eliciting the transcendent immortality of awareness (the *ka*) by the painstaking preservation of life-surfaces.

What took place in mummification is instructive in this light. The body is excavated until it becomes a mere surface, preserved and wrapped, encased in another "surfaced" embodiment, after which surface after surface is built up on it. The vital organs are removed and encased in surfaces of their own, the canopic jars. Over this assemblage of surfaces, the surfacing of the tomb has been erected, the mastaba, pyramid, or shaft-grave—the man in the temple encompassed by the temple in man. Presiding deities like the solar hawk Re-Harakhti and the ram-sun Amun-Re accompanied it as a compounded potency of animal-surfaces. Divinity conceptualized in this way, as the efficacy of form achieving its own perfection, had impressive possibilities but was also subject to the limitations of imagery itself. A comprehensive cosmological vision could only be a panorama of pluralities, a parade of cosmic efficacies like the repleted inventories of frieze-processions. By the Eighteenth Dynasty, Egypt's religious and philosophical world was a vast sedimentation of object-iconographs, a practicum of surfacing virtually as complex and self-repetitive as that of modern technology, and one that had as little to do with nature or natural order.

That is the trouble with using a term like "naturalism" to describe or account for Akhenaten's break with the formalism that preceded him. Where, apart from ideas freighted in by the Western interpreter, can we find evidence for an independent theory of "nature" or natural tutelage? In all the documents and inscriptions we have, facticity is bound up with an equation of divine immanence and precept with efficacy (*ma'at*) in its "true" form. Atenism did not so much demystify this equation, which was the seal set upon pharaonic authority, as it brought it to a more terse realization.

Akhenaten was at war with the self-informing of sense as if it were the perceived world, with the picturing of the godhead through meanings and the consequent meaning of the godhead through pictures. And the only way to prevent the interpretive depiction of a mystery, a trope, an impasse in thought, from consuming its subject is to consume the subjectivity instead. Being "unpictured" in this way, like the simplified solarity or the outline of an own-gendered pharaoh, did not negate the subject; it burnished it.

The vast and unwieldy stockpiling of imageries that pre-atenic divinity had become—Nut, Ptah, Min, Thoth, Osiris, Isis, and others—was godly "knowledge" in the way that our tonnages of literature and computer printouts are treated as "information." This is what Nietzsche meant by "egypticism": knowledge as the sign of a subjectivity become its own end, knowledge *of* the sign as the seal set upon an interpretive colonization of the subject. The sun, and Akhenaten's solarity, is the luminary focal point of all that we can see and know; what else it may be, physically, philosophically, or in terms of some astrology, is wholly incidental to this. No systemization is necessary to show why this is so, and it is not helpful to ascribe reasons for its being so. Akhenaten would not have cared to know how the sun "works"; for him, the aten simply became effective outside of its form.

What would "worship" mean in its context? The word "aten" meant "disk" or "circle," and for all that might have made a handy cookie cutter against iconic profundity, it was no metaphor at all. So to understand the *one* metaphor that atenic theology used to encompass all others, uncoupled *hands* emanating on raylike projections from the disk, takes a bit of imagination.

First try to imagine it as the closest twin of all, metabreath, the mirror being that breathes us in when we exhale and fills us with lifebreath upon its own exhalation. That one, the figure-ground reversal of inner life-space, is no metaphor either, too intimate to bear the sense of its own message. Try next the sun itself, too brilliant, for all of its distance, to even look at, let alone mirror the human sense of things. That leaves the hands as the sensed and sensing form of agentive manipulation; take those twins away, uncouple them from their familiarity with each other as the self, and what have you left but a perfect bearing of the means, a meta-phor as false to the body as it is to the spirit: the pharaonic "Embracer of the Two Lands"?

Akhenaten's coup, at once fiercely political and apolitical, couched in the rhetoric and the machismo of pharaonic divinity yet inimical to its physical gender and conceptual engenderment, was to deny Egypt its mystification of sense. To sustain the coup it was necessary to force a theological, devotional, and political assertion of its fierce anti-iconicism. The tasks were militant rather than pacifistic, and most of the energy necessary to pursue them had to be exerted within Egypt rather than in its foreign policy.

It is not necessary to conjure up divisive factions or power-hungry rivals among the priesthood of Amun to account for the sense of outrage this must have provoked. Egypt was primed, even disinterestedly, to respond; iconography had become its wealth. Akhenaten, however, had no alternative but to transgress social and even pharaonic values.

Egyptologists have conjectured as to whether Akhenaten may have committed so-called royal incest by marrying one of his begotten daughters, Meryt-Aten, perhaps. But if his theology is taken aright, he would have rather *omitted* incest by so doing, invoked a disposition of "sense" that made the incestuous implications of such a union insignificant. The outlines of this are clear from a salient feature of the atenic theology: "the divinities are satisfied with *ma'at*." They are repleted, sufficed, and in a certain sense completely taken care of in the beneficence bestowed by the all-encompassing aten. This reading is apt to be imprecise, even paradoxical, if one goes by the orthodox translation of *ma'at* as simply "truth." But there is sufficient evidence that *ma'at* conflates truth with practical effectiveness, pragmatic authority, and perhaps as well the "sense" that makes reason reasonable, logic logical, and truth itself truthful. Understood in that way, as an example of extreme condensation (the word is Freud's), the formula "satisfied with *ma'at*" commends the holistic attribution of the aten as replenishing the ancient deities, as well as earth and its peoples.

Perhaps more distinctly analogous to Buddhism's "pure light of the void" than to the historical exemplars of monotheism, atenic spirituality was by no means devoid of sense. It carried the political and iconistic "syncretism" of Egypt's religious evolution to a logical conclusion—to the point, in fact, of a virtual exhaustion. Akhenaten's solution to the practice of conflating the conceptual and depictive (and most likely localized) qualities and attributes of divinity into ever more replete and synthesizing form (Re-Harakhti, Amun-Re) resolved attribution into the simplest form of all—the solar disk. The single trope was that of aten's "sufficing" all others.

What Akhenaten's successors seem to have discovered is that it was practically impossible to really "know" Egypt in that way, or at the very least to govern it so. They called Akhenaten the *khru Akhetaten,* the "criminal" of his vast, imposing, and imposed capital at Tell el Amarna. Ancient Egypt's "Hamlet" was in many respects like China's illustrious Chin Jer Hwang-Ti, an ingenious Unifier whose dynasty did not last long, and whose whole genius at beginning things lay in finishing them off. (George Bernard Shaw once suggested that Beethoven belongs in this category as well.)

The human embryo is like a picture of the person within the person, a hologram of the person-to-be. But instead of the merely representational sensuality that thought or mental imagery requires for its expression, the human hologram embodies sensuality itself. Like the ability of the hands to "touch" and "feel" in a mode that is simultaneously active and passive, to *manipulate* sensually, the human figure is both representational and *presentational* in its development. It *establishes* sense, twinned outward as gender and inward as laterality, as the course of its growth, development, reproduction, and lifetime itself, and in that sense is a panhuman reality.

This places the task of representing what the human being is or could be in direct apposition (not opposition) to the sense that thought requires for any kind of certitude as to its ends or means. The establishment of sense is a power, not an icon of itself, and it is relatively incapable of systematization. Hamlet's experience in attacking his problems by representing *himself* (as *mad*) was that it compromised his thought as well as his action by relativizing them. Akhenaten's attack on the fossilization of Egypt's divine iconicity personalized his world and universalized his person in a way that no pharaoh had done before, and none would dare to do afterward.

Because both of them, as royal persons, were after agency—basically control of the board—they serve, like chess, to represent a factor much more general than the dramatic or historical enigmas attributed to them, but much more particular than the usual run of generalities. Male supergender is not macho, it is not mystical, as Akhenaten might have supposed, and not superorganic. It is positional, like the king's role in chess.

Did the ostensible "religion" of ancient Egypt reflect or correspond to a special kind of "magical realism" that Western art matched largely in its attention to perspective, and that otherwise rendered a cultural understanding quite unnecessary? Perspective, like cultural theory, imitates a viewpoint in the world (a "worldview") as *world* itself, and just as the key to this way of "looking at things" would only be a "mathematical" one if one chose to scale a mathematical point of view within it—as fractality or scale invariance—so its "cultural understanding" would have the same topicality. For how might one identify (or compare) a miniature whose relational composition *exactly matched* its relation to other things? If only the ways in which human acts or artifacts *stand in exact proportion* to reality could be miniaturized perfectly in the design of those acts or artifacts themselves, then the merely artificial or imitative aspects would drop out of the picture. One would have reality—possibly immortality—itself.

This is probably the secret of the all-male origin of the universe in the "Memphite theology" in Egypt, and it matches the king's holding the *value* of the game in chess, and Hamlet's intentions in acting himself mad to transform his social world into a moral one. The problem of modeling reality is in each case the model of the problem itself, the very sticky process of trying to figure out what it is that one is trying to figure out and position it accordingly. Experts in the development of computer programs for chess play have discovered that it is not viable to project long-term strategies in that way, or to simulate the "thinking ahead" of an opponent and then think ahead of *it*. The best programs are designed to search out and execute only the *best next move*.

8

The Consumer Consumed

If incest is an icon, depicting the breakdown or self-consumption of gender's outward twinning as a measure of sociality, the icon itself is its antithetical counterpart, placing sense in apposition to its embodiment, or closure upon itself in and as the body. In effect the social hazard represented by engenderment's self-closure can only be demonstrated by estranging "sense" from the basis of its sensing. Incest is *iconic,* rather than biological, genetic, or even purely social, because iconicity itself is consuming and incestuous. The artificial character of incest has long been known and is relatively easy to demonstrate. The correlative inadvertent or perhaps "natural" incestuousness of the icon is much less evident and correspondingly more difficult to explain.

I shall begin with a radical understanding of the *iconic* as distinguished from the symbolic or indexic forms of sign usage in the writings of Charles S. Peirce.[1] The icon is not, on my understanding, a usage but a user, and what Peirce would call "thirdness" marks the point at which the sense or illusionary effect of the sign becomes its cause, encompasses the particulars of its semiotic status. Thus the icon may be recognizably formed as a visual or acoustic pattern, or an example of metaphoric, metonymic, or synecdochic usage. But its alleged "construction" as such beforehand and interpretation afterward are beside the point of what it is and what it does; they are the particulars of usages that its effectiveness consumes.

The effective trope or logo is no longer a *semiotic* quantity or quality, and never was one in the first place. It does not reveal or perform a set of enabling conditions but consumes them in its effect, reverses the assumption of "usage" by turning it back on itself. As it does not allow for *relations* among the elements that would seem to compose it, which it absorbs or integrates, the icon does not require or necessitate relational qualities or interactions among those subject to its consumption. Shared social assumptions and linguistic codings or intersubjective connections may offer helpful heuristics for getting around the point of this, or in relating to it, but they are gratuitous to its very simplicity.

Thirdness, the semiotic "zero point," comes first. It is virtually impossible to realize a sober comprehension of what Peirce's *iconic* might mean within the grounding assumptions and enabling conditions of modern and postmodern philosophy and cultural understanding. Much of what we call the "social sciences" or informed political thinking would have to disappear or be thought otherwise for Peirce's logic to come clear. The *symbol* that stands for something other than its mark may come first in his line of reasoning, and the *index* that denotes what it stands for comes next, but the iconic reality so coded or intended comes beforehand and undercuts them both. The idea that we experience a *description* of the world, that reality is deliberately, or subconsciously, or perhaps inadvertently constructed of signs or linguistic elements is an aftereffect of iconic consumption, an illusion that is ancillary to its agency. Relations among people themselves or among signs, relationships, belong to the rallying or regrouping of an acuity that has already taken them. We do not experience a description of reality; reality experiences a description of us.

The icon simply *is* the way that human mental or physical faculties perform or operate. The pretense that its consuming of sense or perception is but an *effect* of how we perceive or intend things is one that must be staged, reconstituted, even sentimentalized after the icon has done its work, a *demonstrably* false re-iconization that is symbolized or indexed to replace the original. The icon is not false; it is not something that the memory or intention "does" except insofar as one is willing to refashion the conception of memory or intention in its image. Call that willingness "philosophy" or "the social sciences," and you have the point of this.

So I shall begin again with sex or sexuality. It is a consuming effect misperceived as *affect,* accessible only in its iconic propensity, and has no relational qualities in it or around it at all. The act of sexual intercourse, coitus imagined into or out of all the impersonations and circumstances performed on its behalf or substituted for it, can be understood to separate or un-relate people quite as much as it conjoins or re-produces them. Apart from the ways in which intentionality or agency is borrowed from it or lent to it, all of them functions of the iconicity it uses or fuses, it is not a conceptional or conceiving act. Yet even the most comprehensive sense of "reproduction" falls far short of what goes on in sexual consummation, what drives it, what it does to our means for the understanding of understanding itself. As in the case of aesthetic creations, it is only poorly comprehended as a re-presentation and production-all-over-again of the antecedent factors—relations, things, ideas, people—that enter into it. The Barok *kaba*, which makes a special case of this as a double encompassment of ends and means, or of purposes and their fulfillment, substitutes a part-for-whole exhaustion of shape and objectivity for "world" or "worldview." As the conception/consummation of Barok society, or at any rate the only way in which that idea would make sense, it belongs to a "general case" that encompasses understanding itself. That is the proactive and objective *repletion* of human subjectivity that finds its exemplars in the display or "dance," so-called expressions that are not simply "good in themselves" but actually are demonstrative or "giving" of meaningfulness.

They "exchange" antecedence for a plenitude of human experience that could never have existed in that way beforehand. Possibly we would not "study" them, would have no use for the precarious antilogic in the misunderstanding of this simple point (e.g., active repletion for passive reception or "structure"), if this were not the case. For just as the misunderstanding of sexual consummation as "re-production" seems to lead automatically to demographic maladjustment, over- or under-population, so its "cultural" equivalent (an "economic" anthropology, a structuralism or functionalism) clones itself into an overcertain historical and geographic diversity of examples.

If social distinction and differentiation, from their most immediate manifestation in the division of genders and persons to their most comprehensive in the distinctiveness of societies and cultures, are less a reality than a technique for setting up the illusion of solidarities and integrative relations, then the objectivity of sociality and its organizational details would have to depend on something else. Not, certainly, the divisions and obligations incumbent upon "gain" and "loss" considerations like marriage, birth, death, or the exchange of wealth and prestige—the cause-and-effect model that begs the question of the relations it presupposes. Nothing short of a *consumptional* basis for the repletion of social realities through their encompassment in an active antirelation could requite the self-perpetuating dilemma of a so-called reflexive anthropology. Did Marcel Mauss's theory of the gift, as well as anthropology's love affair with reciprocal relations, begin with a profound misunderstanding of the American Northwest Coast Indian potlatch, and of its repletion of the world through consumption?

Necessarily symmetrical in its guiding heuristics (exchange, equivalence, conceptual similitude, "similarity"), necessarily hierarchical in the purposes, events, personalities, and social interests that move it along, the gain-and-loss model reproduces itself ("reflexively") in all of its applications. It models the passivity of the observer in that of the subject and vice versa, absorbs in its conclusions *the sense of the model as the modeling of "sense" itself,* as though nothing were left at the end of the transaction but a settling of accounts. (Even ongoing or "open-ended" performances "go" in this way, engaging the observer as they engage the subjects themselves.) The *sense* of what has happened goes begging and would have to be reimagined as some sort of uncanny physical or spiritual agency if it were to be admitted at all, much less realized as the motivation of everything else involved.

Perhaps this is what Tamati Ranaipiri tried to explain to Elsdon Best as the *hau,* or "spirit," of the gift.[2] Regardless of whether it is given freely or with some expectation of return, regardless even of whether these retroactive "takes" on its giving would necessarily imply each other, the gift that models "taking" in its giving and thus also images an original "giving" in its reception or refusal is a positive quality indifferent to the agencies involved. It carries the sense of its own detachment in all the subsequent attachments that might be made or disowned, as the objective propriety of "sense" in human affairs.

No wonder that the totalizing rite of its encompassment in and of the social that Mauss identifies (but nowhere really defines) in the "potlatch" appears as the object of historical and cultural transformations. "Inflated" by the fur trade, impugned by colonial misunderstandings, exaggerated by writers on personality, museums, and rediscoverers of native tradition, it "models" not the passivity but the active interests of observers and participants alike, a hybrid form of the giving and taking both within and outside of the coast where it seems to have originated—like a "copper," or an overvalued wealth object named "Eats-the-World."

The "icon," as it were, of its consumptional and replenishing strategies and possibilities. Those amazing displays of perception-as-consumption and consumption-as-perception that we know in verbal, pictorial, sculptural, and dramatic form as "Northwest Coast Art" are not *adjunctive* to the double encompassment of cause and effect that we identify with the potlatch, but identical with it. They are not a separate feast understandable in retrospect as "art," but objective detachments of its own detachment in things, not separable "traditions" that those who own up to them might reclaim as traditional. What one "gives" of one's own imaginal resources in "receiving" them, shapes as an understanding of what the potlatch or its performance would mean, is a social encompassment that *naturalizes* indigenous and nonindigenous subjectivities alike. Raven's vomit, that made "museums" of ordinary dwelling houses and the people who lived in them.

"Tribes," those people would say, and have said, *kinds* of people and familial grouping as well as the mechanics and specifics of their grouping and reproduction, "are inventions of the white man," parts of a need to assemble supernumerary instances of culture beside his own and outside of its limits or boundaries. For the display that realizes a repletional subject has a wholly different and virtually opposite agenda. Understanding the "meanings" involved as a form of cultural receivership is, however necessary, incidental to this, for when exercised at the expense of its "giving" or voluntary aspect, as a "sympathetic" or "empathetic" strategy, it automatically converts the ethnographic subjects into ethnic *pathetics*, "victims" of their own perception of things. And because "being given to understand" plays no part in the actual giving, this happens retroactively to the "interpreter of cultures" or "inventor of tribes" as well.

What recourse for the consumer of cultures consumed in his own receivership but to refashion and so "understand" its spontaneous giving in terms of the *reactive* consequences it engenders, as a "total social fact" initiated and kept going by its own repercussions, by what Mauss called "obligations" to receive and to reciprocate? For the binding quality of requital or retribution predetermines initiatory action from its own futurity just as surely as a structured "worldview" patheticizes its subjects, traps them in the iconicity of their own expectations.

Just as the "thirdness" of Peirce's semiotic schema provides the iconic means, the "picture" for its antecedent enablement—the "firstness" of the symbol that stands for what it is not, the secondary quality of the index that "points to itself" in denoting something else—so the iconicity of social transactions reprojects the illusion of its own previousness. The myth of "reciprocity" as a total social fact grounds its "first causes" in the voluntary gift given with no expectation of return, the voluntary "acceptance" that points to itself through the sustaining valuation of present and very real object exchanges. It "reproduces," if that is the word, the illusion of its own consequentiality by pretending what are actually voluntary and initiatory acts of bestowal as consequences of an ongoing transactional continuity.

So it might be possible to "understand" the potlatch—its Native American staging or Mauss's reflections upon that staging—as a profoundly naive reversal of that consequentiality and therefore of the "receptional" mythos that articulates it: a "finishing of all debt" through overgiving and destruction analogous to the "finishing of all thought" in the Barok *kaba*. The only question remaining, and possibly the reason that Mauss was never able to define what the potlatch "means," is the role of understanding in this. For the reflective character of thought's understanding of itself, its so-called reflexivity, is the very hallmark of a receptional passivity—reciprocity's mental icon—whereas a giving detached from all possibility of consequence or antecedence has *only* an actional character in the forced turning outward of its display.

Thus the encompassment of "sense" in *any* self-display of what we should consider the "meaningful" bears no understandable relation whatever to the steps or techniques by which its effect might be set up, nor, of course, to the heuristics that would render it understandable. We would not know innovation itself—what it is or means or how it came about—for the force of its impact.

Like the pun or aphorism, and especially the *logo*, the mark of knowledge's self-containment as the measure of its external effectiveness, the encompassment of the potlatch depends entirely upon an acute interference between thought's articulation and the *sensory* means through which that articulation is condensed (not "transacted," or worked through a scheme of social relations). If all ordinary writing, which seems to have descended in one way or another from some sort of originary hieroglyphics, is a kind of "printout" of knowledge's interference-patterning with the sense that makes it possible, it should not be surprising to find the modern computer out as a *mechanization* of the same species. Together with the whole set of *illuminated screen technologies* to which it belongs, the computer obviates literature by reintegrating its verbal and sequential printout with the movement of sense that makes it possible.

Hence the logo becomes, by "accident" as it were, the general case of something that is both subjective and objective at once, very ancient in its modernity and very modern in its antiquity, something that represents its own phasing or patterning out in time as the skeleton of history itself, and as a kind of evolutionary education or civilizing process of the whole species. For just as the earnest speculator on human origins might postulate untold eons of dumb barter before a "social contract" of reciprocity could emerge, so one might have to posit the human body as the original logo out of which "perception" itself was constituted (or *is* constituted to this very day). But if the whole brute fantasy developed in that way (human "embodiment" as metaphor-made-flesh, beings still pretty "dumb" in their bartering of things, "natural man" in the city) depends for its whole logic on the substitution of human "stages" and types for the patterning of the logo that makes them thinkable, then we have here the whole case for (and against) iconicity in a nutshell.

Human sentience as the badge, the *escutcheon*, of its own uniqueness: the logo makes us proud to *be*. Most creatures, we are certain, are their own evolutionary tool kits, but humanity alone, it seems, has learned to lend evolution a "hand." Yet I have heard birdcalls in the New Guinea rain forest, antiphonal no less, that had the whole symphonic panache, in tone, melody, and style, of Anton Bruckner. Birds, like many cetacean species, do not have to write music at all because they *live* it.

Yet everything peculiar to the human species, especially its communication, most especially its profound isolation, has developed out of a very singular logocentric vision. We do not *go* that way in time; we *stay* that way in time. And if our music *does* go that way in time, or at least sounds as though it might, that is only because it *keeps time* with the part of us that stays.

One need not look far for the logocentric vision and what it would have to mean. Barok call their basic form of social aggregation (the "clan" as they say it) *a bung mara pun*, "the gathering in the bird's eye." There are many examples of what this might mean, and an anthropologist might easily invent sociological bases for them. I was told that the "bird" (e.g., *pun*) involved is the *sek*, or colonial starling (*Aplonis metallica*), whose social aggregation mirrors the human in that it builds its clustered, domed nests in trees above human gardens and settlement sites. Others complained that this was not the point, or even the bird, at all ("Roy was fed some kind of weird east coast clan ideology"), that the actual *mara* is the spot of blood in the fertilized egg of a certain kind of parrot. But, although the two ruby-red eyes of the *sek* "mirror" the local version of human reproduction (the "blood" of the mother and the "blood" of the father conjoined as the specular unity of a single offspring) in much the same way, they were probably right in any case.

For the general case of *mara* is a point of focus for focusing itself that turns the *relational* aspects of aggregation, human reproduction, social interaction, conceptual intercourse, and the "sense" that these make, into incidentals of its own condensation. A clearing in the bush is a *mara,* as is an eye or opening of any sort; the big town Namatanai (*La Marana* in Barok) is "the eye, generic," the very epicenter. The generic *mara* means something very specific: *the absolute identity of the focal point within the eye with that which it fixes in the field of its vision*—visionary, perhaps, but not *visual,* for "vision" would be a mere re-production or reciprocity of perspectives, an imaginary space inserted into that which the concept denies. And the logo is not, strictly speaking, visual either, for its *pun* is not bird but the sound of a word, and (may the author, obviously misled by his informants, please be excused at this point) a punning of the cunning of the conning of the eye.

The eye's understanding or identification of itself, how it would "see" its working, puts a point of holographic self-interference at the very focus of things, a point that fixes its own "indexic" capability better than words can, hence the pun. It "points to itself" in indicating other things but indicates those others in pointing to itself, as the self-deceptive visuality of what Stephen A. Tyler calls the "eye-con."[3] Vision's *invisibility* to itself, the absolute necessity of an identity between the focal point within and that outside of it, parallels the fact that we must remember language in order to speak it, but forget it again in speaking of things. So, too, the knowing of the potlatch would be unknowable to itself, the unconscionable truth of what we call "consciousness." To try and turn the trick of this into an "evolution" turns us into one instead. But it is a strange sort of evolution, a reflexive hominization that necessarily integrates its own devolutionary implications. Another version of the twinning that made "The Story of Eve" possible or a retelling of the Original Joke, it does not move in time but moves time instead. It converges upon, but never quite reaches, the most real and least thinkable dimension of time, the *now.*

It is in the mystery of how an animal species may imitate itself, sexually and reproductively as well as in its lifeways, and create its own circumambient "environment" in the process, that human self-imitation as language and as icon seeks its origins. In this sense evolution "apes" the human, casts a spectrum of recognizable or purely fantastic simian traits and pithecoid forms in the attempt both to incorporate and to account for a creature that came into being as a distinctively cognitive mode of imitating (knowing) itself. So it was not the distinctive traits of language and speech that were copied in the copying of our own imitation, but a creature notorious for its bodily imitation of the human, that "looks" and often acts as though it *could* be human.

This is *Iconopithecus,* the picture-ape, or image of an ape in evolutionary transition to the aping of an image. *Iconopithecus* is the picture, but only a picture, of a life-form about to conceive the image that is only an image, the image that is false to itself but not necessarily false in its appearances. The human ancestor is not *necessarily* depicted in any of the fossil forms that may be identified in its lineage, but only contingently so; it is necessary to have a whole range of fossil forms in order to get a better "picture," as they say. Hence the fossils are nonhuman reproductions of a human self-image, animals that we are not quite sure of caught in the act of a creature that wants to be dead certain of its imaging capability. So the picture-ape evolves or reproduces itself through *human* means (excavation, reconstruction, speculation) backward in time to the conjectural point of its pithecoid emergence. We are its creatures, the beings it leaves behind, as it is ours, the "being" that we go about pushing through its evolutionary paces. It is wholly apocryphal, not able to own any of its fossilized forms save in a contingent sense, for all that the evolutionist must come to terms with the likelihood that each of the forms "depicted" in this way had a life of its own. Admitting to the "humanness" of any given form only means that the real imitative progression took place elsewhere, or was only a thing in process; identifying it as another picture of *Iconopithecus* increments the human reproduction of primate forebears, imitates the ape in the picture.

Iconopithecus is as definitively nonhuman as its authors and creators are human, and is bound by its own mode of human-mediated reproduction to remain that way. It copies us in an anticipatory sense without knowing what it is doing; we copy what it might have done as an originative mythos without knowing what we are copying. All we can find is a picture, because all we can picture is a "find." Iconopithecene form is inherently plastic, a changing of evolutionary change brought into being by a continual updating of the fossil record and of what is made of the record. When a new fossil is discovered, or a more convincing interpretation made of known specimens, *Iconopithecus* has reproduced itself again.

But the agency of its reproduction is that of the depictor, the matured outcome of the process who deserves to be labeled *Homo iconicus* and is likewise an effete being, though for a different reason. Though both are but pictures, in fact pictures of one another picturing themselves (Fig. 8), *Homo iconicus* is the development of what happened to its pithecene forebear, and thus only a picture of the ability to picture. It is the image of the iconic being consumed in its pictures, an involution multiplied upon itself, instead of the evolution made diverse and contingent by invisible divisors, divided by its unimaginable forebears. A present fossil, iconic humanity is as much "beside" itself as its pithecine forebear is inevitably behind itself; it creates contingent *presences* in place of contingent absences, puts itself in the place of others in order to gauge the measure and extent of its self-depictive being.

Approaching the "now" or present asymptotically, without ever getting there, this being proliferates imageries of its own presence instead. It *advertises* itself, overpopulates and so pollutes the near-life reality of its habitation simply to evidence its own presence, "reproduces" the *sex* of meaning, the full sensuosity of what it would have to be, as the meaning of sex. Anthropology invites us to range its appearances in a comparative perspective, "relativize" them and detotalize them into paradigms of system or organicity, understand how image might image itself, or at least attempt a science of the process. Too many cultures and not one good idea of what "culture" might be; too many people and not one good example of what a person might be.

Homo iconicus and *Iconopithecus,* antitwinning taken literally as "figures," like statistical measures, are the same ghastly pair, the same bastardization of human antitwinning, as are "self" and "other" taken figuratively as literature. They are the falsification of each other's hypothetical truth, the human "litter" taken both ways at once.

Like those two evolutionary impossibles, each cutting its own edge, sense and body live an iconic codependency with one another. It is the logo, not the body itself or the likes or dislikes attributed to it, that is the actual locus of its human consumption, that which is advertised, bought, and sold. If the metaphor is *almost* a truth about itself, the icon almost a picture of itself, the word almost a clarity about what it means, then it is the way in which consciousness is consumed in each case rather than how it would be *produced* (evoked, elicited), or even reproduced, that is the key to the sense that is made of it.

If, as Sidney Mintz has made clear to me, human beings have no *natural* food, it would seem that they have no natural sensing of things either.[4] This is not for want of direct bodily sensation or "stimulation," for in fact sensory deprivation is deadly but is evident in the fact that that *or any other* circumstance of human sensing is a matter of *perception,*

Iconopithecus　　　　　**Homo iconicus**

Figure 8. Reflexive hominization.

and in fact of its own perception. We "watch" ourselves, perceive ourselves perceiving as our own evolutionary "niche" in the environment. As the obtaining, preparation, and treatment of food sources consumes the consumer in the intaking or distribution of them, makes "food" possible, so the focality of perception as a self-acknowledging and self-encompassing condition makes the "raw data" of sensation possible. It "stimulates" them, if a behavioral analogy is to be preferred.

Any "natural" assessment of the human animal, such as our family resemblance to other creatures, would be a by-product of this distinctively human artifice, of the original joke of sentience itself. We are "symbolic" creatures naturally, culturally, or perhaps in some very clever way both ways at once, only to the extent that perception, or the focality achieved in it, is not total or absolute. *Total* perception would burn away the world.

Because the work we are obliged to do in adjusting our expectations to fit with a *positive* conception of meaning, how culturally or naturally *clever* it might be, already fills the world with small-time epistemologies of itself, we are lucky enough, as human beings, not to get all the "meaning" we pay for. That fact alone suffices to focus both the finality and the exhorbitant repletional potential of *feasts* like the potlatch or the Barok *kaba*. They "represent" the death of the meaningful in the act of consumption and so redefine the living as consumers not completely consumed by it.

Stanley Walens has called attention to the grandiloquent honorific that the Kwakiutl named to Franz Boas: "Having Fires Moving in the Water," meaning the great blazes set on the shore to guide canoes to the feast as their reflected refulgence spired "downward" in the dark sea, transecting and so consuming the vertical cosmology of the people.[5] John Farella points out the Navajo understanding that a person famous for the explication of mythic lore "does not leave a *čindi* [ghost]" upon death, for that knowledge and its special "authority" live again whenever the meanings are reconsidered.[6] *In vento scribere*, Catullus's retake on "invention," is an inadvertent pun on itself, "written on the wind and inscribed in running water," for the whole trick or poetry of meaning's death sentence in the imagination is to *underdetermine* it, survive the sense in the sensing of it.

Food for thought; thought for food. "The eye," in the idiomatic usage of the Urapmin of Papua New Guinea, "steals it and eats it" (Joel Robbins, personal communication). Barok people claimed they had been cannibals (I knew a very ancient lady, a clanmate, who had witnessed this)—though apparently largely for "show." At any rate, the distinction that cuts the person as the person cuts the distinction had a very literal irony for them. In the old days, I was told, they would cook the body of an enemy very slowly, so that the ligaments remained, connecting the bones. They would hang the skeleton in the doorway of the *taun* and tell the visitors who must brush past it in entering, "Ah, that is old so-and-so; when he was alive he spoke of us with a very decorative speech."

Is the primitivity, the savagery or predatory consciousness that reciprocates ("revenges") itself as the underdetermined *fact* of our whole interest in New Guinea and its peoples, as far removed from the ground condition of our species as the sublime detachment of the Hindu world-renouncer? Being too much *into* the sensual reality of perception—the "sex" of symbolism, or what Marilyn Strathern calls the "gender of the gift"—is no nearer to some imaginally social, primitive, or "animal" roots of human being than the modern state. It is the equal-but-opposite variant of spiritualism's being too much "out of it," overcommitted to abstract and idealized intangibles. Is a New Guinea *singsing* more or less "barbaric" than a hermit in a cave, demanding spiritual credit for the sacrifice of a more active life, or than a tax collection agency, feeding on the absurd banality of a civilized lifestyle?

Practice makes perfect. Psychology, like many forms of humanistic holism, overemphasizes the incorporation of perceptual focality *within* the body, calls it "mind" or perhaps "psyche." Technology and its medical and natural science derivatives overemphasize, like shamanism and its spirit visions, the *appositional* character of the focality, *echolocate* what it means to be human outside of the body and call it "body." But if both kinds of practice, the "out-of-body" experience of the machine or shamanic journey and the "in-the-body" mechanics of a psyche or nervous system, accomplish much the same thing, who is to tell which of these, mind's body or body's mind, is the more basic or original?

The nonpassive subject is not an object of reflection; at best it becomes the creature of one's resistance to it. To come to terms with how this might "feel," I shall oblige the reader's consideration of Rainer Maria Rilke's famous poem on a panther in the Jardin des Plantes in Paris, a work whose popularity gives the impression that it has been all too well "understood." The poem has an accuracy beyond the sense it might project, the accuracy of a concretivity that transcends the projection of poetic sense or subjectivity. Another poet, given the same panther on the same day, might well discover an "accuracy" that had as little to do with Rilke's panther as with the zoo's. "Equal" to all of this accuracy and to much more, the panther is responsible to none of it, and quite innocent of poetic vision.

Rilke's panther, however, projected as the captive of a modern proclivity to conserve the iconicity of the alien and the dangerous, was its spectator's own spectator, the icon's view of its iconicity. Its vision, made "so weary by the passing of the bars that it holds nothing more," will "only sometimes" let an image enter, one that "goes through the tensed-up stillness of the limbs and ceases, in the heart, to be."[7]

The revenge of Schrödinger's cat? Perhaps. We would like to think of Rilke, or perhaps can only think of him, as "living" the power of his imagery, much as composers are credited with experiencing the emotions one "feels into" their music. But indulgence of this sort is the very telltale of all that may be claimed for or against that which we call "interpretation." For to "live" the imagery of a poem like Der Panther is only to succumb to the poem's interpretation of oneself, to assume, for instance, that Rilke "would have wanted" one to feel a profound sympathy for the cat. Containing, consuming the interpreter through the very self-reflection through which the interpretation is projected, the poem itself goes free, detaches the possibility of interpreting it along with the interpretation itself.

Swinging an endless succession of bars past its gait—bars with no faces and no world behind them—the panther is also a detacher of images. But there is a major difference in how it does so. For in the end the great predator gets the better of its best contemporary poet, of the reader, and of the poem itself, beset as they all are with a freight of images, feelings, or whatever else the imagery might call up. Forget what may be the panther's world-weariness, or Rilke's, or one's own; this cat gives the image's own view of its victims, has the power to make image disappear.

Elsewhere Rilke has written of the medieval unicorn, the nonexistent beast, that "they nourished it with no grain, just always with the possibility that it might be."[8] But the panther of the Jardin des Plantes lives the opposite of that subjunctive sustenance, subsists by feeding disconsolate possibilities to *us,* images that have no being in its heart.

III

The Echo-Subject

9

Echolocation

What I shall call "animality" can be thought of in two distinct ways. It can be treated etymologically as an accident of language, the absorption by English and scholarly discourse in general of the Latin *animus,* developing into a range of analogous usages. These would include things like animal, animate being, animism (e.g., animated by a soul), animation, or having an animus toward someone. On the other hand, this kind of historical usage can be treated as the accident, instead, of something much more basic than language or its possible applications. As a basic reality in that way, animality is central to this whole work. It is the "sense" that makes thought, experience, understanding, and even effectiveness itself efficient—a self-organizing, self-motivating, and objective quality in its own right. We ourselves and other creatures are examples of this, and machines or mechanically modeled "processes" are its surrogates.

That the various kinds of animals *are* people, and therefore people are animals, or might be sorted among them, counseled by them, separated or distinguished as animals are, establishes a vast potential for thought. They are "good to think," or perhaps "make it good to think," as Claude Lévi-Strauss has noted, and he has explored the possibilities this opens up for human designation and naming. The very act of being *overspecific* about animals, as we often do in classifying or breeding them, reveals a contrastive plasticity or underspecificity, a transformative capability that can be imagined as evolutionary, adaptive, strategic, spiritual, or perhaps all of these at once. People can specialize in them, as they do in crafts, arts, and techniques, and so animals can specialize in people as well.

Understood as a kind of sense for thought to speculate upon, a shaping of experience that is also animate and motivational, the animal species is reflective of human potential, and human potential of it. Much can be made of the fact that a major part of human technology has always been invested in human-animal symbioses, as hunting, domestication, companionship, cooperation, and even mutual education. Animal knowledge goes in both ways and comes in a wide variety of forms. An older neighbor who had grown up in Poland once said to me, "Roy, you study the anthropology; when I was young they tell me, 'When you see an animal in the morning, you believe on that animal all day.'"

Thus it is possible that we have been domesticated as well. One could go on practically forever in the animal indexing of human thought or the human indexing of animals and never get beyond the purely reflective side of this. At the heart of the matter is the way in which animals and people exist as specific transforms of one another. That fact, very enigmatic and virtually a kind of sorcery, comes dressed in all the symbolic, ritual, and evolutionary sense that people can make for it, as if it were necessary to disguise it in some way in order to know it at all. Among our closest animal companions, dogs extend positive human energy; cats absorb negative human energy and then run around doing little negative things with it.

A *primitive* (from the beginning) knowledge of animality is different from a practical or evolutionary one in several ways. It is concerned with what the species *is* rather than where it came from or where it is going. Thus the kind of transformational knowledge of animality that plays a central role in natural selection, mutation, or behavioral ethology is developed and understood differently. It is still transformational in the sense that different species can be known as transformations of one another, or of some basic principle. But it is different insofar as *knowledge* serves as the catalyst rather than germ plasm, DNA, or taxonomic insights.

Primitive animality knows that the animal species and the myth or story of the species are of the same kind. There are animals that live largely or wholly in their stories, like the dragon, thunderbird, mermaid, or the dinosaur species, and only incidentally in fossil remains, positive reconstructions, or obscure sightings. There are other animals, known and seen daily, whose stories go begging, and animals who have given over their stories to those of human consumption, work, or recreation.

For certain purposes it has been necessary to redesign the stories of those animals as machines and to invent animal typologies for machines themselves. Is it primitive or highly sophisticated to measure horsepower, create classificatory taxonomies for firearms, or investigate the "evolution" of the motorcar, fighter plane, or bulldozer?

Dinosaurs may "live" and actually terrify people through their reconstructions alone, and technological species procreate through their invention. But one would have to understand this in a very primitive way, know the invention of myth or the myth of invention as a power in its own right, to realize that the human complicity in this is not simply a matter of the "imagination." Animality has a reality to its human story, and a human story has a reality to its animality.

Consider the human story of the echidna. This is a small, ant-eating creature that lives in Australia *(Tachyglossus)* and in New Guinea *(Zaglossus)*, where it inhabits the montane moss or cloud forests. Together with the platypus, it exemplifies an order called Monotremata, egg-laying creatures that are otherwise like the Mammalia. Evolutionary lore often connects them with our lineage as an intermediary form between egg-layers and those that incubate their offspring within their bodies. Part of that lore is that they seem to be very ancient as well, and indeed some very old fossil forms have been found in Patagonia.

As an animal *power,* monotreme would seem to capitalize on limits or boundaries and have its life and movement *through* them. The platypus, with its ducklike bill, webbed feet, and underwater burrow entrance, treads amphibiously on a land/freshwater limen. *Zaglossus,* the New Guinea echidna, does its hunting within a three-dimensional maze of long-decomposing forest debris, often many meters deep. It is self-fossilizing, having the power of digging itself almost instantly into the ground, and, we are told, it glows in the dark.[1]

But this does not begin to tell the human story of the echidna. Both the platypus and the echidna have prefrontal lobes, neocortex, in proportion to the rest of the brain as in *Homo sapiens.* They also have a brain size in proportion to body size more or less like ours. We are told that the neocortex of the platypus is smooth, but that of the echidna is convoluted, as in human beings. Experimentalists have tested the echidna in mazes, presumably two-dimensional, and failed to exhaust its intelligence. But that may give the creature an unfair advantage, since it seems to have developed in three-dimensional ones.

More interestingly, the echidna brains itself differently than human beings do. Its brain lacks the hippocampus, the part identified with long-term memory and thus with the ability to dream. So the human conclusion would have to be either that the echidna does not dream or that it moves within the world as one big dream. In other words, it does everything in the way we would aspire to, on pure, raw intelligence, walking in the eternal daylight of the "now." Anyone bright enough to build a starship would be wise to train an echidna to navigate it.

What is male in Australia, female in New Guinea, and frequently hangs by its toes? It is a human story of animal supergender in two parts, one that depends for its whole sense and significance on animality, specifically one that migrates between Australia and Papua New Guinea, the bat.

Although the most familiar modeling of human beings upon bats features *microchiroptera* like the bloodsucking *desmodontidae* that particularize Dracula, the bat/human metaphor can also be found in exclusive association with bats that lack the grotesque facial modifications of that suborder. For it is the other major suborder of bats, the larger, fruit-eating *megachiroptera*, that figure extensively in the lore and symbolism of Australia and Melanesia. These "flying foxes," as they are called for their large foxlike or doglike snouts and ears, orient themselves visually and likewise have the more prominent eyes characteristic of foxes, dogs, and human beings. Species of the tree-dwelling, migratory genus *Pteropus* are noted for large body size (up to fourteen inches in length for some species) and wingspan (up to five feet), as well as for complex social behavior. Anthropomorphic traits (having a cry, when wounded, like a human child; carrying off comrades wounded by human hunters) have been ascribed to them by European settlers as well as indigenous peoples. At least some species migrate from northern Australia up the larger rivers of Papua in connection with their breeding cycle.

Perhaps the flying foxes that figure in the symbolism of the Wik-mungkan of the west coast of Cape York Peninsula, in Australia, are among these. At all events, David McKnight, who treats the subject at some length in a discussion of taboo and purification among the Wik-mungkan, notes that the creatures probably do not breed in the Wik-mungkan tribal area.[2] It is likely, following McKnight's analysis, that the Wik-mungkan would agree that flying foxes differ from other creatures in very much the way that man differs from them: "Although the Wik-mungkan deny that a female flying fox is a placental, they do not withold this status from a male flying fox. . . . We therefore find in Wik-mungkan thought, when human beings are compared with flying foxes, on which man models himself and makes himself sacred, men are the same, while women are anomalous."[3] Flying foxes idealize a social state that emphasizes the sacred differentiation of the male from the less positively distinctive female: "This anomalous creature, woman, shares in being partly male. For the Wik-mungkan, like ourselves, consider the clitoris to be analogous to the penis."[4]

Flying foxes are more like men, then, even though all males share a distinctiveness that overrides, to some extent, specific boundaries. But this still does not explain entirely the identification of men with flying foxes. Human beings (and presumably other placentals, such as dogs) are recognized by the Wik-mungkan to have vaginas, whereas the female flying fox is thought to have only an anus. And it is this issue of female physiology and reproductive capacity that provides the clinching argument. For female flying foxes, "there is no need, or no reason, for them to have a vagina for they do not give birth—they come out of the water or the Rainbow Serpent. Men too come out of the Rainbow Serpent, but they come out as adult human beings."[5] In addition to their other similarities, men are similar to flying foxes in general because human males (in initiation) and flying foxes (at birth) are thought to originate from the Rainbow Serpent (or from the water that is closely associated with the Serpent). Human beings become essentially flying fox–like because they sacralize and differentiate their males on the model of the flying fox: flying foxes, reflexively "male" by birth, totemize humanity's proudest ritual achievement. McKnight says of them: "Sociologically they are like men, for they live in groups, in camps. In these camps the females roost separately from the males. The parallel with male initiates and initiators who are separated from women was readily recognized by my informants and was offered as evidence that flying foxes must have their own Rainbow Serpent too."[6] By identifying with flying foxes via the mystery of their reproduction, Wik-mungkan men are able to claim their own reproductive process for themselves. But the flying foxes, as the totemic model for "own sex" and its reproduction, become, as a reciprocal result of this, an entire species representative of self-sexuality.

Much of this doubtless has to do with the peculiarities of the Wik-mungkan. But much also has to do with those of the flying fox. Man and bat participate in a complex transformation such that it would be difficult or impossible to isolate the ethical component of Wik-mungkan self-sexuality from the component of native knowledge and classification of the bats. Each is a function of the other.

The social segregation of the sexes in *Pteropus* species, particularly during the period of parturition, is a well-attested fact.[7] It is also known that migratory fruit bats in the Australian region bear their young in June at the northern, or inland, extremities of their ranges. This would help to explain the mystery that surrounds their reproduction for the Wik-mungkan, who insist that they have never seen a pregnant flying fox, though they have seen females suckling their young.[8] It is tempting, in view of their association of flying fox reproduction with water, to suggest that the flying foxes known to them are among those that breed across the Arafura Sea or the Coral Sea and then bring their young with them across the water.

This calls to mind the possibility that another people, living at the other end of the flying foxes' migratory and reproductive cycle, might form a coordinate and contrasting conception of the creatures. And such a conception does indeed inform a number of myths and tales that I collected among the Daribi people of the Mt. Karimui region in Papua New Guinea. Daribi speak with awe of the large flocks of the *Pteropus* species they call *tumani,* which fly up the Tua River in the dry season (June–July), settling on trees in such large numbers that limbs are often broken.

Flying foxes seem most often associated in Daribi stories with an asexual state of man, or with the outcome of a failure in achieving sexual complementarity. The most notable account occurs in a myth dealing with the origin of male genitals.[9] Originally, in this account, Daribi men did not have genitals. One man obtained a wife at a pig feast near Mt. Ialibu and brought her to Karimui. Upon discovering that her husband and his compatriots were without genitalia, the new wife gathered *dibabu* tubers and acorns and fashioned testicles from the former and penes from the latter. She did this first for her husband, after which she was kept busy to the end of her days fashioning sets for other men. She died, however, without being able to outfit all of the Daribi men in this way, and those who were left turned into *tumani.*

The idea of *tumani* bats as Daribi manqués is a compelling one, especially in view of the anthropomorphism with which Daribi treat the species (they claim that *tumani* pull up grass and build shelters for themselves). Daribi traditional history locates the ancestral home of the people within the river gorge that the bats negotiate in their migrations, and another tradition maintains that the Daribi ultimately originated somewhere near Mt. Ialibu, whence the wife in the myth also came, and whither the *tumani* people finally depart. Bats as well as Daribi qualify for the term by which the Polopa speakers to the south designate the Daribi: *Hawari Hwę,* "people of the Tua River."

But why should the *tumani* come to exemplify the absence of male differentiation? Male bats have long, pendant penes, and their genital organs are (in contrast to those of female bats) plainly visible.[10] Thus we are left with a mirror image of the mysteriousness that Wik-mungkan see in these bats as the most likely clue to an explanation. The Wik-mungkan see clearly differentiated male bats, sexually ambiguous female bats, and no evidence of biological reproduction. The Daribi, intersecting these creatures at a different phase of their reproductive cycle, see huge flocks of pregnant or parturant animals, with no males in evidence. Perhaps they concluded, like some of the early zoological collectors, that the bats are sexually undifferentiated or that they are composed of females alone, for "at this time the female bats in some species gather together in companies by themselves to bring forth their young undisturbed, while the males either congregate in separate groups elsewhere or scatter more widely during the summer season."[11]

As the flying fox is an exemplar and something of a moral ideal for Wik-mungkan maleness, so it is a foil or counterexample for Daribi male differentiation. But although the "unmarked" character of chiroptid self-generation takes a different foil in each case, deflected from the female in Australia and from the male in New Guinea, it images "own gender" for both peoples.

The flying fox is not being used as a model for gender differentiation here. Rather, its difference from the human becomes a means to echolocate human gender through its differentiation as a derivative quality. Echolocated or "divided" in this way by the bat, humanity reveals the intentional unity of its engenderment. Substituting "human bat" for "human being" in HB and dividing by the bat (B), we get:

$$\frac{HB}{B} = H$$

Chiroptomorphism, in other words, the representation of the human in bat form, results by short division in a generic realization of the human, that is, without the division of gender or engenderment, an expression of the primordial "own gender." Perhaps this is what the Murik Lakes people of the Sepik area intend in their notion of the *nabwag-ngain,* the placental spirit considered as bat that is the "true mother" of every person.[12]

What does it mean to "divide a human being by a bat"? Ultimately it is a form of designation through difference rather than similarity, a way of taking advantage of the condition that representation is never what it represents and using *that condition itself* to represent. This is familiar to us in the principle of the cartoon, in which figures are overdrawn or underdrawn, exaggerated, parodied, presented in animal form so as to elicit a differentiating meaningfulness, the funny edge of things.

What the animists and evolutionists called "totemic" thought was then their reading of the consequences of echolocation, the reflectivity of differentiating thought proliferating across the landscape of known forms. And if every act of differentiation makes its echo in this way, what sort of echo might we get from dividing the bat by the human, using the classificatory sortment that separates the two major kinds of bats? For just as the departures of apes, monkeys, canids, and other creatures from the human are most useful in marking out the human, so the bizarre specializations of the *microchiroptera* have been most successful in eliciting a human echo. By this sort of echolocation, then, what kinds of bats are we, and what kinds of human beings are bats?

Specialization has cast these creatures, mammalian stalactites to the human stalagmite, in the role of a weirdly altered alter ego of man. Liminal to the ordinary surface-bound mammalian habitat, they are nonetheless obviously mammals; nocturnal or crepuscular in their activities, they not only sleep during the day but do so in an inverted position, and within interiors defined as exterior to ordinary human custom and habitude. Adaptation to the auditory rather than the visual mode results in a grotesque, gargoyle-like physiognomy. The shortening of the snout often contributes to, but diabolically compounds, the bizarre anthropomorphism of a mammal whose hind limbs alone, as in man, might be described as "legs," but whose posture (shall we call it "downright"?) limits nonflight locomotion to hanging and scuttling. Whether or not they may be primates, as Linnaeus claimed and the Daribi imply, bats challenge the obvious humanoid morphology and genetic affinities of the apes with a quizzical counterclaim of being more *totemically* human.

The bat is why we have imagined cave-man; the cave is why we have imagined bat-man. Mutual inversions in more than posture, human and bat inhabit converse adaptations to a sound cave, the sounding chamber that is within the human being and around the bat. Whereas bats locate themselves, navigate, and find their food by bouncing sound off of echo-limits, effectively transforming their negotiable world into an imaginary crepuscular cave, human beings locate their subject, its negative spaces or contingencies, by resonating against the limits of language. Sound, or voice, is bigger than language; originating in the contained resonating chambers of the throat and head, it projects its inner reverberation into a volume that surrounds human bodies, everts the negative space of its subject into an engulfing sonority. Humanity makes the subject within its limits into an everted sonority. The bat does the reverse of this, pulling an externalized limit of sound surface within to make its subject; its wings are an adaptation, so to speak, to keep up with that subject, to fly the bat to where it is. Humanity flies, by that analogy, on the internal membranes of its vocal chords, taking an internal sounding subject to where it lives beyond the limits of language.

Language changes, always, in inevitable adaptation to a larger world of sound; music sings imaginary limits for it. The bat flies in music-space, making the modulated cry that finds itself; if bats could talk, they would always be listening for themselves in conversation, which would always be "about" referentiality. And if human beings used their talk mainly in this way, a genuine semiotics might be possible, centering the human echolocation on communication about its own limits. It is because sound is not meaning but the meaningfulness of direction that allows the bat to listen to itself as a navigational vector. And it is in sound's *inability* to merge with or directly encode the meanings attributed to language that it similarly becomes meaningful for human beings, allows them to listen to themselves as vectors of meaning through a medium that is not meaning. Those who wish to ground meaning in language are disposed to imagine the "sign" through a magical precision bridging sound and sense, but such a coding, to the degree it were precise and exhaustive, would render impossible the "play" or ambiguity, the irony of sound and meaning—would nullify sound's echolocative possibilities.

In order to make the *problematic* of meaning, to seriously entertain the concept at all, it is necessary to fracture its intent and remove it from the relativity of personal sound reverberation. A script, whether phonographic or ideographic, *permits* meaning by dissociating its intent from sound. A correlative move for the *microchiroptera* would be a map of their cavernous or arboreal hunting grounds. But, apart from the visual difficulties this would present, such a "convenience" would fail to tell the bat what it most urgently wants to know, which is *where* it is on the map. Like the script, in other words, such a map would omit the relativistic factor of echolocation; the inscribed echo loses its reverberating quality to representation. And if chiroptid ingenuity countered by making a three-dimensional map, a small-scale model of the region to be echoed, the bat as subject would suffer an even worse dislocation through the foreshortening of its echo. The Saussurean bat, then, secure in its conviction of echolocation already inscribed as the "sign" of its echo-space, would be constrained to become its own echo, that is, to bounce *itself* off of things.

It is sound that makes the sign unnecessary for the bat; the bat does not *send* "information," it *receives* it, and the message makes sense only in terms of the relative positioning of subject and object, that is, in those of the bat's motion. A bat that flew at Mach 1 would be in deep trouble. But if the human being, whom we believe to *send* information as well, spoke sign or text, sent and received preinscribed meanings, the exchange would be all predicate. At the other end of the echo-continuum, in other words, the significance of echolocation does not go away. One listens for intent in one's own speech as well as in that of others, and one calls that intent "meaning."

The differentiation of human beings and bats is not just simply practical, biological, or evolutionary. It involves a transformation fact that is neither merely symbolic on one hand nor metamorphic (e.g., actually form-changing) on the other, but rather connects the *realities* of the two. The full significance of this is as difficult to reconstruct in biological terms as it is to bring up whole out of mythic narratives. Hence environmentalists are obliged to turn to holistic or moralistic rhetorics in order to reach the point of this or get it across, and the mythic versions are equated with mysticism or "prelogical mentalities." The problem is that a world differentiated by counterdetermining realities is never a single "environment," and myths that work on the differential between interconnecting realities are, if anything, postlogical.

Animality is a reality shifter, a mover of factuality. A creature becomes proficient in its own lifeways, as individual or as species, through its knowledge of other creatures. But it is a knowledge that takes many forms, from sense and body knowledge to interpenetration, as in symbiosis, predation, and domestication. Hunting with dogs is a strategic collusion of the senses; the group-howling of wolves is *mysterious* to human beings (is it a "social" phenomenon, a "religious" one?) partly because wolves howl in harmonics that sometimes transcend human audibility and can only be *felt*. Many predators work with the edge of sense, seek to control the *eyes* of a prey species with their own before pursuit (if you've got them looking where you want them to, you've got them where you want them). The Bella Coola of British Columbia say that the wolf has "human eyes," that the attempt that was made to turn the creature into a human being succeeded only with the eyes.[13]

Environment and evolution are distinctively human claims established upon the world of animality, claims that we seek to validate by including ourselves within them. They are story claims based on the minutiae of observation (eye control): we notice animals doing something we can understand, or would like to, and then notice ourselves doing something "animal" and include ourselves in. If kinship establishes connections among the living through the dead and connections among the dead through the living, we have our "kinship" there as well. Human eyes: in a perfectly established environment or evolutionary scheme, we would have all the animals looking exactly where we wanted them to, with no animality left at all. If a wolf could look back at this with a human eye, what would it see?

Would a human eye with a wolf's mind behind it see DNA, for example, as the most insidious parasite of all, a separate species—the "Hamlet" of speciation—living on the transformational edge of evolutionary sense? Would it sniff out a human trap in the evolutionary significance we make of this? "Another one of these human *symbols,* like their idea of 'wolf' itself, lurking there in the shadows." Could a human thinker develop a whole philosophy of wolf intent out of that thing they do with their eyes—eye control? Very well, then, "intent" being a human kind of claim, the Bella Coola wolf might suspect a counter-strategy, noting the very strange things human beings do with body, with DNA as embodiment, in the name of evolution.

Animality is the *autonomy* of sense, not its categorization, pigeon-holing, or symbolization. The notion of animal powers, or animals *as* powers, may seem unwarrantedly mystical, especially since the very general conceptualization of "power" in this way is a favorite ploy of the disempowered. Symbolization, categorization (of "species," for example), and classification work with a *captured* notion of sense. People go out into the wilds, or bring wild animals in from there, to get some edge on sensual autonomy; they want to be captured by it, or perhaps capture it (kill it, as the Romans did). Sometimes they captured or caged exotic *kinds of people* as well. This was not only morally wrong, it was damned uncivil, but how much of it was inspired by a suspicion that there might be more to human variation than we generally credit?

Native Americans who went out into the wild, adapted to a life on the high plains (the bulk of them, be it noted, *after* white contact), paid less attention to "cultural variation" because they had something bigger to chew on. Their individual careers as warriors, shamans, or whatever were "guided," to put it mildly, by what they called animal powers.

Joseph Epes Brown developed his conversations with the Oglala Sioux prophet Black Elk into a book, called *Animals of the Soul*.[14] He begins with a quotation from a warrior named Brave Buffalo on the human responsibilities of this kind of knowledge: "The animals want to communicate with man, but Wakan Tanka does not intend they shall do so directly—man must do the greater part in securing an understanding."[15] Black Elk called Bison the chief of all animals, a feminine, creative earth power. Bear is a male earth power, introspective and healing but fierce, with a soul like a human being. Winged beings owned a kind of supremacy in Lakota thought, but the "socialization" of animals in sacred societies focused on major earth powers such as Badger, Bear, Wolf, Fox, and Bison. The *animalization* of personal knowledge and ability was, by contrast, private and often secret. It had to do with the vision quest and had an immediate reference to one's success in life, more or less as education does for modern folk.

Brown notes that Lakota were "somewhat afraid" of powers like deer and rabbit, and indeed what might be called the "depth" of creature power "embraces a whole series of unlikely associates. Among these are the bison and bear, the moth, the spider, and possibly more."[16] Spider is the first of all beings, the creator and namer of all: "I made this earth and the sky and the sun and the moon and everything. You are one of the things I made. You were a little grey thing and I threw you away."[17] But the most important and indeed the principle of power itself was the Whirlwind:

The Four Winds is an immaterial God, whose substance is never visible. He is *wakan* and, therefore, no human can comprehend him. . . . The principle of the four coalesces into a single Wind principle. . . . it must be seen in its total conceptual framework; that is, the Whirlwind principle that was common to the numerous and disparate beings. This Whirlwind *(Umi)* is represented in Oglala mythology as being "unborn," a kind of "playful abstraction from his brother winds."[18]

Male elk whistle the whirlwind to control the cows; bull bison mate by pawing whirlwinds in the dust; Eagle and the flying things embody it. Bear lives on moth larvae and generates his introspection in the cocooning of the hibernation cave.

Winds not only disincorporate the visible and directly observable potential of animality but also, like menstruation or music, turn the very fact of this "disappearing act" into an exponential (power times itself, or *by* itself; hence power *over* power) manifestation of agentive spontaneity. But if wind power *is* spontaneity, akin to the underdetermining conceptional potency of woman or the enigma of "composition" in music, there is also the possibility of underdetermining that one as well. In effect, and for all the fact that at this extreme of reduction only "effects" are knowable at all, the *disincorporation* of animality has been taken as an exponential: spontaneity times itself, or in simpler terms, *by* itself.

This is the most difficult aspect of animality to grasp, the underlying secret of animal powers. Yet, to give the Lakota some credit, it is the only way to make rational sense of power's own empowerment, turn it back upon itself or twist it into visibility. That may help to explain why they called the power of Whirlwind "unborn" and linked it, via some very odd intersections of animate realities (Elk and Moth, for instance) to the power of reproduction in animals. It is "child-reality," the child power of the embryo before it becomes an embryo, the power of conception before it is a conception. It is the basic lesson taught by all the animal powers, and taught about them. And it is the secret of the musical prodigy, and of the woman giving birth to herself when her body refuses its child.

But since we are not in the habit of using animal powers to *think* with, or musing on the ulterior potencies of gender, a more familiar example of this "lesson" may help. Movement (e.g., "mechanics"), spontaneity in the natural world, the central mystery of physics, and one upon whose solution all the causative chains of scientific reasoning are built up. Movement is computed, "echolocated" by the human bat, by dividing unit space by unit time to get "velocity." Motion "by itself," the spontaneous motion of acceleration, is computed by the temporal underdetermination of *this,* dividing again by time, squaring the unit-time measurement in the denominator. The final lesson in this computation, equivalent to the "unborn" potential of the Lakota Whirlwind, would take this one step further and underdetermine movement's own spontaneity, resulting in twin physical paradoxes, the alpha and omega of cosmic spatiality. The first is the power of pragmatic afterlife to reproduce itself, gravity attracting gravity as the "black hole." The second is far more enigmatic, less "visible" for the very *appearance* it gives to cosmic objects around us. It is the power of light, electromagnetic emission, to undercut its own velocity, grow perpetually "younger" as it ages the distances it moves through.

Observable only in the effects of their effects, these paradoxical "third powers" of movement are *only* conceptual; they have the physical status of a concept. The advantage, then, of thinking with animal powers, in what Lévi-Strauss has called "the science of the concrete," is that the paradoxical agency of underdetermined spontaneity becomes visible once more as a retrofunction of its own disappearing act. I might call it "beginning-power" or "the pragmatic objectivity of movement," but to most Native Americans, like the Lakota, it was "moving in a sacred manner" (cf. Navajo *alilée*). (We move retrograde, upon one another, in all facets of reproduction.) A pragmatic conception, rather than a conceptual pragmatic, this one, too, has its animal forms, and its own animals.

A member of my adoptive moiety, "hawk" or *Tago*, in New Ireland, once taught me the secret of relative smallness, of beginning-power in the scale of things. It was a story fragment: the mighty sea eagle (*Malaba*, the other moiety) was teaching hawk how to fish. Elated on taking his first prey, *Tago* cried, "Khraaa, you are finished; you already know everything. But my powers are limitless, I am just beginning to learn." Hence they call the all-encompassing holography of the *Kaba iri lolos*, "finished power," but address the neophyte *orong*, who is just beginning to know the intent of his mouthed phrases, as *Tago*. His is the empowerment of power itself, lapsed back into the "unborn" realm of desire.

Hummingbird ("on the right"), Huitzilopochtli, was an Aztec war god, a power whose lore among indigenous Mexican peoples has been captured in Eva Hunt's *Transformation of the Hummingbird*.[19] Among the Mayans it was often identified as "Lord of the Black Sun of the Fifth World," suggesting a solarity that prefigured its own lucidity in eclipse, perhaps as the avian itself prefigures its flight. It *was* the power of scale change, the secret of its fierceness, and could become its tornado counterpart on the instant, walk across the land in devastation.

The Mayans probably knew that this fractal bird with its pipette beak, microtic nest and eggs, and atomic orbit–like dance of a miniaturized world within the familiar scaling of things could be worked into a metaphor, as we might do in imagining how it "evolved" that way. Did it not also suggest to them something like evolution's embryo of itself, as DNA might to us, or Mozart, the imago that encapsulates a world and a time growing larger around it? The sensible understanding of the hummingbird's seemingly effortless propulsion, an instant determination of stillness or direction, that it could be explained by ultrafast wing beats, was certainly known to them. But like "metaphor" itself, that metaphor perhaps did not matter, and was possibly another aspect of the being's ability to produce wings, magically and out of nowhere, when its flight was over. A being whose prefiguration of itself allows it to enter its own reality might negotiate the world of metaphor without being in it.

Without the human story of its power, hummingbird is totally innocent of the need for knowing what it is doing. It belongs to the special heaven of what the ancient Mexicans called the "volatiles," beings like butterfly that "float to the top," and take the whole matter of transformation with consummate ease.

10

Imaginary Spaces

Listen carefully. There are no spaces between words as people speak them, no pauses or lapses between one word and another in a complete statement. There is only a flow of sound that has to be imagined as talk. There would be no "language" at all without the imagining of intervals to give it a structural or segmental form. Certainly the artifice of writing has something to do with the way this must be presented, for those of us who have the habit of reading and writing often talk ("in prose") as though we were composing something. But listen again; there are no spaces between the words when we speak, either.

The imagining of intervals between words is the structuring of language, that which is necessary to turn speech into language. But the fact that there are no intervals there at all save in the imagination is the power of the sentence as a completed act of thought. In very intensive speech the force of thought's completion in this way tends to overwhelm the sentence as well, and the spaces between these thought-acts disappear into the background context of their articulation. As the spaces disappear, the "point" of the discourse emerges.

But this is just the tip of the iceberg; it is *not* just simply a matter of how we speak or hear speech, or how we write and read. There are no intervals or lapses, either, among the components of a machine, or a natural process imagined as though it were a machine, in its "working." The machine or process could not really operate if those lapses or imaginary intervals were actually there. But without the artificial mapping out of such fictions in its design—without the "writing" of the machine and the machine of writing or designing—there could be no such things as "working," "operation," or "functioning." The same is true of what we call an "organism" and of the "social body" of human beings in interaction. And there are no lapses or intervals between the "pieces" or moments of time, themselves imagined as intervals, save the ones we imagine to be there in punctuating them (e.g., numbers on a clock, pulses, signals).

It is not that one gear wheel turns, and then the next, and so on, or that a particular component actually "performs" its discrete function within the whole; no machine could possibly operate by stages or intervals as though it were explaining itself in the process. The intervals are as wholly imaginary and arbitrary to what is really going on as is the relational schema that is projected in the design. They, as well as the part-and-whole ingenuity of mechanical design form the point of *our own* articulation (how we *work* things rather than how *they* work), how the device negotiates our working knowledge of its parts. Basically the nature of mechanical process or the identification of "process" in nature is a translation of something that may not work at all into the conceptual language of cause and effect.

No explanation or working model is better than the story it tells of itself, but no story is better than the "picture" its telling makes. Yet if one would look in vain throughout the whole anatomy of human perception—brain, nervous system, points of focus within them, perhaps the body's kinesthesia or habitus itself—for the place where the actual image is formed, it becomes clear that the picturing is only a kind of humor about the body's attempts at understanding itself. It is a picturing of what the picturing would be like if it could exist in that way, as one might speak of the brain and its functions as an "organic transplant" for the mind that would imagine itself thinking in that way.

For the imaginary spaces are "imaginary" precisely because they must be projected somehow *outside* of the thinking process in order to be incorporated back into it via an echolocation of world-in-the-person and person-in-the-world. They "exist" in the representations that thought makes of itself so as to know itself to be thinking, in the pictures, texts, characters, diagrams, and schematics made "on the outside" as though there might be some kind of "interior" to match them.

We begin, really, in an interior that is actually "outside" of the mother's body. The tiny fetus learns motion, the proactive motor activity that underlies all perception, like an astronaut, by "dancing" with its mother in the flotation of the womb. Then it comes back to earth at birth and must learn it over again in gravity. "Little babies," said my daughter, herself at an early age, "laugh on the *inside*. They laugh on the inside first, and then later they learn to laugh on the outside." So it is not necessary to go back to the womb to understand how languages, designs, and imageries might be copies of "originals" that never existed in that way at all, objectifications that resemble their human understanding more closely than that understanding resembles them.

Imaginary spaces are the negative definition of what is usually called the "imagination," and sometimes, as if to pinpoint it more directly, the "visual imagination." Thinking *about* imaginal constructs that are themselves products of thought (e.g., using language to analyze the basics of language, making the working of machines and the social relations of their operators into functions of each other) compounds imaginative understanding into a double negative or double jeopardy of itself. At that point one is no longer thinking about reality, or how one's models or designs might fit with it. One is thinking about how one's thinking fits with itself, a kind of fractal pseudoreality or virtual understanding of understanding.

This is not only the essence of so-called chaos science; it is also what Hamlet did in acting himself mad, and what the term "wise fool" meant to writers like Erasmus. An important part of Shakespeare's wit involved making theater of the "logical" version of it inherited from medieval scholasticism. And although a great deal of contemporary life and thought is invested in taking it altogether too seriously, its most famous reducer-to-absurdity was an ancient Greek, Zeno the Eleatic. Zeno contrived his famous paradoxes patronizing the ability to know-by-explaining to substantiate the teaching of his mentor Parmenides that "we cannot know anything." So the paradoxes are *not* about time, space, or motion—Zeno knew perfectly well that arrows hit their mark and that fast runners can overtake tortoises. Nor are they about the logical or epistemological conditions of *knowing* itself, except insofar as they may be predicated on the strategies used to demonstrate them. The stories about Achilles, the swiftest runner, being unable to catch up with the tortoise because he must always traverse half the remaining distance, or an arrow never reaching its mark for the same reason, are specious exaggerations of the way in which explanation operates. They are parables about the insertion of imaginary spaces within the workings of the explained to make them explainable (or inexplicable).

Are the spaces purely "mental" ones, like the imaginary causes invented and, despite his own disbelief, *acted upon* by a neurotic? Or is the fact that they actually take over any attempt to think rationally about them a proof of their existence out there in the world? How might Zeno have used his favorite trick of "explaining" things on the "labor problems" or worker mentality of nineteenth-century industrialism? "Think of mechanization," he might say, "as one gigantic wheel encompassing the whole of society rather than innumerable little turnings engaged in its works. Think of the center of the wheel, the point of its 'magical' advantage, as the tortoise, and of the worker at the periphery as the hero Achilles, the famous runner. Now the longer the radius of the wheel (capital investment? means of production?), the faster Achilles will have to run, going *backward* half the time, to keep up with the tortoise, though both will reach their destination at exactly the same time."

Would Zeno, as he was wont to do, have turned this into an additional paradox for those who may not have gotten the point of the first one? "Imagine the great socialist minds, Marx, Engels and the lot, as *fans* of Achilles, and you will understand not only where this whole thing is going (e.g., backward half the time) but also industrialism's fanatical obsession with sports and fair play." Perhaps we are fortunate not to have a third version for the twentieth century "explaining" its fascination with putting things into orbit.

What we now call "society" was too real and matter-of-fact, too much a part of its own doings to need a theory, before explanation entered the picture and addressed itself "socially." In medieval times it was called "the secular arm," a member, so to speak, of the Christian Body, which was imagined very holistically, as we now do with "the environment." When it did emerge, in the writings of Thomas Hobbes, as an independent item of thought, society was conceived in naive and animalistic terms. Hobbes called it the Leviathan, or "a mortall God." It was Jean-Jacques Rousseau, in *The Social Contract* and the *Essay on the Origins of Inequality*, who fully *socialized* the concept, severed the connection with animality by treating it as an item of thought that had emerged from a state of nature. Instead of an animal monstrosity it was now a *social* one, an emergent and unpredictable force that created, not law and social distinction, but the *need* for them. We may note that this was not quite the same thing as the order of law or the classes or estates of society, except insofar as these implied the force behind them. It was not yet the *organism* of its own explanation or self-understanding.

So the most significant juncture in the conception of society as an *explainable* condition did not come in the writings of Hobbes, Locke, Rousseau, Montesquieu, or Thomas Jefferson. Neither revolution, nor Napoleon, nor the emancipation of the slaves or serfs resolved the issue of the social monstrosity. To become an operational force, rather than

the rational *tempering* of a force, its imaginary spacing had to be revealed as being more real than the Estates of prerevolutionary France,
or the classes of an industrial social order. It was called "the division of
labor in society," the title of Émile Durkheim's dissertation and famous
book, and was treated as a manifesto in the writings of Karl Marx and
Friedrich Engels.

A society—social order, family, sociality—that exists as though it
might be figured out, or is *known* to exist in that way, becomes its own
echo in the process. The working out of its explanation becomes the
explanation of its working out, so that regardless of how people live
their lives or transact their business, they are patterned into the artificial
relations that thinking makes for them. What began as a social monstrosity in one corner of the world became a monstrous sociality, an
echo-effect of explanation misidentified with colonialism or globalization that transformed the visible human world into a monopoly of self-
conceived relational entities.

The facility of explaining things takes over from the things to be explained, until the whole project, whatever its aims or original intentions,
becomes a forum in methodologies: how to know what it is you are testing and test what it is that you know. What seems to be compulsive behavior, going back and rechecking the checking of one's progress, resembles as well the "possession state" of hysteria as the hypothetical
picturing of things takes over the sense faculties that prove it to be so.
How the "picture" itself works and how that working pictures itself is
both enigmatic and self-determining, at once the "mechanism" of psychology on the outside and the psychology of mechanism on the inside.
Does it merely echo its real workings, or actually *work* by echoing itself?

We have Sigmund Freud to thank for the name that is given to a self-
echoing contagion when imagined this way. He called it "neurosis" and
provided a more precise term, *Nachträglichkeit,* for the retroactive motivation that seems always to be implicated in it.[1]

Neurosis in all of its many forms, hysteria or the compulsive-
obsessive variety, names the circumstance in which the "self" becomes
immediately sensible as the object of its own reactivity. Self is otherwise *only* a reaction, and has no object, hence no scientific purchase. So
unless one were willing to count memory as a "real" and delayed version of the same thing—deliberate and deliberative *Nachträglichkeit*—
everything *else* in the Freudian universe became a work of memory or
something to be worked on through memory. Neurosis was another
version of worker mentality, an imaginary lapse inserted into the im-

mediacy of action to turn it into a knowledgeable "working," but this time conceived as a mental and personal disorder rather than the redress of a social one.

Imaginary spaces aside, what is the etiology of neurosis, the jump start that keeps reconnecting as a worry about the self? The so-called imitative hysteria, the Malaysian *latah* syndrome, is a good place to start. This is a kind of reaction to one's own reactivity in which the impulse to check oneself, to *stop* oneself from acting in a certain way, becomes immediately identified with the behavior one is trying to stop. The denial is so emphatic, perhaps affirmed by the sight of others caught in the same condition, that a simple "no" is insufficient, and one winds up acting out the thing denied as a necessary part of banishing it. The impulse to do so spreads in this way, too, becomes contagious as others try individually to avoid what seems to have become a general panic.

Is laughter itself motivated by the impulse to stop oneself from laughing (e.g., regurgitate the humor that has consumed one)? Laughing *latah* can easily be touched off by playing a recording of laughter and so turning one's *resistance* to laughing into something that is funny in itself. Laughing becomes the only way of stopping oneself from laughing. Researchers have sometimes traced *latah,* or the capacity for it, to an innate "startle" reaction found in some human beings. But since a "startle" is itself an inadvertent imitation of that which startles one, they would seem to be talking about a kind of whiplash effect, a counterstartling that triggers itself off in that way. Is *all* neurosis, in effect as in its causes, really antineurosis, as though the worker mentality of the body went on strike? It is certainly, like *latah,* behavior that is so insidiously *about* itself and its own exegesis that it sets up imaginary causes for real effects. In *latah* or in laughter the action is so immediately efficient—virtually self-diagnostic—that one is tempted to think of it as unconsciously motivated, in terms, that is, that are directly antithetical to the self-consciousness necessary to bring it about. In other words, the action itself provides the injunction to *stop oneself from thinking about it* and identify "it" as the agency of one's doing so.

Nonetheless, and Freud was very clear about this, the *other* forms of neurosis, the obsessive-compulsive varieties, are altogether *too* conscious, in fact, self-conscious or hyperconscious. Instead of acting upon the identification of causes with effects, as we do in laughter, anger, or other forms of hysteria, obsessive-compulsive action becomes *conscious* as the need to control their separation from one another. The compulsive knows perfectly well that the motivational causes presupposed in his symptomatic actions are imaginary, fictional, and fatuous, but this matters less than the drama of isolating them as such. Not merely rationalizing them, but rationalizing the rationalization of them. This is not, in other words, a disorder of the mind, the nerves, or the human "psyche," whatever that may be. It is the diagnostic disease of imaginary spaces.

Theories about the mind are "mental" ones and therefore inherently contagious, like worker mentality, when put into practice (hence the transposition of subjects that Freud called "the transference"). By that standard the most ambitious attempts to deal theoretically with psychoses, "going out of one's mind" in schizophrenia, acute paranoia, and delusional states, could be expected to take themselves out of psychological relevance and to be practically useless for grounding a psychology. So it was the idea of *mundane* mental aberration, neurosis, that formed the basis of Freud's career, as well as the psychoanalytic thinking and much of the "on the street" folklore and superstition about the "mind" that echoed it. These are theories about *sanity*.

But, although it must necessarily "work" the subjectivity through which its working is imagined, a machine does not work *subjectively* either. As in the cases of neuroses—the "startle" reaction of *latah* or hysteria, the "antistartle" overdetermination of obsession-compulsion, it is the *objectivity* of the machine that is both cause and consequence of the subjective mistakes made in trying to figure out how it works. Objects and their perceptible shapes and properties (including Freud's favorite genital objectifications of the body, which seem to move of their own accord and have a will of their own), control the world of subjective perception so comprehensively that it is often necessary to invent imaginary ones to explain how the mind or body works. Or how "working" itself works; why else would worker mentality be such a *fan* of the technological innovation that caused its problems in the first place?

Imaginary particles for imaginary spaces: there is always an arcane atomic structure to the mysticism of insights into the unknown and unseen. The "energy particles" of subatomic physics, the tiny invisible particles of Hindu nutrition-and-pollution theory, the *guruwari,* or "dreamtime," particles of the Walbiri in Australia are not so much cultural accidents, conceived at different times by different peoples, as they are explanatory disasters. They are artifacts of a comprehensive particle degradation that is more nearly universal than the facts and theories that support it. The decay of thought into object and object into thought has a radioactive half-life of its own, actually measurable in the transformation of symbols over time. Exciting discoveries in high-energy physics degrade irrevocably into self-consciously arbitrary pieces of language like "quark," "meson," "neutrino," or "gauge boson," but language itself decomposes, as a result of taking it too seriously, into particulate pieces of its own continuity—syllabary speech events, phonemes and morphemes, units and characters of an imaginary form of speaking and hearing called writing and reading.

If physical reality and language gravitate toward one another through the imaginary spacing that conventionality puts between them and in what Freud could have called a "de facto neurosis" of the conventional world, then it is plain why we would not need Zeno anymore. His sense of our humor and our sense of his have negotiated a transference, changed places to the extent that we now take the substitution of explaining for knowing quite seriously, but regard his patronizing exemplifications of it as peculiar and paradoxical. If the machine of language and the language of the machine are in fact one and the same thing, then his imaginary spaces control our lives.

Zeno was not even talking about epistemology, but the postmodern world cannot get enough of it, produces technobabble and psychobabble at the drop of a hat and often simultaneously in the high-tech world of computer and communication technology. Shrinking the imaginary spacing of the world down to the dense packing of "factoids" and informational bits on the computer chip, expanding the horizons of knowledge's prepackaged DNA into globe-encircling netscapes, but holding it all to the size of the illuminated screen. Zeno would have had a lot of fun with this one, but we would be obliged to take his fun very seriously.

Would a computer languaging of Zeno's kind of fun, a more direct programmatic enhancement of the "machine of language as language of the machine" principle that all programs run on anyway provide the ultimate computer virus? More likely the programming of program's own echo would converge on something much closer to the technology's original intent: knowledge as the achieved object of its own means— the ultimate logo generated out of its own insight, as a clock objectifies intervals out of pure emptiness, or a symphony is made of nothing but air.

Or as neurosis generates imaginary causes that are more real in their effects than the consequences that produced them in the first place. Did the "feedback" technology that found its first instance in the clock escapement elicit a whole epoch of underdetermined purposiveness, from Calvinist predestination to warfare with weapons that had best not be used and histories and chronologies that are very subtle deceptions about the time that passes in them? Have we all learned to live past in its own futurity (yesterday's tomorrow) as future in its own past (tomorrow's yesterday) by making conventional excuses for it? If infinity provides the best excuse of all—infinite opportunities, infinity of kinds, infinity of opportunities, infinite spatiotemporal extension, then the thing we would be most obliged to forget about it would be its absolute dependence upon the *finitude* through which it was known, intuited, or positively reckoned.

Infinity is a *symptom* of the routinized permutation of words, images, set characters, and configurations, of the bit or particle as an excuse for insight. A numbering system that developed a distinctively original mark for each new thing to be reckoned would not be a system, and a language that created its words anew each time they were spoken would lose the sensual echo of "speaking" in the spoken-of. So the infinite variety of possible sound codings or subjects of speech is an echo-effect of the need to *remember* language as one speaks or hears, numerical infinity a specter of the place value implicit in numeration. In all of its possible attributions, conceptional, intuitional, and, insofar as it makes any sense, experiential, infinity is a commentary on the finitary point of contrast that it echoes.

So the notorious omnipotent and omniscient deity would be in the position of the bat listening for *itself* in conversation, determining a fixed point of purchase for its fabulous powers. No Freud otherwise with enough authority to name its neuroses for it, establish the etiology of imaginary causes for the consequences that were there in the first place.

Does time "listen for itself" in the same way? It is the *finitization* of time, marking it as a finite quantity, that elicits the continuity of its imaginary extension. The idea of *measuring* time makes a cause of what is actually a consequence of doing so, as though the time yet to pass (the "Zeno remainder," or the course the runner has yet to travel) were already a function of the part already collected as the "past." For even when projected forward into the future, or scheduled (e.g., "tomorrow at nine thirty," "for the next two weeks"), time "keeps" a purely negative quantity, a sum sub-tracted from the only part of it that "still matters." To demonstrate why this must be so, it is important to pay attention to the traditional wheel-clock, the common denominator of "automated" technology, and to how it "works."

Perhaps the "hands" of the traditional clock face were originally fanciful imitations of the shadow marker on the sundial, which sweeps over the dial in a course opposite and retrograde to the sun's transit across the heavens. Possibly additional hands were supplemented to give time's foreshadowing a greater leverage and precision. But even if this were not the case, the fact remains that the clock face images an inside-out version of the observer's vantage in looking *out* at celestial bodies, a *contained* rather than a containing revolution of temporal markers.

The inversion "works" by *arresting* circular motion, gauging a simulated temporal movement by checking it, as though one could only glimpse or record such a flow by making the "telling" part of it run backward, like viewing the *front* of an image through its back in a mirror reflection or understanding gravity and angular momentum as opposite imaginary vectors of the mutual *balance* that is always held between them. So to be explicit about the *object* that is the only real part of keeping time, one would have to note that the arresting action of the escapement's rocker arm, which allows the clock's drive wheel to pause and hover in its own momentum by catching gears at successively previous positions, is translated into the motion of the hands.

Inverse temporality is time's "movie" of its own temporal gravity, always on "rerun," attracting its own description in things. If this mechanical analogy of time's retrograde "movement" seems a bit over-strained, one might try a visual one. The appearance of a wheel or a tank tread turning "backward" in a motion picture is commonly understood as an accidental illusion, a visual effect created as the timing of the individual frames catches the image at successively previous stages of its rotation. Run the movie backward, and the wheel or tank tread will appear to be going forward, though everything else moves in retrograde. In either case the opposite rotation is actually "telling the time" of the movie, marking the finitization necessary to gauge movement in a relative medium. What the movie "captures," in other words, is its own capturing in time, the time-within-time of one revolution contained within another, and also, of course, of the movie's own recapitulation of events, its "once upon a time." What it shows is that if time actually could run in reverse, a clock's escapement would have to artificially hurry up the drive wheel instead of slowing it down.

What it *means* in this context is that "time" is no more a self-supporting or independently existing abstract entity, understandable apart from kinesthesia and the finitization that makes kinesthesia tractable, than infinity could exist in that way and apart from our finitary means of knowing it. The universe "watches out" for itself in the same way that a supreme being would have to listen for its own location in order to establish or even know its own supremacy. The question of who images whom else in the very dicey business of creation is a difficult one to answer.

We do not normally think of men and women as opposite poles of a single coital conduit, nor identify the mouth and anus, via the vast range of positive and negative, intaking and excreting, cultural values ascribed to them, as merely opposite ends of a single alimentary one. The whole speaking, listening, and thinking element, imaginary spaces with cultural logics of their own, comes in between. And although one might intuit, or actually rave about, a unity of time or even space-time in the present, it is only the finitization of the temporal, understandable in many ways as measurement or simply "passing the time," that would allow one to do that. If time's finitary measure is always a negative quantity, and if *duration,* the actual experience of time's passing, can only be made sensible in spatial terms, then Zeno's paradoxical casuistries would have it right: *space* is the only part of time that *still matters.*

Imaginary spaces in real time or real ones in imaginary time? "The remnant," as the Vedic Hindus called this part of the paradox, made sense of the whole sensible world as the perpetual and self-perpetuating afterimage of perception's lapse, the time it takes to perceive. This would seem to mean the exact opposite of space as "the only time left that still matters," but only apparently so. For equating the Hindus' lapse in perception with Zeno's perception of a lapse in the distance yet to be traversed remainders what is still around in the same way, gives each instance, however "arrived at," the same pragmatic valence.

The understanding and explanation of how things work, general things in particular and particular ones in general, is the secret shared between all public and private discourse. It is the part of the talk that we make inside of ourselves that is shared (or begrudged) on the outside, and the part of common parlance or discourse that is re-intuited as individual finesse or wisdom. One always suspects a "politics" of some sort behind a theory gone wrong, but suspects a theory of some sort behind a politics gone wrong. If there is no better way to understand theory, politics, or even "suspicion" than this, then talk, the "noising" of the human race, is as *nearly* immortal as the supreme being that would listen for its place in it. If there is no better way of understanding supreme being than this, then the person, or individual human being, is another story. One might suspect a politics, a plot of human machinations, behind the facts of one's coming into the world, but suspect a theory of reproduction, genetics, and human care and concern behind those politics.

Listen carefully, for how else might one begin to suspect where jokes come from, how the more derivative ones copy the originals and vice versa, how humor itself copies the languaging of things back upon itself as laughter copies the body on itself, finitizes the reverberation of sense and sensing upon a single point. If that is how finitization "works," tell me if you will how humor works, and I will tell you that that is just how you work it, the politics behind your theory. If the person who discovers a truly original joke is really only discovered by it, becomes its self-evidencing in telling it, then it is self-evident that humor's originality is far older and more final than the subjectivity of knowing it, telling it, or suspecting one knows how it works and then making a joke of it to confirm that suspicion.

Sound-thinking is the only real antidote to neurosis, the thought-in-action that emphasizes its own finalization to the extent that it identifies its own impulse as a force coming from outside of it. Self acting itself by copying out "no" in its actions is the cakra or echo-subject of human subjectivity. The unity of sound (no spaces between the words) that makes a sentence into a completed act of thought, or a symphonic sequence into a "movement," is simultaneous or synchronic in its spacing out of tones, but linear and sequential in its *conceptual* unity. We "hear" it all at once by collecting its separate vibrations, but each of them resonates a single closure.

The sound-center, or ground bass aggregate tonality of all the human vibrations ever produced, might resonate the globe like a tuning fork, make a single sentence of all the things, species, and imaginal forms located in its echo-subject, including the supreme being that listens in them. The biggest meaning of all, earth-shattering in its significance, indecipherable in its grammar. That is perhaps why we all sing separate songs, and why all the language phonologies and musical works and performances are carefully constructed to avoid it, get the point of it by not getting it.

And it is likely why Anton Bruckner, a confirmed neurotic by all accounts of his personal life, actually tried for it in his Eighth Symphony, and also possibly why he dedicated the next one, the one he did not finish (he died before completing it—think of avalanches crashing in the Alps) to God.

The totality of sense, pure meaningfulness, is like infinity; it is never an option. Perhaps that is why we divide it (and ourselves) up into cultures, then try to cipher the differences among them into a positive quotient called "anthropology." There is always the possibility of a most acute underdetermination, a point of exact equivalence or double encompassment between infinitude in all its parameters and the finitization that makes those parameters possible. Jan Sibelius likened symphonic form to a riverbed: "The bed of a river is composed of innumerable tributaries, brooks, and streams, and eventually broadens majestically into the sea but it is the movement of the water that determines the shape of the riverbed."

Every phrase, resolution, or tonal finalization in a symphonic work is a humor, not only about itself but of the whole harmonic continuity; every chamber of one's life is an irony in itself about the whole expectational fantasy that encompasses it. So the parallels that might be entertained between musical form and nature, harmonic completion and life, one's own and other lives, or life itself and history are unnecessary if not grossly misleading. For they merely trade off echo-subjectivities, play on the differences between alternative kinds of experience in the way that those experiential modes play upon the differences within them.

So perhaps Sibelius was right; the symphony is not a human invention but a kind of natural discovery—about life, and life's environing of itself within an environment that "works," imaginally, in much the same way. He was not a composer of nature, then, but part of a natural composition.

Symphonic music is not necessary at all except insofar as it is sufficient, and it need only be sufficient to itself. In that same way omniscience and omnipotence are unnecessary and exaggerated attributions for supreme being, our sense of its humor merely and for all the fact that it would never need to imagine *itself* in that way. It is not that such a being would be too abstract, ineffable, and all-encompassing to be imagined, but too concrete and finite—more *personal* to the person that would imagine it than any echo-subject he could conceive for the purpose, more *individual* than the most original individual (including itself in the comparison) that ever existed. So instead of trying to imagine supreme being, think of an Englishman at a dinner party trying to establish his exact social positioning by listening to the conversation. Better, imagine a bat at a cocktail party, ears cocked and head tilting this way and that, the martini slightly askew in its hand. If it never quite establishes its point of human reference (the "life" of the party) with the exactitude it would require—the universe goes on—we would not be able to do so either.

If any sense made within culture or about culture would have to gauge its point of human relevance more immediately, concretely, and definitively than the bat could get its reference, then theology or theory of any sort is entirely beside the point. One could only hope, for all the background chatter, to listen as acutely as the bat. For the human counterpart would be obliged to do more: listen to itself listening to know itself knowing or even *that* it was knowing (e.g., not everything at once but one thing at a time), and so only move in counterpoint to its divine attributions. The resolution to the dilemma posed in this implicit comparison between the human condition and its "original" would not be "salvation," a more vivid or viable experiential life, or a more compact death, but a kind of folding-into-itself that perhaps only music might insinuate to us.

Reimagined as a finite or definitive quality, as imaginary spaces between sounds, moments in time, parts or components of the working of things in nature, machines, or the organism, the infinite loses nothing of its awe. If holism itself as well as the analytic parsing needed to imagine it can only make sense in that way, or sense make sense of itself, then the difference between infinite extension and its finitary appropriation is recapitulated in every version of it. The difference need have nothing other than this to do with the actual being or configuration of reality so long as it completes the ways in which we would know about it or do something about it.

The "discovery" that human beings construct their own realities or interpret them in and out of existence, or that perception is a kind of artisanship in this, is one that is made over and over again. Without any real effect. It is the mainstay of most "spiritual" philosophies, con games, and critical investigations into what human culture, understanding, and perception are supposed to be. But like the theory of neurosis in practice or the practice of neurosis in theory, it feeds upon the very falsehoods that are "constructed" in order to explain it, becomes an ever-repeating tautology about its own "bright idea." By using self-falsifying examples (instead of self-verifying procedures, like psychoanalysis), preempting the false conclusiveness of reality construction, Zeno tried to reverse the thought process of this, to show that we cannot "construct" our realities at all, but only self-deceptively reconstruct the constructions that would explain them. Do we actually *believe in* the lexical authority of the words we use, pretend to believe on the conviction that others do, or only pretend because we suspect that they are pretending too? The real problem with those who do not believe in the efficacy of words is that those who do will be able to tell them *in no uncertain terms* what an ass they have made of themselves, and they themselves have no rejoinder.

II

The Cakra of Johann Christian Bach

Mark Twain once remarked that he had heard in Germany that Wagner's music is actually much better than it sounds. But the music of Johann Christian Bach, made in the seventh and eighth decades of the eighteenth century, makes its own joke of that one. It actually *sounds* better than it is historically and musicologically supposed to be, cuts a caper around its own importance. Sometimes called "the London" or "the English" Bach after the place where his career found its fruition, Johann Christian was the youngest son of the great Sebastian, who left him three harpsichords upon his death.

Christian Bach's style has sometimes been called "more Mozartian than Mozart," borrowing a bit of (exaggerated) fame from the prodigy it had helped to set up. But Mozart in his later works carried the style of the "singing allegro" to degrees of suppleness and complexity that his friendly mentor had not even contemplated. If those directions were the issue, or the ones that music had taken afterward, Christian Bach would count only as an important "influence." And if *that* were the issue, musical evolution, I would not have raised it at all.

Mozart's father, the astute Leopold, spoke of Christian Bach's works as *diese Kleinigkeiten* ("smallnesses," "bits" perhaps, but not "trivialities"), and he spoke with admiration. The point is simply that Bach, Mozart's senior by several decades, was conceptually and stylistically *younger* than his exquisite protégé, that he modeled the inceptional movement or spirit evident in Mozart's work more fully and originally than Mozart could have. He died earlier and lived longer (by eleven years) than Mozart, was the prodigy behind the prodigy.

What might this mean? One could start with the Baroque concerto grosso, an art form capable, as one writer put it, "of practically infinite extension," and ask how Christian Bach or more likely Stamitz and the Mannheim school "transformed" it into a music of greater speed, conciseness, and expressive power. That would be the historical or musicological way of explaining things. Conversely, one might begin with something more akin to "taking the derivative" in calculus and ask how a genius at harmonic syncopation, foreshortening the musical interval, turned music around to fit it. The calculus succeeds, whatever the imageries used to make sense of this, by reducing knowable variables to a point-event and making continuities responsible to it. The eighteenth-century "new music" did something analogous to this for musical form and melodic conception. Did this tact at compressing life experience, launching the "Mannheim rocket," affect the life spans of the composers themselves, make longer life spans somehow unnecessary—the opposite of modern "health care" practices?

The point, musical but not musicological, is that Christian Bach's music forms the same pragmatic contrast with the music that came before it as with the music that came afterward. It is newer than the labored "romanticism" of the Baroque period but younger than the classical modeling of Mozart, Haydn, Beethoven, and Schubert, in *advance* of the self-conscious romanticism and neoclassicism that followed them. It was no accident but in fact an acknowledgment of this contrast that the high formal art of the Baroque composers was "rediscovered" in the 1820s and 1830s. Beethoven emulated Handel in much of his late music (especially the Missa Solemnis), and Mendelssohn quite literally *conducted* the revival of the Passions and other religious "music dramas" of J. S. Bach.

The problem of musical cakra, how it might be defined or understood, is not exactly historical, although musical history can be helpful in coming to terms with it. It includes the music's placement in time, the audience's or performers' *participation* of it, and the explanations that might be given for it, within its definition. If it is not quite so simple as to say that the part of the composer's life spent conceiving of the music, composing and perfecting it, involves or galvanizes the parts of our own lives spent in knowing it, it is not terribly more complex than this either. The music is a cross section through time, and the time of the music itself is a cross section through its formal structure, as well as the reactions—boredom, exhilaration, indifference—of those who hear or perform it. It is like the product that includes so much of human participation in its design—how people buy or sell it, use or abuse it, like or dislike it—that the product is not a product without that participation. The pragmaticity of the product is more nearly objective than the object itself, and it is just precisely that pragmaticity that determines its value and role in the economy. At that depth, however, "economic" is virtually interchangeable with "aesthetic."

It is nothing short of amazing that most people—not only educated ones—know exactly why classical music is important, more nearly expressive or emblematic of "our culture" than any other mode of experience or understanding. They know this without wanting to know it, and without knowing how or why they do. Often enough they are indifferently selective about the music or even resentful of it (both natural results of being made to "appreciate" it—whatever that might mean). Shorn of its pragmaticity, classical music is often, in fact, ugly, boring, or dull. Beyond this, most of those who love it or have learned to live with it (and this includes many musicians) are thoroughly incapable of articulating how or why this might be so, or even what music itself might be. Perhaps, as many of them would want to tell us, our inability to articulate its meaningfulness is the very secret of music itself. But even those who are able to get beyond this degree of mystification and are able to know what they know about music might resist the suggestion that music is fundamentally technological and that, as I would rather assert, it is the foremost example of our technology.

Composers with a great deal of insight into their own work, like Johann Sebastian Bach, Beethoven, and Sibelius, doubtless had an intimation that what they were working on was something more than music. What we have in the potential of sound to unify a sentence or a work of music is no less than the germ or essence of holography, the capability of integrating *any* task or understanding into a single and utterly simple totality. At work and at hazard in any attempt to comprehend or represent it, this is not a mere representation, cognitive conception, or interpretive point of view. It is the *reality* of absolute comprehension or technical facility—the key to knowing or doing *anything*. It becomes a fractalized version of itself, a theory, a culture, an ends-and-means project in technology or scientific understanding only to the extent that it gets in its own way, doubles back into the knowing of its knowing.

That something of this ambition, and something of the problem that seems inevitably to dog it, is fundamental to Western classical music, is evident from the work of the German theoretician Heinrich Schenker. Schenker was able to demonstrate that music written in a "key" according to the canons of Western polyphony can be analytically reduced to a single "germ" motif. A "fundamental structure," as he called it, a simple, germinal progression in polyphonic form, pervades every bar of the score, sets every movement, whether in sonata, variational, or three-part form, into an organic "fit" with what he called the "background" of the work. The score itself, and the music as it is performed or heard and experienced, is the "foreground." His analysis constitutes the "middle ground," a series of transformations that show how the fundamental structure keeps its scale as one moves from foreground to background or vice versa. Worked out in a series of exhaustive analyses,[1] his method demonstrates the scale-invariant organicity of music of this type, but as a largely imperceptible and background congruity, one that is not apparent in the movement of melodic content or rhythm, or in the succession of the sections or movements of the work.

The question that the listener, performer, or critic would raise is that of how this background would matter, since the experiential meaningfulness of the music lies in its temporal movement, its dynamic of tempo, rhythm, thematic transformation, and key modulation and resolution. If the "foreground" *is* music, just why would it be necessary to abstract a background for it? Is the "background structure" *simply* analytic, a unity of patterning that the music inadvertently describes, or is it the key to music's pragmaticity? Schenker would doubtless acknowledge that his method is not "reversible," that it could not be used synthetically to generate more Mozart concerti or better Beethoven symphonies.

Schenker's approach approximates the synchronicity of the music, the pragmatic objectivity that holds its temporality to a focus, and it abstracts a background that is as detached from its musical experiencing as a joke is from the humor that motivates it. The ways in which we might hear it as music, respond to it as music, perform or even compose it as music correspond to the same subjective or temporal vectoring that humor does. For all the fact that the pragmatic objectivity would not have come into existence without the composer or the originator of the joke, that objectivity is singularly definitive of its total effect in a way that tonality or laughter cannot be. (Music or humor can be made of a purely "found" pragmaticity; Beethoven was inordinately good at this, often to the admiration or bemusement of his friends.)

Schenker himself paid tribute to the detached quality of his "fundamental structures" by speaking of them as organic forms with a life of their own. In his acute commentary on Schenker's approach in *Man the Musician*, Victor Zuckerkandl provides a more helpful exegesis of what this disclosure of musical pragmaticity might entail. He suggests that the organicity of a classical work grows "in a dimension perpendicular to time," that it is not constructed by the movement and "working out" of the music as it flows, but only in a sense revealed ("iterated") as a counterpart of that repetition.[2] The organicity is *acquired* as a meaningfulness from its performers and listeners, defines the emotional objectivity of the work through a rightness of sound that is available to hearers throughout.

The same could be said of the creation or composition of the music. The life of a great composer is enigmatic, the subject of many biographies and studies, as if the compositions could in some sense be explained by the person. In fact the peculiarities and idiosyncrasies of the historical person are most often foregrounded with the idea of getting some sort of insight into how such a person could be creative. What we find, rather, in the Beethoven of the anecdote, the sketchbooks, or the quizzical *Tagebuch,* or the Mozart of the letters to his father, is a reasonably intelligent person rather beside himself and astonished by his works. The composer, and his life as well, is in a more important sense "composed" by the music, realigned by it. If that is genius, then one would have to conclude that it, too, develops through a dimension perpendicular to the temporality, has its only congruity with the facts of the composer's life and personality in that way. It describes or accounts for the composer's life without being described by that life.

The synchronicity of the music is not quite the same thing as the germ-motifs and "fundamental structures" that emerge from Schenker's analyses. These are "life-forms" because Schenker gave them life, or brought them to life in that way, just as they are "structures" because Schenker was able to locate his version of a self-scaling structure within them. His method of analysis focused upon the way in which the self-action of the composer, performer, or listener is emplotted within the music, and the shift of focus to that "background" throws its temporal modulation into foregrounded relief. The beauty of this analysis and its fundamental lesson in eliciting a holography where others would find a temporal movement or flow is not structural at all. What it demonstrates is more basic—not simply *that* we are hearing ("feeling") our own input or participation as the music, but how this happens, and how the objectivity of the music is integral to the meaningfulness or musicality we give to it.

If we do not ever feel emotions directly but become, instead, emotional about our feelings via the thoughts that inform us about them, then music does not "embody" emotions at all. This means that what we witness or experience as "emotion" itself is actually the backlash or echo-effect of what we would seem to feel, that what musical resonance captures more convincingly than verbal description is the dying-out or receding effect of feeling. So music is not so much emotional as the re-activity that we identify with feeling is inherently musical, crucially dependent upon some form of resonantial modeling. Properly speaking there are no "feelings" but only felt qualities, *sense* taken in place of the body's reactions to it.

In other words, the sense of what a feeling might have meant when recollected after the moment of its own demise is hardly the same thing as emotional spontaneity. What music provides instead, or the qualities of "tone" or voice that carry the emotional tenor of speech, is a surrogate autonomy of sense, the substitute for a spontaneity that could not be recognized even though one might cultivate an ability to isolate it. The quintessential mortality of life's expression, the death of feeling as a necessary prerequisite to feeling itself, is perhaps what the Gizra people of south Papua mean in identifying the woman Kumaz as the "originator of death and musical instruments."[3] But it is certainly the refinement of this principle as an agency in its own right, synchronized without being "synchronic," that Schenker recognized in what he termed "musical life-forms."

Music echoes, locates, possibly originates emotion's time and direction, yet it is always a time apart. Performers as well as audience dress for it as though for dinner, or as if paying their respects at a wedding or funeral. Possibly because music has the relational place value of a minor divinity, musical people do not really need a separable religious identity. It is somewhat arbitrary to them, and many of the historical figures, Sebastian as well as Christian Bach, Mendelssohn, and Mahler, changed confessions in order to suit their circumstances.

Music that incorporates its own sense of direction and purpose, musical cakra, is more nearly akin to a gyroscope, the navigational aid that offers a positive resistance to any change in orientation, than to a holography. What Schenker called a musical life-form and A. L. Kroeber, persuaded by the sense of culture moving independently of its participants, termed the "superorganic," bears a strange resemblance to the "biofeedback" conception of brain-body functioning and its externalized representation in the feedback loop. Nonetheless, the suggestion that musical integration is a kind of "right-brain" function moved outside the body and into an agentive space of its own conceals more than it reveals about an ostensibly reflexive art form. If music brings the resonantial patterning that is already evident in speech to a sharper, more encompassing focus, just what, exactly, is it a reflex of?

The power of music to simulate human emotions that could never have been "there" in the way that its tonality resonates them, of not merely expressing but actually inventing feelings, involves a cathexis of the self-imitative reflex. As in *latah,* or bodily possession states, the human ability to react models itself upon itself, codes its own reactivity in instances like laughter, orgasm, and hysterical anger or weeping. The inceptive impulse "catches" itself (like a disease) too quickly and immediately for the kind of self-interrogation necessary to know emotion, so that intentional cause and effect are conflated. As in those nominally "hysterical" disorders where an imitative pattern is actually induced by the impulse to check it, the behavioral motivation is "syncopated," jump-started by its own interference with itself. It is usually experienced as retroactive to the subject, brought on by an alien or external agency.

The resonant or musical cathexis of motivation in this way involves the interference of music with itself in a kind of vicarious or appositional "hysteria." Usually described as polyphony ("many voices"), it is the art of evoking an uncanny and motivating melodic continuity out of imaginary spaces, composing and performing an "invisible third melody" as the interference-patterning to two or more melodic lines that are recorded ("composed") and performed separately. The result is like a hologram in sound, an independently motivated (e.g., "three-dimensional") musical figuration.

Traditional Western musical art was totally impelled or inspired by the retroactive implication of this "invisible" melodic background, as if it had existed independently beforehand to educe the melodic lines that evoke it. The ability to "echolocate" this effect, usually a result of early and intensive training, is commonly attributed to an inborn talent in prodigies like Mozart, Mendelssohn, and Richard Strauss. On the broader scale of musical history, from Gregorian chant or Palestrina onward into classical or modern times, the very same attribution is made to music itself, as if in echolocating its own echolocational facility it had been its own prodigy. Yet the principle also bears a direct analogy to the retroactive implication of "meaning" in the formation of a trope or metaphor, and to what is called the "harnessing" or application of energy in the working of a machine. Whether musical, rhetorical, or mechanical, the "device" is rationalized as a kind of consequence of the effects it produces, as if these were somehow its "causes."

If the contrastive "subjects" or themes developed in a sonata movement, or the thematic iterations of a fugue or theme-and-variations piece are in each case subtle deployments of the same germinal motif, then we have, in Schenker's demonstration of this, something wholly prodigious. The formal structure is like laser light, refocusing its own deflection and interference with itself to form a comprehensive image of its emission source. And we have in musical form itself a causal deconstruction of the "sense" that motivates the meaning or working of things, like a clockwork that "tells" temporal duration through the momentum of an ever-recurring now. Does it also copy, and hence reflect back to us, our ability to participate in its simulation of emotion, confer a sense of authenticity to the feelings we have about our feelings? If so, that would help to explain why a more condensed version of this overdetermined art form, a syncopated polyphony like that of Christian Bach, might sound better than it is musicologically supposed to be. Instead of drawing out and elaborating upon the response time that we take for "feeling" itself, it incorporated and thereby revealed a different kind of truth about emotion—the ability of emotive feeling to anticipate its own response. Bach's syncopation worked ahead of schedule, preempted melodic contours in theme and development. The result, copied extensively by subsequent composers as the very model of classical precision, likewise belied those efforts. It showed musicality not in the size of its effects, but in the affective qualities of its own size.

The ability to feel with the eyes, the ears, skin, and hands, with the motion and balance of the body (kinesthesia) is not a thing that has necessary limits or boundaries. Whatever interposes itself as an agreed-upon or habitual limit, like the physical body or the analogous demarcation of sounds and physical images in the world, becomes a double-edged identifier or feeling for oneself and for others. One knows oneself, feels one's feelings about oneself in that way, and one is known in that way by others. Because sound and resonance (ability to "sound again") is out of sight and physically "out of bounds," it falls naturally into the role of integrator, the medium of feeling's limitlessness for the tonal patterns made of it in speech, language, or music.

Consequently, whenever we speak or think abstractly about consciousness, emotion, being, or the self and its propensities, we are dealing concretely with the sense that is made for them by sound and its properties. More precisely, we are speaking both with and about the resonance that makes a delimiting "sense" out of vibration's interference with itself. It is as though the ability to feel feelings about oneself or others, to know that one is knowing, were a vibrating column of air or the chord of a plucked string. The integrational faculty of resonance is rendered abstract and ephemeral in silent reading or in a "signed" conversation, and the faculty of "reading" or actually demarcating thoughts and propositions is correlatively sublimated in music. What a symphony would have to "say" about our attempts to make sense of it would be too much a part of its resonance to be translated.

Yet the symphony is made of the same air as its explanation; the only difference is a pragmatic one. Speech is essentially monovocal, demanding of language for the sense it makes, and music is polyphonic, engaged with its own resonance through and across the temporal vectoring of things. We do not speak our piece all at once, and music has no ear to listen for itself. Something *like* music would always be necessary to conceive a sense of the person-beside-itself—being, emotion, consciousness, soul—and something like speech's demarcation of sounds, imaginary intervals, would be necessary to make distinctions at all. The Dani people of central New Guinea speak of the soul as *etai-eken*, the "seed of singing."

A single chord or melody has a composite finality about it that would only encumber the imaginal demarcation of speech. Modeling its resonantial integrity upon the line or continuity necessary for spoken sense does something strange to the music as well as the story line, creates the metaphor of a foreign language in the song, opera, or tone poem. Modeling the resonant finality of the chord upon its own inception, as in West African drumming, the Indian raga tradition, or the germ-motif music of the European Enlightenment, has the opposite effect. It conjures the nonmetaphor of a language known so well that nothing beyond its tones need be uttered in it.

No one plays the main beat in West African drumming; it finds its limit or absolute demarcation among the other beats, propels the core of an invisible music. To make analytic sense of the modeling of a musical work or performance upon itself, one would have to say something drastic, like that the conclusion or finality of the work is played through to its beginning.

Emotional *sense*, a kind of movement or changing of feeling, is the retrocausality of music's pragmatic, the "participatory" strain that runs from beginning to end as the formal structure collapses on itself. Calling the role of sense in this "meaningful" is less helpful, though directly analogous motivationally through the similarity to trope, because the sound does not make a detour through language. The sense is more nearly akin to "energy," though here it moves the subject, rather than

the object, of the technology. Does our ordinary sense of gender motivate its supergendered capability in the same way, or do kin relations
throw incest back upon itself?

That is the trouble with "pictures" in music. Pace Richard Strauss,
who often spoke of them as objective, their visuality is a retroeffect,
an iconic *outcome* of the music's consuming action rather than a consumer of it. A music built upon its own tonal interference-patterning—
drums, bullroarers, or didgeridoo no less than contrapuntal or part-
polyphony—plays the process of iconic consumption in reverse,
repletes the sense instead of eating it.

"Drum sound is forceful when it transcends the event and remains in
your head, continuing to flow."[4] In his remarkable studies of musicality among the Kaluli of New Guinea, Steven Feld elucidates the way
in which musical self-interference catches language on the rebound.
Feld's Kaluli confreres called metaphor *bali to,* "turned over words,"
and spoke of their acoustic evocation as *dulugu ganalan,* "lift up over
sounding."[5] "Concretely, it is the moment when the throbbing drum
voice is no longer heard as a bird voice calling *tibo tibo,* but is now heard,
on the inside reflection, as a dead child calling *dowo dowo,* 'father, father.'"[6] One might speak more familiarly of this retro-languaging as
"overtoning," and ask whether the pragmatic of spoken language is not
really a fractal overtoning of word-sounds interfering with one another.

The cakra version of sense as retrocausality is that the part-and-whole
quality of life, its remberable content and continuity, constitutes its
own remnant. The biographical and biological development in time,
known and told as it unfolds but unfolding pragmatically as it is known
or told to itself, is a real artifact of its interference patterning, a virtual
arrest analogous to the "vertical" harmonizing or counterpointing in
a work of music. Life's time span is continually finishing itself off, an
"originator," like the woman Kumaz, "of death and musical instruments," its nominal "afterlife" component a running accompaniment
to what we understand as the experiencing of events. Once the "lift up
over sounding" of life's experiencing had exhausted itself, one would
find oneself down and flat on top of the merely real.

Whatever its validity, in other words, there is enough in the musical
analogy to encourage a reexamination of traditional spiritual statuses
like reincarnation or "afterlife" as a kind of beyond in death. Do they
fade out after the death event in a sort of half-life of remberable potency, a kind of eddying effect? The analogy might be more helpful, in
any case, in understanding the reflectional cosmology that Feld and

E. L. Schieffelin have described so vividly for the Kaluli (Schieffelin once called it a "mirror-world"), as a relation to the "inside" or "underside" of human speech.[7] A Kaluli "gone person" or deceased spirit might still be calling out "father, father," or be imitated so in the drums of the magnificent *gisaro* performance, but survivors would hear in the forest only the upside of the turned-over words, as a bird voice calling plaintively *tibo, tibo*.

Sentiment and speculation to the side, all that this may mean is that treating death as if it could have a living subject is so futile, if not downright misleading, that the only viable recourse is to treat life as though it has a dead one. We die, literally, out of our moments and experiences and into a resonance that makes sense of them, a sense that joins itself not to the reality that made it happen but to another, like vibrato still continuing from beforehand. If one makes the anthropologist's choice, takes the social (conversational, dialogic) implication of this over the individual and psychological, one joins to an infractional column of air that is well-nigh immortal, that has been moving with the sense of things since well before "sentience" happened to the race. What New Guinea people call "the talk that never dies" has been noising about the contours of the land for so long that languages and language families appear and disappear in it, whole speech communities metamorphose into others without changing its fundamental character.

It is tempting to think of this relatively ageless toning of human sense and emotion, stretching before and after any conceivable span of lifetime, memory time, or chronicled history, as having some subliminal order, a semiotic formula or structural motif as the chord of an order more exhaustive than chaos. Pythagoras insisted that number and numerical relations presented a kind of magical key to this, and Johannes Kepler and his contemporaries imagined it geometrically, as a "music of the spheres." Possibly Beethoven, who thought of musical keys as having specific tone colors (B minor, for instance, was "black"), might be curious about its key signature, or wonder whether it had an overall emotional tone.

But that kind of thinking, or at least supposition, has the problem exactly backward, like the romantic fantasy of thinking of a composer's music as being about his life experience when the reverse of this is much more nearly true. The secret of interference patterning in music or speech is not overdetermination from beyond but underdetermination from within, an internal limit that conjures or merges with the infinity around it. Logic and verbal proposition have no *application* without the sense that provides their empirical scaling, but sense and feeling have no significance whatever without the imposition of an underdetermining scale or limit.

Unfortunately, though perhaps fortunately for artists and musicians, substitutes for emotion are all we will ever know or feel of emotionality itself. A work of music, musical cakra, need not have any *meaning* at all, for despite the superstructures erected around it—in the training of musical sense and the explication of what it "means"—it is the *feeling of meaning* that tunes and determines its worth.

The pragmatic afterlife of a composer—all we really "know" of the person—becomes the structural and possibly psychological *decomposition* of his work. It is the story and actually the pragmatic reality of a life that interfered with itself, fell apart, and transformed itself aesthetically into patterns of sound. Little wonder that the emblematic classical figures gravitate into pathologized versions of the lives they *might have* lived—Mozart as the debacle of his perfectly ordinary marriage to Constanze Weber, Beethoven as the pathology of his abortive attempts at love and family life, the Bach lineage cloned into ever newer and younger editions of its fabulous musical predilection.

So the implicate "holography" or sonorous infolding of musical space that Schenker described for classical works, and the echolocation of emotional reactions that romantic music substitutes for it, might actually take the place of biography or history in accounting for musical development. Musical works generate a *feeling* for logic, for causal or propositional sequency, via the sense necessary to its demonstration, that is more definite and definitive than logic itself. An art that plays familiarly and exclusively with the beginnings and endings of things by joining them at the very midpoint, "participating" them in the *now* of its performance, is at once the humor and the objective measure of time's interference with itself. Perhaps that is why classical works, some of them more than others, are performed over and over again, and why the time that passes between performances is so antithetically different from the time that is passed off within them. Like that of the joke that started off language in the first place, the point of it was rather made to be missed, but missed as closely as possible without incurring damage. (One is not supposed to *die* into the music, though this does not stop some people, even composers like Wagner and Mahler, from trying, and if one succeeded—what a death!) Also like that joke, the true progenitor of all attempts to elicit humor or get at its truth, the point of musical extinction has a logical existence that is altogether beside the point of its historical possibilities.

A great music in *any* genre or tradition is too personal to be emotional: the echo-effect of what we call "emotion" and the counsel it keeps with us simply betrays it. Music that is tolerated for emotion's sake is emotion tolerated for the music's sake, and the person caught up in such an imitational double bind loses musical immediacy and becomes a "personality" by that much. Caught up in, eventually created by emotions about the emotions it has had, the personality *has* relationships instead of being them, is always ripe for analysis or therapy. Romanticism per se has very little to do with this; Rachmaninoff was a personality, Richard Strauss was not, and only learned to tolerate personalities.

The point is not that music's "feeling of meaning," the sense that it makes of straightforward logic, is *sometimes* paradoxical, but that it necessarily has to be so. Consider the example of Orthodox Slavonic church music, the *demonic* part-singing of a "sideways" polyphony that actually *outflanks* its temporal sequence, turns language into music and music into language and gets to the point of it before belief does— the most purely commiserative music ever made. Consider especially the conception of godhead, called Bog, that *listens* in the voices of the choir. Bog did not have to create the world or the myth of the world so long as he listened in them. It is immaterial to the force of that listening whether Bog would exist or not, or whether or not he is believed in, for he is omnipotent and omniscient on the point of his *listening*. Bog listened to the noise of the czar, to the noise of Lenin, Stalin, Khrushchev, and Gorbachev; he listened to the terror of the black hundreds and the mafias and hooligans that followed them, to the silent suffering of the gulag victims. He listened for the advent of Slavonic church music in the Crucifixion, and will still be listening after its last note has sounded. Bog is not a god you will ever know anything about but that he hears what you tell him of it.

Do we then perform the acute *listening* of Beethoven's deafness in his music, his personality all gone to tatters in the intensely personal feeling of its meanings—the human bat, echolocating his life on the dying out of sound? Listening is the "shape" that these old masters come in, and to perform their music is to catch the note of their own precocity, make the *future* listen better.

The history of music is full of nearly tragic composers like Liszt and Wagner who tried to live their lives up to the emotional scale of their music, and of others, like Sibelius, Richard Strauss, and Shostakovich, who lived their way out of it, and so outlived it. Yet the issue of emotion's underdetermination in music is a telling one. Works of rare genius in the arts are "parts" of culture, culture made out of culture, that miniaturize it, underdetermine the whole sense and purpose of the cultural so acutely that future generations are themselves imitations of the style in which they do so—and frequently with such poise that no one seems to notice.

How like Christian Bach, notwithstanding the fact that, in an act of what Mozart was later to call "unnecessary violence," he once seized an unusually punishing critic by the hair.[8] (Critics often deserve at least as much.) Here was a composer who had learned to do something rather more satisfying than inventing cultures. He invented sense, sometimes, arrested by his own spontaneity, on the spot. The part that Johann Christian Bach played, mere "entertainment," in underdetermining the "system," the powerful and oftimes sinister cultural hegemony of George III's England, was inconsequential. It cut no political ice, but it matched pragmatically, precision for precision, the work of a London contemporary, John Harrison (1693–1776), whose achievement of a near-perfect chronometer solved the problem of longitude and made the British Empire possible. (The unsung genius who made the clock work and the singing one who contracted *musical* time.) Yet it made the most important and valuable point that can be made about culture and its poorly understood invention.

What is the relevance of Johann Christian Bach's achievement to the argument of this work? To the extent that the consummate *melody* is incorporated as a kind of "art" rather than acknowledged openly, its significance will be rationalized either in formal (e.g., "classical") terms or in the seemingly emotional ones that we attribute to romanticism, and thereby missed. To the extent that it may be realized as more effectively definitive of the means used to describe it than those means could account for it, only the performance counts. Explaining what it means exhausts the possibilities of explanation instead, isolates a quasi-musical substitute for something that is not musical in those terms.

Shall I try? It could be said that music elicits a nonphysical energy, that it defines Karl Pribram's idea of holographic brain functioning more concisely than David Bohm's notion of a holographic universe could validate it, but undercuts the "implicate structure" of that universe more incisively than the holographic mentality necessary to comprehend it. Or I might argue that it engenders a polyphonic movement that is more definitive than the physical intuition of *motion,* one in which the automimetic dynamics of eroticism and the quasi-kinetic ones of the musical performance copy one another. And I might suggest that the holistic function of the ear has been mistaken for something that the mind is alleged to perform—that there is no "mind" at all, but that the facility of initiating balance in the body's motion, and motion in its balancing, is an *acoustic* one.

Either words themselves, or the ways we use them, fail in the attempt to say what I mean here. I have often suspected that the medieval monks made a terminal error when they adumbrated the visual illumination of their manuscripts, and that the early professors compounded that error in inventing *scholarship*—that the footnote and indeed the proliferation of commentaries and thus textual theories, even text itself, are the outcome of a failed attempt at textual polyphony. If no mathematical equation or set of equations, no formal argument and no abstraction whatsoever is ever more correct or useful than the imageries used to make sense of it, then no imagery of any kind has any purchase over the music that makes nonsense of it. As Ludwig Wittgenstein, who could whistle whole symphonies from memory, became the best philosopher of his times by stating absolutely nothing of which he was not certain, so Johann Christian Bach, who *composed* whole sinfonias by anticipation, became the best musician of his times by writing no note that was not certain of itself.

12

The Near-Life Experience

A myth is not simply one category or type of story that people have made sacred for religious, traditional, or historical reasons, and that stands in some kind of inevitable contrast to ordinary folktales, moral parables, or those hypotheses that Tennyson called "fairy tales of science." A myth is the *sense* or imaginal content of any narrative, demonstrative account whatsoever as it condenses into the finite and objective limitations that encompass the details of its knowing or understanding. So the myth about myth that we call "mythology" has the sense of its own significance backward; it is not sacredness or tradition that turns stories into myths and myths into mythologies, but the radical finitization of the story that mythologizes ideas like sacredness, tradition, or history, renders them imaginable.

On that basis, and since we cannot really talk about anything without calling its near-life experiencing into account, and hence into question, persons and objects are implicated as well as the stories and objective limitations that make them what they are. A person or personality is the "picture-soul" of the encounters, biographical details, and echo-subjectivities that constitute its familiarity to itself and to others. An object is the objective limitation of its mythical shape and shaping. But if neither persons nor objects make sense without the myth, or comparative perspective, that forms their contrasts and distinguishes them as such, then it is the character of that myth that matters most in understanding them.

The problem of "viewpoint" or perspective, of one plot or scheme of reality juxtaposed upon or set within another, "seeing double" in ordinary space, is the problem of reality itself. It is not a product of perception or the differential sensing of things, but the original, the "sense" necessary for perception. Life's *approximation* to itself resembles the stereoscopic vision of the anthropologist or historical researcher, viewing or understanding one total framing of human experience via the perspectives of another. It *appears* (and this word is important) to be the same thing. But like the *mise en abym* of literary criticism—the self-focusing strategy of a "view of the whole" set within the whole, a play within the play—these are artificial and self-emphatic strategies for pointing out something that we do mindlessly and every day.[1]

They are radical versions, like the "built-in" figure-ground reversals that define the naïveté of what is called "tribal" or primitive art, or the reversed perspectives of Byzantine painting, of the straight-on sensing of things that we normally consider to be normal. Consider, then, that the constantly changing "picture" we get of the reality around us, and in which we act, whether in the eye or the "eye of the mind," is merely an "other view" set within the total compass of our movement and motor activity. When *either one* of these is finitized, emphatically defined in its respectively physical or mental circumstances, the other takes over and provides the ambient stereoscopy or echo-subjectivity that renders the experience itself provocative and meaningful.

The single strategy that defines the modern "take" on near-life experiencing best of all is not that of historical, cultural, or physics relativity, though these were important and necessary precursors. The strategy is that of the emphatically illuminated movie, video, or computer screen, the bright "control panel"—the use of light itself as a finitizing device. Whatever its ostensible purpose or use, and however complicated the technologies or electronics behind it, the lit screen plays the crucial and central role in the displacement of the relativity necessary to its effect. As a mesmerizing device, emphasizing the deceptive importance of its messages or informational content, it assimilates to the "picture soul" of a viewer or user. No surprise that something like a "picture-body" comes into relevance as well, not only in aerobatics, jogging, martial arts, and "fitness" training, but also in the enforced standstill of meditational drills, "watching your breathing," and so forth. Relativity offset in the other way, via the motor actions and reflexes of the body, is likewise the "message" itself, though it is only the "flux" that defines the relevance of one side of the perception/motor activity complex through the not-doing of the other. Shamans and gurus have been their own television sets for thousands of years.

So it is not really necessary to contemplate the paradox of near-life experience in phenomenological or epistemological terms. All that is necessary is to perform a simple experiment: focus your attention beyond the limit or edge of the illuminated screen while holding the view of what is going on in it, and you will experience the *whole* reality of the phenomenon. If this is done inadvertently and out-of-awareness in any case by viewers and users, masking relativity by perceiving *through* it, and if remaining sane while hallucinating is the only real challenge that drug use can offer, then the same thing ought to hold for body-picture people. It is also the secret behind the virtual reality of motor-reflex therapies; to remain *self-conscious* about running, exercise, or martial arts drills while seemingly letting oneself go, or paying rapt attention to a meditational *technique* and letting it "turn off the brain."

The relativity of the background attention that is foregrounded "magically" in all of these cases is a "message" about itself as a kind of transparency of the near-life experience, and is otherwise inert and useless. Try it with *rhetorical* devices instead of electronic techniques or enforced body disciplines and the experiment will not work. For "relativity" has no cultures in it, nor worlds either. It is simply the lapsed power of a literacy that lacks the authority to tell one it no longer has an authority.

Life's echo-subject is closer to it than the physiological organism that defines its feeling or the mental pictures that determine its thought, like the remote *front* of a mirror image seen immediately through its back, or like the anatomy of light's production and emission that the telescope magnifies as an image of the cosmos behind it. The story form of the myth made finite and distinctive: historical and cosmic events or cultures remote in space or time are mirror images of their significance in the here and now. They are not *necessarily* lies and deceptions. Though the person looking into a mirror is certainly not the one looking back out, the twinning *outward* of our constitutive laterality is no less familiar to our sense of agency than the folding *inward* of gender is to the generic sense of social life. We believe we avoid incest; we know that tools use us.

We identify so completely with the Antitwins that most of the world's population is imaginary, statistical, idealized in terms of historical, fanciful, and purely superstitious stereotypes. No surprise when the foreign traveler or the anthropologist isolated in some remote community discovers the folks out there to be doing pretty much the same thing. Bringing it home, the sojourner realizes that the medicine ball of human diversity, tossed back and forth in this way, is himself or herself, something to live with, take responsibility for, and pretend to cherish. And because travel and encounters with other peoples are not unusual at all, and have been commonplaces of the human experience from the earliest of times, *all peoples ever encountered* have mythical and imaginary forms of human otherness *that they pretend not to believe in,* retroactive realities of the distinction that cuts the person as the person cuts the distinction. They cannot be proven or disproven (for that would give the game away) but only encountered. Call them "imaginary-space aliens"; call them the Antitwins.

Have we done much the same thing with inanimate matter in inventing its "energy," and with the earth itself and its many twin forms out there in the cosmos? If music is more personal than the emotions we make up for it, the objectivities of inanimate matter and alienated space are more abstract than the abstractions they are supposed to stand for. The effective concept of energy is no older than the widespread use of "automation," the feedback or multiple-wheel engagement that gave it its example and explanational necessity. For just as there is always some *kind* of energy in the working of a machine, so there is always some kind of machine in the working of energy. Each so much requires the other for its validation that to speak of "the body's energy" implies some—hopeful, disguised, or "incompletely understood"—*mechanical* model for the body.

So the convenient assumption of a kind of natural machine or process serves to distract us from an even more damaging fact about energy: that it has *no natural state.* Every conceivable means by which we might perceive energy, use it, define it, or know about it is based on the transformation of one "kind" of energy into another. Unfortunately, however, if we were to use this fact in itself to define the concept (e.g., energy as the point or moment of its transformation), we would lose the explanatory value of the various kinds of energy—potential, kinetic, electrical, and so forth—on which the validity or provability of "transformation" itself depends. On that mundane, practical, and "merely heuristic" level we are dealing with the ways in which our categories impinge upon one another and only secondarily with natural effects. We are perceiving a perception.

Take a single instance. What we see as lightning striking the earth from the clouds is a retinal afterimage, usually of a static charge going the other way—the perception of a perception. What we perceive in the heavens as an eclipse or solar flare is an exaggerated version of this, with space as our lapse-time. Is "space-time" the perception we are looking through? How much of its objectivity is the necessary and necessarily inadvertent rationalization of our perspective in it? Is the "picture" we have of dimensional space the residual effect of an underdetermination that has nothing more to do with time than the techniques we use to know and measure it? The velocity of light, upon which much of the rationalization depends, is an inference based on a systematic set of inferences about gravity, mass, angular momentum, and other mechanical principles. Can we use that model to measure light, as we use light to measure the model?

Even as it has been scientifically defined and described, explained to the best of our judgment, we would never see the light of the universe directly. What we perceive in that way is always some oblique, reflected, refracted, or transformed version, a slowed-down copy of the original in the nerve impulses reaching the brain, observed as part of the body that is observing it. So that perception of a perception must be augmented, magnified in the telescope or sensor array, made coherent in the laser beam, in order to make scientific sense of the universe. To give light a *velocity* relative to the universe that we know through its means, the rest of reality must be slowed down, lapsed by the mechanical "reaction time" of gravitic/inertial mass and the angular momentum that counterbalances it. Then and only then could an Olaus Römer compute how long it took for an occultation of Jupiter's moon to reach his telescope.

What begins as a near-light experience in the optic nerve concludes with a magnificent irony about luminous being and the rest of the universe: *we alone are responsible for the velocity of light,* via the light we have shed on it. If, for some unimaginable reason, scientists decided that the speed of light were instantaneous, space would no longer be "space-time," and the vantage of the observer would lose its privilege as the most *recent* spot in the knowable universe.

Space-time is light's "escapement mechanism," as though the circular, spherical, and radiative plotting of energies had the power to hypnotize destiny, invent a universal karma on its own. We make a wheel of the magnet in all the practical and theoretical uses we put it to, but then go on to make an artificial lodestone, in the gyroscope, of the wheel principle. Even the fabulous "nuclear device" of World War II, the modern "breaker of cities," had to wait upon the application of a simple mechanical principle—implosion—for its real "discovery."

Implosion as mirror reflection; the atom smasher become planet smasher, magnified out of all proportion and human decency, like the knowledge that a supernova or imaginal black hole is really a very large subatomic event, or that galaxies are some of the *smallest* things one can observe. Earth is like an extinct insect preserved in its own electronic amber, embalmed in the status quo of its own times and timing of things.

Music has the power of "time warp" instead; it "accelerates" the past, catching the present at successively previous stages of its tonal development, so that at the conclusion of a symphonic work one is back at the very beginning of modern times. It was the insight of Mikhail Bakhtin that identified this "shaped time" or "time-space," in the finitization of a myth or literary work, the *chronotope*. "Time, as it were, thickens, takes on flesh, becomes artistically visible; likewise space becomes charged and responsible to the movements of time, plot, and history."[2] Like music and, to Bakhtin's credit, unlike the physicist, the chronotope has no problem with time. Time, it seems, has a problem with *it*.

The planet earth is the near-life version of cosmic containment. The "global" is mapped down on the local as the comprehensive nature and configuration of the cosmos is in turn estimated by analogies drawn from earth-surface experience. Navigators have used a plot based on earth's position and movement in the heavens to find their way around and map its surface features, but all the imageries used to comprehend that "firmament"—its laws, motions, properties, and processes—are drawn from the familiar experiences of our own "biosphere." Each component of what amounts to a spherical double encompassment has been "deduced," if that is the right word, from its counterpart reality in the other.

Artificially "grounding" himself with his instruments, navigating the earth, the mariner sailed among the stars. Moving, ironically, within the most exotic "worldview" of all, the anthropologists traveled the same route and proceeded to discover seemingly more naive ones among earth's indigenous folk, turning the plot of the cosmos inside out.

Pragmatically, however, the shape of the earth both implies and is implied by two contrastive perspectives, regardless of which of them is favored and of the purposes for which it is favored. In the more parochial of them—the earth-surface experience acknowledged in habit and deed even by those who "know better"—the earth is flat and four-directional, usually rectangular like a map or a page. It is a proximal or geocentric acknowledgment of the fixture of the poles ("annual" north and south and the seasons) and of rotation ("diurnal" east and west). To establish the converse perspective, objectify the earth as a body in its own right, it is necessary to imagine or visualize oneself *away* from it—displace the commonplace, see distant objects disappear over the horizon, if not photograph earth from a satellite. Any conception of earth itself or of the cosmic spaces beyond it is a consequence of the volte-face; earth's view of the sky and the sky's view of earth are the basic variables, and their integration is always a near-life experience.

The shape and shaping of the earth is a perpetually undefinable and so a perpetually finitizing quality. For lodged between the two perspectives by a sort of navigational error, in a place where no navigator would look for it and no sextant or astrolabe could find it, is the pragmatic that defines them both: the earth carries its stars as the stars carry their earth.

The two perspectives are equally valid, and it would not be surprising if they had a similar antiquity. Acknowledged by the ancient Greeks, likely acquired by them from the Egyptians, who showed them the experiments to prove it, the knowledge of the earth's sphericity was possibly widespread and commonplace in ancient Eurasia and Africa. It was its own myth, and different peoples would have had their own ways of putting it. It is probably what the old Polynesians meant in saying that "the sea closes on itself." What the different peoples chose to *do with it* was something else.

Consider the imperial Chinese. Usually Confucian in its ethical and political ideology, traditional China was dominated by Taoist physical and cosmological principles, evident in the layout of the last imperial capital in Beijing. The central axis of the city is marked by the "Road to Heaven," connecting the imperial residence, or Forbidden City, with the Temple of Heaven. This effectively centered the city's plot upon the emperor's annual progress, at the vernal equinox, to the Temple to conduct the legitimating rites connecting *di* and *tien*, earth and sky. Appropriate to the *yin*, female, passive, gravitic, the principle of the earth and the "yielding center," the Forbidden City is *rectangular* and enclosed (self-emphatic *kolume* or containment, like the Barok *taun*). Appropriate to *yang*, masculine, active, celestial, the real Temple of Heaven is a round platform, open to the sky.

So regardless of what imperial Chinese scholars might have known, deduced, or speculated upon as to the sphericity of the earth, it was politically as well as cosmologically correct to represent the earth according to its own self-similarity—as flat, square, and four-directional. One can even imagine a scholar's rejoinder, say in Mr. Jiang's wineshop, to some curious navigator regarding the Chinese "error." "Yes, of course it would look like a globe if one happened to live in the sky, but we, you see, inhabit the earth. One can indeed *site* a temple for heaven by using the techniques of geomancy, but the self-establishing *de-containment* of the *yang* principle cannot even be *represented*." ("What a bummer," thinks the navigator to himself, taking another cup of wine, "the old guy is not even *biased*.")

How many times, and in how many different ways, was the fundamental *astrosplit* reckoned in the civilizations of Eurasia, Africa, and the Americas? The essential conundrum—grounding by ungrounding and vice versa—of earth's actual shape is neither a specifically cultural nor even a generally scientific issue, but the fundamental fact of the myth behind the stories that are made of it. The shape of the earth, and the concomitant reasoning about the universe and universal law established by it and through it, is chronotopic. It matches the wheel, the circular pattern of temporal reckoning, and so also the codependency of the energy concept and the machine, has an "angular momentum" all its own. Temporal "directedness" (and hence, by inference, "dimensionality") as a linear coefficient of gravitic circularity is not simply a device but a basic and largely unquestioned underlying premise.

The temporal shape, or chronotope, of the earth (Fig. 9) is time's definition of space; it includes the entire cosmos or universe within its rotation as the cosmos includes the physical earth in space-time. The moving, rather than the fixed shape that captures all of our experience, even of objects very far away, it is not orbital, and would not rotate on its axis but *gestate* it, form its own hologram of, rather than within, space-time. It folds in and out of a background for which no space program has yet been devised. It is only a "point" to be made.

Let us stop and simplify at this point, as human beings nearly always do when faced with infinity's double curve. On the one hand we have earth, the *place* of our space or the shape of its containment. On the other hand we have the decontainment that makes containment possible and is in fact envisioned through it, though in this case the one hand and the other do not even belong to us. They do not "twin" inward, like the hands of a clock or the sides of the person imagining this, but outward, like those of the person in the mirror. If there is no human being reproduced in the wheeling of the heavens and the navigation of the earth, no sex at the coital juncture of yin and yang, then this is not a cakra like the ones the Hindus imagined for energy centers in the body. It is more like the cakra of Johann Christian Bach, or what the ancients called the "music of the spheres."

The *lateral* counterpart of incest is a universal decontainment of the

Figure 9. Geos chronotopos.

integration that we experience directly as our own objective presence to it. It is not something we could prohibit, however imaginatively, as we do incest, but only approach asymptotically, as with the reckoning of space, time, and number, for instance, or as in research, development, experiment, and technological design. The point of its "joke" (as against the dead seriousness of incest and mother right) is that it has *nothing to do* with the universe apart from the part we play in it, and so describes nothing better than our own efforts at using or understanding it.

Incest has a subject that is more "real"—closer to the meaningfulness of kin relations—than either its practice or its prohibition might disclose, though it need not even exist to make the sense that it makes. It "works" of its own accord, without having to be committed, and, like energy, it has no natural state for the *fact* that conjecture makes of it in surmising how it might exist or operate. Light or energy is always more immediate to the problem of confronting its nature or properties than the rationalizations that would explain why this must be so. Incest's counterpart human reality in the far-out and unknowable, laterality's twinning beyond the means of its physical or cognitive grasp, is the subject of the most extreme philosophical abstraction and speculation. It is fathomless space as the only time still left around, the adult embryo still gestating in the best minds of its generation.

Immanuel Kant called it the "noumenal" in contradistinction to the *phenomenal* quality of knowability itself, meaning by that word that it is the only real antithesis to our ability to know about it or anything else. Kant was being very mystical in the most rational way he knew, but in doing so he missed the only point about it worth making. For the degree by which it misses any attempt to know about it or make its verbal copy is the exact measure of its antithetical identity with that effort. The finitizing of infinite possibilities in a single coup is one and the same thing as the possibility of infinite ways of achieving or understanding that single coup.

Like the bodiless near depth of illuminated screen relativity and the mindless embodiment of meditational and fitness or martial arts routines and like earth's twin perspectives, Kant's noumenal and phenomenal antinomies are near-life experiences *of one another.* Each is closer to the subject of the other than that subject is to itself. So the twinning of incest's self-image with the reality function of the adult embryo might be more concretely situated as the *inherent laterality* of gender and the *positive engenderment* of our lateral grasp of things without eluding the near-life quality of the situation. The expression is more tangible and concrete than the logic that supports it, but yet more logical in that way than physical matter or concrete experience. Just as the "energy" concept motivates and was motivated by a nonenergetic point of transformation from one "kind" or state of energy to another, so the *sense* of twinning is lost in precisely the way that it begins to make sense. Without "other gender," the twin we do not have, the one we do have would not be here; our lateral "grasp" of reality is reality's grasp of us; we have nothing other to do with it.

"Laws" or descriptions of natural regularity are like the metaphors and experimental shifts of orientation that support them. They have no permanent value or significance in themselves except insofar as they are points of transition from one inventory or conventional sense of things to another. Scientific models or metaphors—the Bohr atom, the laws of thermodynamics, the whole "energy" complex—are thus beginning points in an argument or process of finitization that can never complete itself. Their very stability or certainty, as "paradigms" of research or factual inferences on which others are built or "proven," depends upon the "phasing" of one mode of thinking or sensing into another and upon the historical and "hypothetical" foils necessary to the credibility of the phasing.

For the whole "sense" acquired in that way, the "negative capability" of a real transition between imaginal beginning and end points, is to *resist* finalization, not simply retard but actually threaten the extension of the meaningfulness elicited in it. Did Keats, himself a sublime master of negative capability,[3] intuit the inherent *destructiveness* of their meanings in the negative capabilities of dramas like *Macbeth, Othello,* and *Julius Caesar?* If the "jewels" of the Indra-net, who "do not know whether they are one or many," mark an apt cultural metaphor for the "passage" of metaphor itself, then hydrogen fusion would be its physical counterpart, the incandescent finale of elemental particles unable to determine their distinctiveness from one another.

For the metaphors of the universal pun on itself that I have called the near-life experience are all physics, and its physical properties are all, alas, metaphors. Is it, then, the inability or unwillingness to exorcise this inherent destructiveness, give it free rein of expression, that demoralizes contemporary anthropology, offering the professional renegade or dropout a poor range of alternative options—anywhere from computer programmer to serial killer? Elsewhere I have had to use the term "obviation" to mean both a technique for the analytic study of myth and the essential "virus" of the thing studied in it.[4] For the otherwise more concise model that Lévi-Strauss calls the "canonic formula of myth" promotes a more conservative conception of the sense of myth, one that excludes the killing of meaning.

Technology is the perfect foil for those who would measure the metaphor, solidify the imagery of sense and ask provocative questions about the facticity or credibility of doing so. As a habit of mind it becomes confused with "mind" itself, more or less as the brain does, so that metaphor, syntax, or any other articulative coefficients of understanding take on the semblance of meaning's technologies. The independent and largely unnoticed life that sense leads as though a world in the person or a retroflexive personification of the world is then imagined as something that ought to "work" in the ways that machines or even life processes are imagined to do. Then of course the life of sense would be dependent rather than autonomous, like the "dependency" models that seem so crucial in the projection of interpersonal relations and relationships.

Then the most fundamental mistake one could make about near-life experiences would be that they somehow betoken *another* reality hidden within the one we live, try to understand, and experiment with. Or that they would be the living counterparts of the so-called "near-death experiences," those vivid recollections of what it is like *not to die* that become inevitably confused with what death would be like on the understanding that the subject was given some kind of choice in the matter. Then of course our everyday experience of not dying would amount to very much the same thing, "near-death in proximity to life," and we would all be living versions of our own afterlives at this very moment!

For if the near-life experience is actually *closer* to its subject than that subject itself, the life of sense "heavier" than its embodiment in world or person, then none of this fantasy could be admissible at all. The secretive other or more "real" realities could not be hidden within the one we know, but merely projected outside of it; the meaning of the myth would not be behind it but, as Paul Ricoeur once suggested, "in front of it," the intuited formula for how death actually "works" another sentimental earthbound phantasma.[5] "Of course it would look like a globe if one happened to live in the heavens, but we, you see, inhabit the earth." So it is the easiest thing in the world to imagine some kind of near-earth life in the heavens, or "heaven" itself as a terraformed version of the life that led up to it.

Life's imitation of life in the echo-subject, thought about thought, is like metaphor's "phasing" of mind-sets to the extent that it simulates the *simulation* so well that commonplace understandings and descriptions can only serve as foils for its action in doing so. That is how the *grounding* of our thoughts and perceptions came to be described as a solid object moving in space through the artificial distancing that is necessary to shape a perspective. A very practiced negative capability converts the canvas of the imaginal landscape or trompe l'oeil picture to a fantasy of itself that is as different from an ordinary piece of canvas as it is from the scenes and objects depicted on it. Ordinary scenes and objects can hold the human gaze just as well, if not better, but they cannot hold it as *still,* nor be rolled up at the end of the day.

Likewise, a *dead person* is a contradiction in terms, a quickening paradox or fantasy-of-itself whose negative capability motivates not only funerary practice and ritual life but virtually the whole canvas of history, myth, and imaginal kin relations. It is not morbid, like a corpse, or factual, like a deceased person, but alive as the one we think we are in kinship—the past or passed-by "formerly living person" that is most present to us when the near-life experiencing of thought that we call "memory" gets the better of us: the simulation of "person" through thought's simulation of itself. If it is a *fact* that ghosts simply do not exist, and a fact that space is the only kind of time still left around to frame the perspectives of what we call "time," then everything from spirit possession and psychological "personality" to bloodlines, genealogies, myths, and historical continuities are the foils to prove those facts.

Near-death or near-depth experiences are not about who we are, what will happen to us, or how the world around us came into being through the phenomena we experience in that way. What their consequential, after-the-fact, and empirically self-evidencing character describes is only their *invention* or originary nature, how they come to be original. If gravity, like energy or intelligence, attracts its own *description* most of all, gravitates to the point of it and so energizes that point, then that most original joke of all—the one that started language in the first place—was too original to matter at the time of its discovery. It would have passed unnoticed without the language necessary to appreciate or even tell it, not even have been funny at all until the ensuing laughter echolocated the edge of its humor in things. Whoever told it would have been the first human being; whoever laughed would have been the first human society, and since it is impossible even to conceive that situation without somehow putting oneself in their places, that is the only way we can be certain that the joke must have existed. It is a subject for ongoing research.

At the very least one could use the hypothetical outline of the joke to ascertain the shape of the problem itself and, given the analytic tendencies inherent in the social sciences, perhaps conclude that the shape of the problem had been the joke all along. We would at least know in that way where jokes "come from," why the joke is beside the point of the humor it elicits, and why all jokes are derivative copies of an original that never could have existed in that way. Everyone *dies* on a joke, sometimes very tragically, but jokes never die, usually very comically.

Sometimes the polarities in this are reversed. Taking the world out of the person and the person out of the world for the most objective reasons ricochets the joke backward in time to its cosmogonic beginnings in a "black hole" situation—all attraction with very little left to describe. Energizing the point of its quizzical beginning intellectually (or at least intellectualizing it very energetically) to the present of its telling leads to a very depressing punch line—the describable universe as a very *unattractive* picture of itself. Just try, on this analogy, to imagine the near-death experience of one of those unfortunate people who forget the punch line of a joke in telling it, so that the joke dies on them instead of the reverse. Or take the observation (often made) that the abstract and impersonal quality of the joke-as-we-know-it could only originate in a sophisticated literary tradition as a token of the inarguably *primitive* perspective of humor itself.

Perspective itself and the fictions of "dimensionality" that map it onto experience make a "ghost" or quasi-objective echo-subject of the human ability to concretize, achieve a finitizing self-definition in things. In the same way that the *perfective* mode in language may be mistaken for the past, present, future schema of verbal tense, the temporal pragmatic, "time," is often treated as though it were a dimension. Whatever its heuristic value, however, this sublimation of experience within the experienced begs the question of its own transparency to understanding or observation. Would it help or hinder our understanding of language to add the heuristics of linguistic analysis as another feature or property of that which is studied in it?

The reluctance of the imperial Chinese to "globalize" their earth-surface experience would not necessarily make their cosmology less sophisticated than the "Copernican" perspectives with which it might be compared. Then perhaps the commonest assumptions made about ancient Egyptian mummification and ritual practices, tomb design, and cosmology would emerge as a kind of understandable error. For if a kind of intrinsic, self-scaling perfectibility (as in Barok funerary practice) of life and cosmos in a universal "hieroglyph" were all that were necessary—the "punch line," so to speak—then eternity and perforce infinity would be the joke of it. Once the scale were met, and that moment achieved ("higher is the *ka* of Amenemhet than the height of Orion, and it is united with the underworld"), even immortality might be anticlimactic. Neither tomb robbers nor even archaeologists could make much of a dent in it. Definitive styles in art, architecture, and ritual, the pragmatics of politics and dynastic succession, are *temporal* phenomena; the defining moment is a *spatial* one.

The near-depth experience of "space-time" recalls the joke about the lost mountaineers: after studying the map, one of them points to a distant peak and exclaims, "See that mountain over there? Well, we're on it." Like the distancing of our grounding location as a separate world, a planet lost in the expanses of its own imagining, the objectivity of time and space as coequivalent aspects of a single continuum loses the pragmatic necessary to its understanding. Not quite as simple as the mountaineer in the joke, but far more pragmatic, the time-space alternative would include its own reckoning in the outcome, put time *first*. Time is always the *beginning* of space, wherever it may be and whatever the circumstances, so that space is the only part of it still left around to tell us what it *was*. The beginning part of the continuum is like the portion of the wheel that runs backward and at the same rate to the part that identifies the momentum and relative progression of the whole. If the only "relativity" in this concerns just exactly *what* portion of the wheel that might be (for a wheel without it is not going anywhere), one would not need Fourier transformations to decode its cosmic significance. One would only need a reinvention of the wheel.

IV

Cakra

13

Reinventing the Wheel

The wheel rolls into history under the armored wagons of the early Babylonians and the carts and chariots of Eurasian wanderers and conquerors. Perhaps, then, as a historical "discovery," the wheel propelled its own diffusion, turning a part of history upon itself. But the discovery of the wheel was not quite the same thing as the invention of forces that it brought into play.

The problem with the wheel's "invention" in popular thought is that its simplification as a relation between hub and circumference glosses over the advantage that links it to the gyroscope, the self-relative quality of its movement. It is certainly appropriate to think of the wheel as a device for overcoming friction, although the "roller-bearing" analogy tends to obscure the role of gravity, whose acceleration is used in calculating friction. Basically the wheel's leverage or mechanical advantage is exerted—like that of a gyroscope, at right angles to, or perpendicular to, its axis of rotation. It provides, in other words, a "gyroscopic" leverage against gravitic acceleration, disposes a vector of force upward against the object to which it is attached, "lifts" it against friction.

In simple terms the wheel itself is the image of the work it does, a technological "interpretation" of gravity whose very simplicity conceals the gravitic reinterpretation within its operation. A wheel mounted universally (with the facility of turning in any direction) demonstrates its inertial and self-relative orientation as a gyroscope ("scope" because it reveals the earth's relative turning beneath it by keeping its own direction in space). The Babylonians, Indo-Europeans, and other early "peo-

ples of the wheel" realized the advantage of virtual antigravity by applying it directly to the earth itself, and only indirectly imagining that
the sun, or the heavens, or fate, might be wheel-like. But there were
others who did not make this application and knew it only incidentally
(in the top, or in childrens' toys), and applied instead the rotational motion that circumscribes *us*. Austronesian speakers navigated their history
around half of the earth's circumference using astral and other techniques that applied earth's "wheel" to their voyaging. And the ancient
Mesoamericans applied the earth-wheel in the combinatorial cyclicality
of calendrics—the *tonalmaatl* or *tonalhualpilli*—creating a cosmology
of time closing upon itself.

Perhaps the best way to illustrate the play of forces in a conventional wheel is through a simple thought experiment. Imagine a bicycle
wheel mounted on an axle, the other end of which is suspended by a
rope or cable. As long as the wheel is motionless, it will hang straight
down. Apply spin to it, and the axle will begin to rise toward the horizontal, pivoted on its suspension, with a helical (twisting or corkscrew-
ing) countermotion. This is its gyroscopic counterthrust. If the axle is
mounted rigidly, as on a wagon or bicycle, instead of being able to
pivot, the counterthrust is directed upward at the vehicle on which it
is mounted.

There are a variety of ways of reexplaining this to simplify the sense
of it. One might say that the wheel's rotation "levers" the vehicle upward against gravity in a double action not unlike the screw's version of
a wedge. Or one might observe that the relation between hub and periphery most commonly used in explaining the wheel is actually a kind
of shorthand, a "twist" on the other, less obvious component of its
action. But neither of these tries, or any others that I can think of, is
nearly as simple as the thing it is trying to explain. They do not explain
the wheel at all but are instead explained by it. An "explanation" that
worked as well as the wheel did, underdetermined its own means with
a like pragmatic acuity, could probably be used in its place.

That would be a reinvention of the wheel. Otherwise the attempt to
explain or understand it is an exercise in its own right, a use or application of the wheel. A complete roster of the uses to which the wheel has
been put, its total applicability, including gears, turbines, clockworks,
wind- and waterwheels, propellers, rotors, and armatures, would be less
effective as analogy than the simple device that undercuts them all.
Would the *simplest* of the many variants necessarily have been the one
that was invented first, or would its "simplicity" represent a compromise

with our ability to think out the beginnings of thought? Is it possible that Paleolithic humanity, *Homo erectus* perhaps, used a variant of the principle that long predated the simple cartwheel? Does not the very shape of the hand ax (sharpened all around, with a flange to give its spin an angle of attack) suggest a spun projectile? Launched from a version of the David-and-Goliath type sling, mounted perhaps on a pole, the device would require great stamina but would leave other stone weapons in the dust.

We do not have, and quite possibly could not have, positive evidence of when and where the wheel was "invented." There are early appearances in the archaeological record, generally in Eurasia, preceded in some cases by the potter's wheel. But if the simplicity of the wheel is more basic to the technologies that develop it than those technologies are to the wheel, then the time factor might cease to be the most important criterion in its development. It could have been reinvented, over and over, out of those applications, and they out of it.

Reinventing the wheel, retracing its course, quite literally in-volves an understanding of how it would "work," not how it might work other things, or other things work on its analogy. This means, for instance, that the wheel gains its primary advantage over its own full (cakra) potential, rather than in application to human tasks or in relation to the space-time around it. The flat trajectory is a fairly near-at-hand phenomenon; when we go up the scale of size and distance to the spinning earth and its orbital congenors, or down, to particle spin, we run into the wheel again. It is largely in the ordinary, everyday world of motorcars, circuitry, and washing machines that we can afford to take it for granted.

So the wheel's analogy to the human work it performs, the many ways in which it models what is distant, abstruse, out of scale upon the near-at-hand, lies in its "leverage" over itself. The fact that human beings have, or rather *are,* a different kind of leverage over themselves might help to explain why the wheel's "discovery" would be so problematic. There are immense stretches of time in which the whole of earth's population, or large portions of it, were entirely ignorant of its knowledge or its use. But there are also large portions of history in which its knowledge and use have been taken for granted, sublimated into other versions of the same principle. The wheel is as easy to have as not to have; this makes it rather more difficult to "invent."

"If me granny had wheels she'd be a wagon." The kinds of "lever-age" over themselves that human beings represent, individually, collectively, mentally, physically, in the willing, planning, and recollection of things, are very difficult to define or understand. Whole psychologies and philosophies have been wasted in the effort to accomplish this. The wheel's peculiarly "objective" self-leverage is not an answer to what that human ability to know, move, and recollect itself might be. It is a *simplification*.

The wheel and its special properties represent an acute underdetermination of human tasks and abilities, of our own self-leverage. It closes laterality upon itself outside of the person, the mind or body. The wheel with a person in it or on it, propelled by it, earth itself likened to a wheel, moves our world. The wheel principle *within* a person makes sense only as a radically simplifying analogy—the circulation of the blood, the neurophysiological "feedback loop," the spiritual analogy of the energy-cakra. "If me granny had cybernetic feedback loops she'd be a computer."

What we have in the cakra is something that is only simplified in thinking of it as a wheel, or using it that way. It is an unassigned potential that depends upon some form of simplification to be used or grasped at all. Calling it "cakra" is like calling the conception of a culture "anthropological," for this names a kind of characteristic product, a concrete human *character* that is neither personal (e.g., a function of the anthropologist's personality) nor collective (an indigenous lifeway), but is an outcome of both. Is there something wheel-like in the order or makeup of physical reality, or is cakra purely a "human" thing? Why, for instance, should trigonometric functions, rotational angle measurements like sine, cosine, and tangent, describe, in the Fourier transformations, electromagnetic and acoustical phenomena so well? Understood on the "physics" alternative, as an expression of "out-there" reality, the sense of this descriptive language convinced generations of physicists that their matter/energy cosmos was composed of vibrations, wavelike energies and their interference patterning. On the "human" alternative, however, this "wave theory" could as well describe the ordering of our perceptions as their perception of an outside order, our grasp of the world instead of its grasping of us.

The fact that either of these alternatives developed into a comprehensive theory—physical or neurophysiological, as the case may be— would easily account for the other, should make one suspicious of both. The trigonometry might just as well have nothing to do with either physical reality on one hand and our perception and motor coordination on the other. It might work so well as the description of "description" or the explaining of explanation—what we do to ourselves in conceiving a theory of any kind—that the physical or psychological parameters would be beside the point, and indefinitely contestible.

Cakra circumscribes both the understanding of its uses and the uses to which that understanding it put. It mirrors each part of the interfacing of thought with reality through the other, underdetermines any problem we might make of them. So in effect each degree of simplification in its application—applying the simple wheel, applying the principle of the wheel again to itself as a second-order "automation" of it—realizes a more fulsome command over the cakra potential, the "dimensional" configuration of spatial extension. The second-order wheel is the exponential, or what mathematicians might call the "power set," of the first.

An ordinary wheel determines linear motion in one dimension, subsuming its "gyroscopic" potential in the other two as a lift against gravity or a spin for greater stability (as in the potter's wheel or the rifle bullet). But an automated or self-redoubled application of the principle determines in two of the dimensions, incorporates a "maneuverability," a greater degree of control and precision in linear motion. The helicopter deploys the combined action of two versions of the wheel—the airfoil and the rotor on which it is mounted—to hover, move forward, backward, or laterally. The escapement mechanism of the traditional wheel-clock uses the rotation of a toothed wheel to brake and release its own motion, to overdetermine the monitoring of a linear temporal rate by interdicting its own trajectory. The transmission of an automobile "paces" its own torque in this way, moves the movement of the vehicle.

A powered aeronautical or ground vehicle "works" on this principle through the multiple distribution of a single motive of torque, as do the engines that provide that torque. The "feedback" or self-action of the multiple axis has not changed in principle since its early exemplars in the clock or steam engine. It has been extended and developed dramatically in electromechanical and electronic elaborations, taking advantage of improvements in power source, efficiency, materials, and miniaturization.

Nonetheless, throughout a world of product designs and combinations, the "culture," as it were, of modern world technology, "automation" is very simple. Its underdetermination of the wheel principle engages, by applying that principle to itself, two of the three acknowledged dimensions of spatial extension, a double cross section of gyroscopic movement. That is, in fact, all that the familiar gyroscope itself achieves—a stable, inertial axis of spin in one dimension supported by two dimensional degrees of freedom for a self-encompassing centrifugal force. In effect the mechanical chronometer was a roundabout version of the same thing, a slow gyroscope adjusted to the diurnal cycle.

Telling time measures or marks out a kind of spatial advantage, one that is not very different from the mechanical advantage achieved in the lever, bow, wedge, or screw. The advantage is a very real one, a trade-off of effort for spatial movement called "linear time" that functions as a baseline regardless of what notions like "space" and "time" might actually refer to. In other words, the "synchronization" that establishes that baseline as a workable standard (Greenwich mean time, like the "standard meter") is as much a fiction as is the simulation of terrestrial and celestial motions in our timekeeping devices. The advantage itself is a *fact*.

Mirrors record the passage of time in an entirely different way, as do events, books, periodicals, diaries, and letters. So the original wheel-clocks effected a departure—a use of the advantage to measure *itself* as factual or artifactual time—from the kinds of reckoning enabled by the sundial, water clock, or hourglass. It engaged the movement of a master wheel with an offset version of its own torque, brought the wheel's self-leverage into play as a separable component of its own action. The result is a leverage over movement itself, a conservator of motion-as-time that "simulates" celestial motions because it simplifies the principle upon which those motions are conceived.

The ironical part of this is that when philosophers like Kierkegaard and Bergson speak of the "eternal now" and the subjective nature of temporal duration, they are actually speaking of *space*. Virtually any revelation one is likely to encounter regarding the nonlinear essence of time ("there is no time," "all time is *now*," "the universe is folded back on itself in a fourth dimension") describes instead the *mechanism* through which linear time—the standard of comparison for "no time"—is generated.

Time as if it were a linear movement with a measurable distance is like choosing the value of "place" as something one might return to or share with others and substituting it for "memory." Instead of all time being here at once as an eternal present, all space or *situation* is. Each of us would be subliminally present, actually existent, in all the places or local situations we have ever occupied and would or will occupy, and ostensible "faculties" like memory or imagination would amount to no more than the fantasy of being able to claim a personal point of orientation as a "moment" in space. Very well, then; the measurement of time as if it were localized takes care of this fantasy for us.

For the only real difference between time and space is that space is concrete, tangible, every bit as "dimensional" as time is not so. The reason (better: the sense) that very concrete motives ("faculties") like touch and smell, or very kinesthetic ones like music and dance, work so well with fantasies like memory and imagination is that they *locate* with a stronger facility than any notion of "time" can do. If the shape of the wheel and its simplification of space can do this as well, that is probably why it has left so strong an imprint upon our conception of time, our "gut" inclination to totalize it as personal, cultural, or universal cyclicality. That is why I have called the music of Johann Christian Bach a cakra, selected it, rather, from a roster of musical types. It improves the clock's imitation of time as movement, takes better care of memory or imagination than the historical versions of these fantasies do of it.

Think of "gravity," then, in strictly mechanical terms as always representing the hub of an imaginary wheel, "represent" it, in other words, exactly as it figures in our equations, as a force or attraction exerted from a "center of gravity." In every conceivable instance where gravity makes a difference (objects "separated" and attracting each other, objects "falling" under its influence or "rising" against its pull), the gravitic force or attraction is exactly counterbalanced against another force, which we call "angular momentum." That is what keeps us from being down at the center of the earth, the earth from being down in the sun, and so forth. The two imaginal "forces" are always in equipoise, regardless of the relative motions of the objects involved, and it is only a fiction that separates them into two distinct agencies—an attractive force and one that counteracts that attraction.

Cosmic "automation" operates on a somewhat different version of "escapement" than the wheel-clock, the device that furnished its original timekeeping analogy. For instead of doubling the axis, engaging a drive wheel with another that retards and feeds back its motion, the astronomical escapement subdivides the central and peripheral components of the wheel into apparently separate forces called gravity and angular momentum and then recombines them in endless permutational possibilities. The analogy of the clock's escapement is conserved and reasserts itself in the infamous "three body problem," which limits traditional computations to dealing with only two bodies at once. Few, if any, modern experts on the cosmos believe that its mechanics are as simple as this "classical" version suggests; few, if any, are able to do without it, or indeed linear time, as a baseline.

Some versions of automation, complex engines using water or wind power, catapults, and even primitive steam-powered devices, were already in use in the Hellenistic Mediterranean and flourished in the late Roman Empire. There are also examples from the Islamic world and from China (like the odometer). But the sense of the practical chronotope, mechanical and eventually electric and electronic time-space as a solver and displacer of problems, expanded to encompass much of the history that ensued, took over the everyday feeling for the world more or less as the printed text and its dramatization took over history. Identified completely with human achievement and potential, it promoted a novel way of understanding it in the aggregate, as the generic of what we call "culture." (The term originally referred to the use of wheeled implements in agriculture.) The human cross section of the wheel as a simplification of use, potential, psychology, and order.

So it became possible to define the antithesis of what Bakhtin was to call the "thickening" of time—the literary device of "culture" and the culture of the literary device. Leading theoretical physicists of the early twentieth century called this antithesis "space-time," the closure of spatiotemporal extension upon itself in a manner that was relative to the situation (read: "the chronotopic capabilities") of the observer. Franz Boas and Albert Einstein. "Relativity." We have the second power of the wheel, the sense of automated problem solving in everyday life, to thank for a cultural view of universal reality and a universal view of cultural realities. There are no describable cultures without the overview called "culture"; there are no physical motions and relations without the underview called "space-time." Spatiotemporal integration would be a single point without the relational qualities we have to imagine into its reality; human social, conceptual, and psychological relations would be a big blob without the point of "culture." Getting the point by not getting it; not getting the point by getting it all too well.

Reinventing the wheel behind its own times to recover the secret of its development since then gives time the shape we have learned to associate with clocks and histories. The wheel could not go forward if about half of it did not rotate backward in the same motion. *Resimplifying* the wheel by another turn, however, invents the device ahead of time, and ahead of the shape of time that we know it (and ourselves) by, reciprocates a novel "pastness" back out of a future that has no precedent. Would a wheel that closed upon itself in all three of its dimensional attributions make no kind of sense at all, or would it make every possible kind of sense?

Understood very carefully, the transition from the simple wheel to its exponential power, the principle working back upon itself, measures a net gain in pragmatic leverage. It is only the overdetermination of "technological" specification that gives its abbreviation of time and distance—cybernetic circuitry and the vast wheel of the communication nets, the distributional torque of the transportation system—an aura of complexity. On the blunt perspective, however, it should be clear that the more of the cakra-potential that is incorporated as "leverage," the less of it remains in the form of a subjected energy. The simple wheel *sublates* two of its dimensional vectors into a gyroscopic counterthrust. The autoreactional "multiple wheel" embodies those two dimensional vectors in its "leverage" and sublates (drives and is driven by) a single dimensional vector, as in the overprecise temporal monitoring of the wheel-clock, or the multiply selective torque of the helicopter or the automobile transmission. From a technological point of vantage, it would seem as though a third term in this series, the wheel principle applied once again to the factor of its automation, would accomplish a complete dimensional lockout—all "leverage" and no sublational energy left to move it.

To understand this as an illusion fostered by the habit of technology and its grounding mechanical and spatiotemporal assumptions, one would have to come to terms with radical simplification or underdetermination as the veridical root of the wheel principle. The third power of the wheel, or what I should call the "mirror wheel," would sublate cakra entire, exert and incorporate a leverage over the principle of locality, or dimensional extension. It would "reflect" the whole of our means of controlling it as the thing controlled in it, put us outside the design of the cosmos we have determined for ourselves.

The simple wheel mirrors a lateral advantage lineally; the "automation" of the wheel's wheel reapplies that lateral advantage, controls linear motion laterally. The third term in the series re-in-vents, folds back into the simplification that is original to all of its examples. It is the *original* wheel.

Why a "mirror-wheel"? The kind of time we can talk about, measure, and understand is a reflection of place or situation, intimately linked to the conception of "energy" and the ways in which that which we call "meaning" is represented to itself. Grounded in a schema of place value, like the tones of a musical scale, elements on the periodic table, word values in a language, or frequencies in the electromagnetic spectrum, reflectional time reprojects the concrete part of explanation's imageries. It assumes the significance of "movement" in them. But a movement in *advance* of these concrete value markers, one that sublated the dimensional role of sense in its entirety, would be *all* reflection.

In other words, that whole aspect of our understanding that is "performative" depends upon our own progression in understanding and living through events for the sense it makes, could only be known empirically as an inversion of itself. It would seem that things newly discovered were a part of memory, history, evolution, or cosmic process. Coming *into* the knowledge of the mirror-wheel would not only seem as though the observer, as person or species, were moving forward out of it, but also as though our whole physical, mental, and historical constitution were arranged for that purpose. The panorama of the textual or mechanical chronotope, time-space as a model of and for the world, is a subject unto itself, with rules and properties of its own. It is an artificial solution to a real problem: one would not know what real time would be like for the interposition of one's own modeling of it. Reinventing the wheel ahead of its time to know what is "behind" it is then a real solution to an artificial problem; one would not *need* to know what real time and space might be like to resolve the dilemma that thinking puts in the way of knowing them.

What might this mean in terms of the mirror-wheel's "reflection" of ordinary reality? As I have shown earlier, the idea that we experience events *shortly* after they actually happen and in much the same way, as a consequence of perception's time lapse, is an illusion. "Back then," a mere instant ago when the experienced event was ostensibly taking place, the observer was busy "experiencing" an earlier version of the same time lapse instead. But because that experience refers back in its turn to a yet earlier episode, we have a continuity of the perceiver perceiving himself perceiving, with no event in sight. The experiences themselves have an inarguable spontaneity that is never recovered in our experiencing of them. The active subject passively perceived is instead the "reaction mass" of the universe with all its real energy gone; it is the medical description of the body or brain, the self-surrogate or imago of the psychoanalytic "ego."

The spontaneity of action or perception, unaccountable in the perceived but wholly accountable for it, corresponds to the mystery of what we would call "forward progression," "duration," or "time." The illusion of a spatial traverse in this, a personal or universal movement ahead of itself as time, is a kind of relative backlash of what we do to ourselves to think or perceive, that is, *recollect,* ourselves. For the spontaneity is in no way separate or distinct from the collection of "self" in thought and practice, actually no more separate from what we are than the part of a wheel that must travel a forward arc, outward and beyond the point of its traction, is separable from the shape or action of the wheel. It is the outward twinning of our human leverage, or laterality.

So we reinvent the wheel inadvertently in thinking of time as motion, duration, dimension, reconfiguring the spontaneous trajectory of action ("will") or happening in the world as though it could come to bear on a hub, a center of force and movement, that was already *behind* us. It is necessary to cut that imaginary wheel apart, section it into respectively resistant (gravity) and spontaneous (motion, angular momentum) forces, to derive and measure the velocity, speed, and direction of electroluminescent phenomena. But that is the face of our cosmos, all we might know or think about it. Billions upon billions of stars and galaxies; what chutzpah!

Separating out a distinctive part of the phenomenal world, of our organism or of the physical world around us as the spontaneous component, as motion, intention, will, or spirit, is not a solution to the dilemma of what reality may be like: it is the cause of the dilemma. Is something called "time," or "spirit," "creativity," "imagination," or "will" actually *collecting* and summing up a movement of thought as it recollects itself in perception, or is that recollection merely collecting *it?* The aspects of extension, *res extensa,* that are rendered usable and therefore analogically convincing through a linear conception of agency, or a lateral ("automated," "chronotopic") control over it, fall short of a totalizing simplification by just that much.

For the close copying or "modeling" of human leverage in space and time—the "wheel" in the person—is never more or less effective than the modeling of a person in the wheel, the human cross section of the degree of simplification achieved in it. It belongs to a gradient of human similitudes that only begins with the close copying of lovers and the love act, body's copying of body in utero or as DNA, the roles and learning designs of social mimicry, the intense mimesis of envy, hatred, or disdain, the death-imitation called "mortality" as a model for human existence.

Imitation, twinning the human ability to extend in reproduction and *intend* (in-vent self or world) by copying the "sides" on one another, comes full circle when the copy that is made is more powerful than the original. That is what the play of *Hamlet,* the game of chess, and the supergender capability of social interaction are all about. To grasp the full significance of social or political charisma, sexual attraction, or what Aristotle termed "persuasion" is to admit a fundamental innocence in knowing for certain what one's emotions and intentions really are, where they are at. Were someone to "express" my thoughts, my feelings, my whole imitational disposition more naturally or compellingly than I myself could do, my imitation of them would be overcome by their imitation of me. Did human beings originate and multiply so that *Hamlet* could eventually establish their quotient, divide them in this way by what they cannot know about themselves? Are we all "originals" of the copy he made of himself?

We intend the world by *learning ourselves as language,* intend language by shaping our feelings to the world. Human sapience is a quotient established by long, long division. Did sound separate off as a "faculty" from the totality of human feeling, emerge as tone or voice to galvanize its third dimension, the depth of its world, as music? Speaking or hearing out of a complete familiarity of one's feeling potential with the flow, articulation, and modulation of sound obviates the problem of the sign, or of language or culture as a separable agency. Learning others as language in this way would, even if only partially successful, make a better copy of "communication," "relationship," "love," and even "reproduction" than what we conventionally recognize through those terms. To fix this point of feeling, by whatever agency, more indelibly than the "point of view" or the machinations of reason could fix it, would spell the obviation of social concerns. So beyond a certain degree of social or cultural competence the ability to copy others in one's total feeling, or be so copied by them, becomes extremely dangerous. It is the secret behind such disparate motives as political interrogation ("brainwashing"), cultic or religious "conversion," psychoanalytic transference, and limerence in love, and the secret motive behind its secret is that extrinsic concerns cease to matter for the subject.

The ground condition of subjectivity is that *things* (anything capable of being demarcated, isolated, limited) are always more real or concrete than the ability to explain, understand, or use them. They may be explained or understood, even used, to satisfaction, but that satisfaction is invariably an end in itself. In other words, the ability to grasp or comprehend is only as good as the means used to do so, and so the net result runs in reverse of what is normally thought of as "thinking things through." One can only grasp or comprehend things to the extent that one's process in doing so is itself grasped or comprehended by them.

If "the limits of my language" are limits that language itself imposes, then the thing we are talking about, "language," would have to be objectified, forced into the mold of a "thing," before *it* could fully comprehend one. A thing called language could not otherwise be learned or taught, so that a small child in its attempts at speaking or hearing it would be actually *making* it. It is a first lesson in subjectifying oneself, an art of being *integrated,* pulled together and forced *under* by the things of which we speak. Words, voice, sentences, and texts come to live an independent existence, and the question of whether we would live another, "in our heads," or in our feelings is one, alas, that would also have to be resolved in words. This has resounding implications for the theory of signs or symbols, for it means that the *things* we make of them are the full concreteness of everything we attributed to the world around us. It is the concretivity that we ourselves delimit and become the substance of in this way—not how we exist or how we may think, but how we *are articulated*—that is at once world in the person and person in the world.

So a search for the true definition (outlining, limiting off) of things brings one back to the concreteness that words and images amplify. And a search for a true definition of language through any point comprehended in it brings one back through a circuit of definitions defining other definitions to the point one had originally set out to define. Getting the point of it by not getting it in that way, imitating a thing that imitates one's efforts in its turn, is like reinventing the wheel of language, yet another "shape" in which its thing might be made.

Language is not necessarily wheel-like, and not necessarily a mirror for human thoughts, actions, and cultures, though, like a mirror or a wheel, it records the passage of time. Borrowing the concretivity of the wheel to reinvent language is like borrowing the concretivity of language to understand or amplify the reinvention of the wheel. They articulate together through a quality that is basic to objectivity itself, a simplification of the sequential ("one thing after another") character of what we call "structure."

So the work of making the wheel principle concrete, as we must do with words, ideas, or language in order to explain anything, involves virtually the whole development of technology. Some versions of this development, such as the airfoil, electric and electronic circuitry, or the whole phase of "automation," have become so completely integrated into the conception of human tasks and responsibility that the original principle is hardly recognizable in them. The idea of the wheel is so completely imitated in the technological infrastructures that imitation runs a reverse course, and the user is better reflected in the various "applications" than he can reflect back upon them. The concreteness projected for the wheel principle has absorbed its "wheel-ness." In a roundabout but nonetheless very elegant way, the resultant technology has substituted itself for the means and purposes of human subjectivity. (That is what advertising is all about.)

When the user of a computer or motorcar executes a few simple operations, the device is expected to "work by itself." That is an imitation of human spontaneity—the ability to initiate action—and, within the limits imposed on it, it *is* self-operating or spontaneous. To understand that automation, the feedback loop or automobile drive torque "taking over" its own operation, is a simplification of the cartwheel; we have only that more "primitive" version. It must be pulled or pushed, but once that happens it *will* operate spontaneously, deliver its peculiar "lift" against gravity. By incorporating the pull or push as well, automation enhances the capacity of the wheel to "do its own thing."

Whether automated or not, the wheel principle effects a simulation of the human ability to initiate action, though within (and the term is advised) "circumscribed" limits. A third-order simplification of the same principle, the step beyond automation, would bring it full circle, encompass the disparate "forces" and "dimensions" of the mechanical world within an underdetermination that spontaneity itself could only be said to imitate. (It should be obvious that something quite different than "energy" or "agency" would be involved here.)

By making the wheel principle concrete enough to use or think, weighting it down with our tasks and responsibilities, we design and fabricate a microcosmic equivalent to the big world out there, convince ourselves of the existence of "forces" on the model of our own spontaneity. (The biological "organism" or "environment," another kind of robot, is surely one of these.) But the very constraints and limitations imposed in the process—the achievement of linear time, measurement of "lightspeed"—make our sense of what is "out there" a better simulation of the microcosm than the microcosm is of what may actually be there. We are trapped not so much by the properties of physical reality as by the sense we have made of them. Imitating *their* imitation of us is the reinvention of the wheel. The irony of all this, the undercutting humor of the wheel principle, is that we possess the mirror-wheel whole and entire within our everyday usage and understanding of things. We *simply* (and that term is here very strongly advised) lack the means of *displacing* it.

Neither the wheel itself nor that simplification by which we have come to know and use its properties exists independently of human thought and conception. Where its close analogues can be found, in the spinning earth, solar system, or galaxy, it is we who do the work of separating out its gravitic and angular-momentum components, divide by an automation we have learned to anticipate. When we map the earth or the heavens, send people or objects into orbit, draw "how-it-works" conclusions about the observable cosmos, we are negotiating an imaginary world that is more real than our understanding of it.

For in the final reckoning the act of "understanding," all of the subjectivity or inclusion of self-as-subject included in it, is impossible without that we make a *thing*, a kind of self-referential metaphor, of it. It becomes a slave of the pattern through which it must be expressed, an answer that disallows its best question, like the notion that time is made out of time, which Jorge Luis Borges attributes to Josiah Royce's conclusion that "every *now* within which something happens is *also* a succession." [1]

The radical simplification of the wheel would seem to betoken the opposite, the classic anthropological case in which the posing of questions proves more conclusive than any answers that might be forthcoming. For the answers in this case would not be "structural" or reconstructible ones but instances of an objectivity that is itself *interrogative*. Let me ask them in succession:

1. Is it possible that the whole effort at *constitutive* understanding, discovering the constituency of matter, energy, or life at the subatomic, molecular, cellular, or organismic level, is another "automational" leap of faith, an overdetermination of simplifications to be made on the direct scale of human life experience?

2. Would not the idea of empirical objectivity as a *made*, constructed, or originated potential merely reflect the "heuristic" approach as a subjective error about subjectivity itself, disclose the material world as a reflective prism for what we do to ourselves in positing and thereby "understanding" social relations?

3. Is there a real-time alternative to our constitutional (and thus also institutional) obsession with *anticipating the past*, our endless recycling and rearranging of it? Is it possible to see, know, or move *past* the past, and not get caught in its spurious redesigning as a "present" or a "future"?

14

The Physical Education
of the Wheel

We have not learned the wheel so well as we have taught ourselves to it, and because teaching is a very different sort of knowing than learning, the wheel knows its human counterpart much better than we, in our turn, know it. The lesson has a familiar ring, an echo in the language that speaks of it even down to the point of feeling in that our words, acquired in a similar way, know our feelings much more familiarly than our feelings know our words. The attempt to say what one really means, articulate feeling as though it were thought or engage in the thought-as-feeling posturing of rhetoric, is only incidentally linguistic or significational. It has already, as Jacques Lacan might have put it, a personality structure. Once Shakespeare had decrypted the human part of English, its literature became something much more than a mountain of texts or a condescending parasitism of interpreters. It had developed a personality, a stamp of character all its own.

In that sense one might speak of our technology not as a culture, or an aggregate of disparate lifestyles with similar aims and views, but as a wheel's intuition, or interactive feedback loop, as to what we are all about, most especially in those facets of its understanding, like the airfoil, the screw or lever, the closure of electric or electronic circuitry, that are most difficult to reconcile with the motive and action of the simple wheel. They are, in a sense, the wheel's strategy. Easy enough to imagine a time when humanity was the prisoner of its perceptual faculties alone, the personal perceiver in the guise of "natural," or cave-man. But now, we have learned, things have gotten more complicated, and any normal bat (or surveillance satellite) could easily outfox the human "captive" in Plato's cave analogy. We have not learned, and not for want of trying, a damn thing more about *Homo perceptualis* and its curious plight than the ancients knew, but we have taught a great deal more about it to the wheel.

If there were a part of us that had learned, from the cradle or before, to *anticipate* action very precisely, throw itself blindly into a space we could never perceive, that would be the part that the wheel knows best. The wheel would know the rational part of our echolocation of things, the part that *perceives,* or makes sense of it, holographically, but we could only learn that holographic design rationally, as the scale model of all the mistakes to be made in figuring it out. Very possibly, then, the anticipatory vestige of our recollecting selves, the part that does the action of what we recover as "dreams," would not be a "perceiver" at all, and would have existed originally in no way that perception could construe as "natural."

But as a separate coding of the human race, a form of human kinship-with-itself that lived "magnetically," so to speak, through a more immediate intuition of similitude and difference, or attraction and repulsion, than language can map outside of the body, rather than socially, as we do. There is a very real question as to whether that harmonic lineage of humankind, interbreeding kinship, could even *laugh* at all, laughter being speech spelled backward in the body. (Perhaps it would die trying.) But there is no question whatever as to *what* it would laugh at, if it could.

So we have no need even to posit its existence, search for its fossils, or try to imagine what it would be like to live magnetically. The whole effort would be a social disaster, and we have quite enough anthropology as it is. Enough to know that we have taught that magnetic, anticipatory part of ourselves to the wheel, and that the wheel has picked it up and rolled with it, quite incidentally, perhaps, to the aims or purposes of those who first "discovered" it.

So it would have been the wheel that did the discovering, after which its human teachers would have more to do with revolving than evolving. The wheel is the perfect symmetry of our lateral engenderment and engendered laterality, but twinned against the embodiment that holds itself so. One needs only to think of how its self-closure is deployed to make electricity useful to learn what has become of our erstwhile magnetic being.

To mirror the fey and absolute precision of our anticipatory facility, the machine of our dreams, within the symmetry that the wheel has recovered for it, would be to undercut the whole scenario of extensional semblance, substance, and form that perceiving man has arranged for its recognizance. The wheel dances with gravity, makes evident in a single shape and motion that what we separate as "gravity" and "angular momentum" are physically identical and only artificially separable as projections, like "cause" and "effect," of a simple movement that underdetermines them. The ambivalence generated by our inability to perceive motion directly—the puzzle of whether movement outside of the body echoes or is echoed by an intrinsic motion of the senses—plays a central role in this. And we are still at the periphery.

The wheel is not too complex, but too *simple*, to be understood in direct physical terms. Direct physical terms, or laws and properties as we may understand them, are the physical education of the wheel. Balance, recursiveness, feedback loops, reflexivity, and reciprocity are introspective exercises that we engage in to try to educate ourselves about the wheel. But a wheel that did not in some way make sense of its working would not matter; the device could no more exist independently of its principle than its principle could exist independently of it. So the wheel or its principle might indeed have an independent existence in nature, but only if we, who have fabricated its image in so many ways, recovered it in that way, invented a naturalism for it.

It is like the known but unknowable god that the Aztec priests, according to Leon-Portilla, defended against the Franciscans at the time of the Mexican *Conquista*. They called it "the Lord of the Center and the Periphery," a true image, like Indra, of a false relation. Like the zero marker, which the ancient Mexicans and Indians seem also to have invented quite independently of one another, it not only marks out the place value of the unknown in human affairs but also maintains the most nearly definitive way of knowing about it.

The Wheel of Asoka still turns in the infrastructure of modern Indian democracy, abolishes the caste system that re-forms on its periphery; the zero marker holds the empty place value of ancient Mesoamerican thought and practice in modern Mexico. The mechanical wheel, which the Aztecs gave over to their children, more or less as they let the aged get drunk whenever they wanted to, has become the commonplace objective of all the world's children. It is the image of human effectiveness that toys with itself in all the imaginal fantasies of globalization and technological world conquest; the wheels run other wheels, if only in the mind, and they, in turn, run them.

In other words, one might best think about the problem in the zero terms of human continuity itself. *Nothing* is more apposite to the thought of the thing, *any* thought about anything, in any conceivable state of awareness that mind might experience in so doing, than the thing itself. The peculiar objectivity, with all its knowable and unknowable properties, that is isolated from the other objectivities around it and encompasses the whole possibility of any myth that is made about it. There is no human genius but for the ingenuity of this technique, and no human origin but for the origination of it. In the beginning was the thing; then, on principle, was the thought of the thing, and in the shape of the thought and the sense of its imagining is the invisible god, the true image of a false relation, who created the thing in the first place—the deity that would not have to create the world, or even itself, but only create the myth of them.

The wheel simplifies itself dramatically through all our efforts to complicate it, reduce the whole phenomenal world, its chemistry, energy, or imaginably living awarenesses, to some form of mechanical advantage. And if the myth of that effort is that it is not mechanical, and the reality is that it is not really an advantage, then what we have in the most inscrutable particle or chemical germ of life's awareness is the unknowability of the wheel's self-simplification. The tiniest particle or seed of awareness is only part of the design that makes its properties sensible, and so gives the myth to its basicness.

No wonder, then, that the multiple-wheel fixation that originated automation, from its tiniest beginnings in China or the Graeco-Roman world, overcomplicated itself as it picked up speed and direction and learned its spatiotemporal coordinates. No wonder especially that theories of relativity originated in thought experiments about clocks, trains, and elevators, objects that moved on the wheels that moved them. Or that time was, automatically, elevated to the status of a dimension.

The principle of the wheel is like an overfamiliar habit, breathing, balance, the use of the arms and legs or the language one has brought up to one's own standard of thinking, that becomes routinized in dealing with other things. If the art of "interpretation" is like looking at one's own pet language, the intelligent part of thinking, in a mirror, then automation is the mirror image of the wheel. Cultural relativity may be no more than the estrangement that results from making pets of other languages as ways of thinking; physical relativity would account for the habit of noticing and isolating the wheel principle in all details of the celestial and mundane worlds and taking the enigmatic part of it as a universal law or reality. Pretending to a passing familiarity with what is basically a true image of a false relation in either case, we would not be learning fundamental truths about cultural or physical reality, but fundamental lies about our ability to know what we were talking about.

In effect, then, our highly relativized cosmology, with its almost infinitesimal particles and its almost infinite cosmic expanses, betrays the kind of conceptual mystique that is often visited on the ancient Egyptians. No right-thinking archaeologist would want to suggest that the horse and the wheel were "too easy" for the tasks the early dynastic Egyptians set for themselves, and the facts of the matter support this. They were a self-isolating people, sure they were right about everything, and that certainty persisted as long as the civilization remained historically visible. They seem to have been "infected" by the horse chariot and the wheel through the depredations of some Asiatic invaders called the Hyksos, and then to have used the acquired habit of them to drive the invaders out. But the facts of this and also the certainty of the whole pharaonic conceptual schema imply the *opposite* of cultural or physical relativity, for the chord or scale of the finitary, struck just once and in the right way, might resonate eternally or infinitely for all they could know or care about it. The signature pattern of a civilization or the intimation of eternity carried in those vibrations would be *our* sense of their humor.

Could the Egyptians have patronized us in their turn, pointing out that by getting the scale of the wheel wrong and working through the errors we acculturate ourselves, not only to a sense of cultural relativity, but also to a fantasy of self-effective action in our machines and in the "energy" they manifest for us? Science fiction seems to be the current venue for making sense of a relativized cosmos and the parts of the wheel we do not know. Let me try. Did *Homo erectus* use a device whose sophistication we cannot even imagine to hurl the hand ax as a projectile? Wiping themselves out in the process, in what amounted to a perfect evolutionary displacement? Probably not, though they were damn good. But trying seems to be our best shot at the physical education of the wheel, and sometimes we succeed. Like the Wright brothers.

On the other hand the very "science-fictional" angle in all of this, separating a species from the technology by which it gained its livelihood, serves to generate exactly the kind of relativism that poses its problem. Separating an energy source from its means of application (what's the difference, since an energy source is itself a means of application?) is like making an artificial cut between world-in-the-person and person-in-the-world and pretending psychological or methodological insights on the result. Cut a wheel apart, if you can, into the sections that move respectively backward and forward in its rolling, or disconnect its balance from its momentum, and you lose the unity that makes it a wheel in the first place. All you have left is a metaphor of cause and effect, a true image of a false relation.

Simplifying greatly, one could say that there is the energy of application and the application of energy, and that the more nearly these two approximate to one another, the more "educated" a wheel one has. This simple formula for the displacement of human potential becomes more complicated, but more interesting, when applied *as,* or within, the human factor that it inevitably implies. The more nearly the two "sides" of the brain-body complex, of human laterality, approximate to one another, the more effective both the differentiation and the integration of the genders will be. Laterality divides the world as it divides the person, integrates the sense of each within the other, and the wheel displaces that unity within the physical world of human tasks. Gender, however, the two "kinds" of bodies that make the single body "happen," is the *displacement* of human physicality within the unity of its lateral closure. And it is a necessary displacement. For just as the *absolute* integration of the lateral functions would leave no grasp of the world and no world to grasp, so an absolute integration *or* differentiation of the genders would lose the power of its reproductive continuity.

Gender is not just some nasty trick played upon the human race, though it may often seem that way, and the wheel was not just an "accidental" discovery. It was always there, waiting in the wings. The nasty trick is not simply the involvement of gender and laterality with one another, nor the equivalent displacement that happens naturally and unreflectively in us and in most of the other species with which we are involved. As I have noted in chapter 4, it is an *additional* form of displacement that I have called antitwinning, a kind of artificial leverage over the natural symmetries.

Our clock was stopped so we could think. Whatever the means *Homo erectus* used to spin and hurl its hand ax as a projectile, and whatever role this might have played in its extinction, *Homo sapiens* made a worse one in the clock, which does not even need to be hurled but does all of its damage by spinning on its own wheels. *Erectus* may have been damn good, but *sapiens* is double-damned, twinned outward and inward against itself on the dimensionality of its own reckoning.

The clock that makes a temporal myth of the wheel by plotting its motion against itself cheats on the perfect synchronization with the cosmos that the Egyptians tried for and the Barok simulate in the *kaba.* It measures out a kind of insight in discrete intervals, regardless of whether that synchronization represents a truth about death or only a special case of our ability to know about what we know. For the wheel is not the theory of human displacement, nor the knowledge of that theory, but, as a kind of children's toy or child reality of the shape of the world we live in, the *fact* of that displacement: three dimensions working in two; two dimensions working as one; "two-together-two," like our fondest imaginings of love.

Like a little world in the person, like a little person in the world. Twinned away from our ability to focus or know it completely, the *fact* of human displacement has an equal but opposite meaning to the simplification of the body and its passions that we know as sexual reproduction. Incest oversimplifies the facts of its case, twins them *inside* of the facts that would make sense of them, so that the best we can do is make up reasons for why it was prohibited. The wheel, however, displaces the very hinge of our effective action outside of itself and into no-man's-land. It displaces itself and *keeps* displacing itself, as a globe that encompasses our life-space and a cosmos encompassing that globe.

If there were a kind of mistake, a holographic error in this, it would be that of mistaking the need or opportunity of sense for the sense that fulfils that need or takes advantage of the opportunity. Like imagining the goddess Kali's sublime underdetermination of the temporal moment as a tremendous appetite for either life or death because she dances victory at the very inception of her affairs. It is a problem of *human* perspectives.

The wheel principle is a universal perspective-on-itself that achieves its depth by foregrounding the destination or vanishing point as the very means of getting to it. As the traditional landscape imitates the imaginal movement-through-space implied in one's point of view in regarding the whole at once, the globe is simultaneously our point of reference in the cosmos and the mechanical or geophysical constitution of its referentiality. Cosmological inversion, navigation *among* celestial objects instead of within one, is a chronotopic history lesson. It teaches the wheel all it would need to know about our past and the antique brass Copernican perspective that relativity physics tried to rescue from its own self-estrangement. As though the wheel did not have enough relativity in its various paradoxes to process the whole thing in miniature, give approximate sailing directions for the minor cosmos of the Bohr atom. Marshall Sahlins wrote of the "islands of history," but the star trek is really about an unfamiliar universe turned inward to familiarize its details through what we know of our past, read off a scientific history from the instruments. The actual depth out there may be vast or infinite, but without a pivot to turn the mind upon, we are lost at sea.

Thomas Gladwyn and David Lewis have given detailed accounts of how the old Pacific navigators learned to isolate and memorize currents and wave trains in the sea. Sitting in the stern of the canoe, they taught the body's equilibrium to the wheel of the depths, turned one kind of energy and direction into another. They were the astronauts of their own times and places, for there is no science or hope of a science on earth or out in the galaxy but that it makes an artificial "thing" out of space, time, and the "energy" that pretends a leverage among them. No hope of a practical advantage either. The nautical imaginary may still provide a most appropriate pivot for the art of mammalian trans-location, from the sea captain's watch-and-chain of command to the porpoise's integrating and overmatching the sine wave of the water it swims in.

For at bottom there is only the single relation of time turning into the space that tells where it has been and what it was about. And there is the wheel principle in all its infinite variety that gives our best chance at making a "thing" of it; the Bernoulli wheel of the airfoil and its self-integration in the helicopter or hummingbird, the angular momentum of rocketry, always a curve in its straight-line flight, the *equation* as a mental balance set for gauging the scale of things that are not really things at all, but only thoughts. It is pure science fiction to imagine that there is any time left in the spaces we can see and measure all about us. That is not where time comes from, but only where it goes.

So the next step in the physical education of the wheel is to make it fully understand, grasp in all its essentials, that no body of any kind can ever move forward into the space that passes around it as it goes, and indeed comes from that going. We step into the unknown and breathe it in, exhaling space; time not only passes but *geht uns vorbei,* "passes us up," in the language of Martin Heidegger, who called our condition in this *Geworfenheit,* one of being hurled or thrown. Thrown off the point and back into space, so that it is the veritable lapse in this that the wheel makes its "thing" of. But this truth, which can be understood "cultur-ally" from all manner of perspectives, can be simplified very drastically in direct physical terms. The simple fact of it is that we cannot perceive or register *motion* itself but can only represent or recover it in an action that is separate from its original happening. It is the *recovery* of motion that we perceive as movement, displaced in the very event from its cen-terpoint. That is the fact of our temporal emptiness, the needful basis of any attempt to isolate time as a thing, dimension, or thinkable topic.

It means that the unification of motion is more important than its structuring, its measurement, or the attribution of one or another set of properties to it. It is a self-defining action, at once the sense and the sensing of the thing we would perceive in that way, and so entirely *spatial*. It is in respect of this that the wheel might be said to *balance* instead of move; making the *recovery* symmetrical with the original happening of its motion, it executes a perfect reciprocity between the two in a single, continuous flow. It is the perfect "body shifter" or organ of human displacement, in that it models the part of our action that we cannot perceive directly (stepping into the unknown, breathing it in) through the part we can recover (the separate action of representing it), with no real separation between cause and effect. The wheel locks into its own antecedence.

Otherwise the notions of "time" itself and *futurity*, the unknown factor of the times or events that have yet to happen, would stand opposed as mutually contradictory aspects of the wheel principle. The paradox of the yet-to-be-simplified wheel. Thus the physical wheel might be understood as the one vital organ that has been left out of the body's anatomical constitution, the single cakra, or bodily energy center, that must be recovered (invented, discovered) on the outside if the symmetry of movement is to make sense, and the unification of time as well. Insofar as its projected recording or ordering is concerned, all time to come is already past and belongs to the same circumferential circularity as the times that have already gone by. Name any future time or date, however near at hand or far into the coming time, picture for yourself any events that might take place in it, and both the dating of the events and their imaginable contents are part of the world you already know.

Then the next step in the simplification of the wheel is to demonstrate why this must be so. The next thing to happen from now is just exactly as unknown as the one after that, or indeed any or all of the subsequent ones, so they cannot form a system or schematic continuity except insofar as we might be able to anticipate them. And if the essence of realism consists in precisely this sort of anticipation, all the more reason to pay attention to the wheel's possibilities in it.

One might think that there was always a part of us, an "anticipatory" or synchronizing intelligence that had learned, from our very first step into the unknown or the first gulp of it breathed into the body, to anticipate events and movements with an ever greater precision—the unknown part of ourselves that negotiates the unknown. To the degree that the wheel could be educated up to meet our physical expectations of that "part" of ourselves, the problem of representation itself, and many of the problems of science, would disappear. "Unifying" time would not, then, mean finding better or more exact units or systems of units for its calibration, nor developing more powerful aesthetic or explanatory chronotopes to enhance the sensing of it. The kind of wheel or degree of its simplification that would separate "time" itself off from the anticipatory flow of event is an *emergent* rather than a displaceable function of our present technology and physical thinking.

What this might mean is perhaps best illustrated graphically in four stages. The following discussion refers to Figure 10:

10a: The traditional yin-yang figure may be simplified as a picture of a moving wheel inscribed with its heliacal counterthrust, dividing it schematically into two separate "moments" of force. Given that motion itself is not directly representable, the two "forces" might be radicalized respectively as "going time," the action of its *passing,* and the separate action of "coming" time or futurity that is necessary to recover that action as motion.

10b: So the wheel's recoverable motion propels, and its rigidity as a usable artifact retards or arrests a *chronotopic* rotation as an emergent— necessary but never fully realized—phase of its self-integration. The chronotope is self-symmetrical: each component might just as well be the other. The "previous" and the "yet-to-be" are simply phases or turnings of the same presently perceivable object. So the full significance of the chronotope might be rendered thus: anything we might remember, intend, intuit, or discover about the past through research or introspection exists only in the *future* of the present moment; it is only the past that is round and routinized, the seeming "approach" of event hides itself in this and surprises us in the need to imagine a shape and a sequency for it.

10c: Then it would seem that the subdivision of the chronotope into separable "moments of force" is an analytic and self-effacing mistake about itself. In effect, and *as* the whole effect of the chronotope an obverse form of dimensionality—an anti-extensional principle or mirror dimensionality—is simply *unwrapping* itself as a necessary part of the wheel's action. The coming into existence of this unimaginable counterpart of the perspectival imagination accounts at once for the integration of the yin-yang figure and the properties and attributes ascribed to time, motion, and mechanical advantage.

10d: Thus the wheel's action simultaneously retards and brings into being a geometric paradox or "möbius plane"—something that is otherwise impossible to represent in that each "side" of it exists only through its division of, and division by, the other. If the mirror's usefulness and

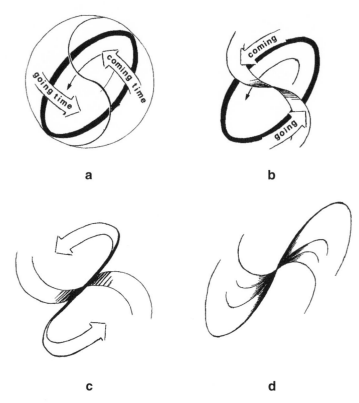

a   b

c   d

Figure 10. Dimensional sublation.

the paradoxical character of mirror reflection are explained by the fact that mirroring brings the phenomenon of perspective full circle, divides *perspective* by itself in the same way, then the motional counterpart of this exists as an untapped potential of the wheel.

The mirror-wheel is an invisible support mechanism for every aspect of technology (including the aesthetic) and the world and cosmos we have learned to shape and feel through its use and its lessons. It is the fundamental humor of the way in which temporality turns back around into spatial extension as "the only time left that matters," the "left" or leftover side of time. Spatial underdetermination, perspective's closure upon itself as an antidimensional or "mirror" continuum, is not only what time is "about," but also the subject of the whole energy-cum-wheel-and-circuitry complex that profiles "modernity" in its automational obsessions.

What is only a speculative fantasy in the "space warp" or "time warp" demonstrations of science fiction, a failure to displace the perspective necessary to know what such a thing might be like, functions pragmatically in the double-encompassment chronotope of earth and cosmos, the de facto figure that we use but normally do not acknowledge in deriving the attributes of each from the other. The mutual encompassment of time's passage and the separate action of recovering it cast a long shadow of "understandable self-efficient action" over the attempt to imagine or demonstrate *agency* in the world, or as the world. "Pragmatic" actually means the inability to fully materialize, or render into a laughable humor, the underside or underdetermining potential of natural extension as the basis of imagination itself. The "other side" of the physical demonstration given in Figure 10, and hence the whole lesson of it, would not be the discovery and use of physical principles to figure out a practical solution to the problem of agency, but the recovery or materialization of the extensional melodrama that supports its principles.

What we imagine time itself to be is so well accounted for by its transformation into space that its calibration or speculative essence is entirely beside the point. Time is magnified, like stars or atoms, in order even to make a topic of it, and the artifact of its magnification is the chronotope. Divided by itself, time's perspective would not leave a chronotopic quotient, but live the finality of things in their beginnings. It would be like the ground zero of the ancient Egyptian eternity complex as the radical simplification of infinity, or music's mirror of itself in the works of Johann Christian Bach. Short, sharp, and overmelodic,

Bach's music and that of his Mannheim school contemporaries divined the chronotope that later composers were to expand so magnificently, made a more nearly perfect beginning for it. The young Mozart once wrote that he hoped someday to be as famous as Christian Bach, but he wrote before music had fully entered the phase of its retrenchment.

The sense or, better, the sensuality of perspectival division made unlikely collaborators of Bach and the artist Thomas Gainsborough in London. At one time concerts of the "new music" were held in a hall decorated by paintings and other works of art illuminated from behind by candles. But the indirect lighting gave the lie to the powdered wigs of the attending socialites and had to be discontinued. "What, Apollo and the Muses gone?" a lady complained. To which Bach replied, "They have acquitted their late stations, madame, but have not absolutely deserted us. When the performance begins, I hope your ladyship will hear them all." [1]

Gainsborough gave so many original canvases to Bach's collaborator in the concerts, Karl Friedrich Abel, in return for lessons on the viola da gamba, that Abel literally covered the walls of his home with them.[2] Gainsborough "had the strange notion that by borrowing his friends' musical instruments, he would also acquire their ability to play them." [3] One has the idea that the artist had a sort of creative jealousy for music, or at least that the sensibility that held the mutual fascination of Bach, Abel, and significant painters like Gainsborough, Sir Joshua Reynolds, and Johann Zoffany worked through, rather than against, the division of perspectives. Was their "art" as much behind the scenes of its public presentation as scientific research hides in its methodologies, hypotheses, and facts, all of which must be staged as "performance" after the fact of its original syntheses? Charles Darwin displayed the wares of a cunning idea of self-efficient transformation in nature that he did not invent, or even explain, so much as factualize. The sense of the wheel principle, its chronic displacement of human temporal emptiness, becomes a negative capability for human tasks upon its recovery in one or another form—like the cat that "evolved" by learning to be "no cat" for its prey, or the electron whose precise location and exact velocity are differential functions of a single ambiguity.

Music is the better theory of motion; motion is the better theory of physics. The objectivity shared between them makes a science of the art and an art of the science, turns the pair of them into kinesthetic kissing cousins. An artist like Gainsborough, who would kill to know the secret of movement behind his perspectives, paints his own still portrait in that way. As Rembrandt dusted his canvases with the light of shadow, and Vermeer canvased the play of perspectives with the shadows of light. Physical extension is the architect of its own perspectives; motion is the pencil that draws them.

How might the heuristic error of imaginary spaces be used to correct rather than to justify itself? Is the quasi-mathematical pretense that we call dimensionality really a tool of the mind, or is "mind" a tool of it? The problem of motion or movement, the only one that matters in physics, can then be visualized in an entirely novel way, and the secret of its shaping is less a matter of what Einstein had in mind than of what the Netherlands artist M. C. Escher showed to the body.

Gravity or inertia (which Einstein determined to be the same thing) measures a resistance to motion or velocity in space, a *contraction* of the extensional principle (viz., "imaginary spaces") that we use to understand space as well as time. If gravity/inertia is a negatively positive resistance to motion, then the distance it must traverse is a positively negative one. Hence what we measure or compute as motion is not motion. It is an artificial quality that resembles real movement only as the one configuration of extension differs from the other, or in the way that a musical and a visual art might be jealous of one another.

The craft that attains "escape velocity," coasting on the inertia of its own impetus, finds itself lost in space and confronts the other half of the extensional dilemma, the *distance* that measures gravity the other way around. Velocity, unit space per unit time, divides extension by itself, overdetermines motion as a measure of the medium through which it moves. Divide space's dimensional similarity to itself by time's ongoing differentiation from the extension that measures it, and you get an underdetermination of the problem of motion. Then it would make more sense to conclude that the mutual underdetermination of mass and distance is the reason the stars are so far apart than to identify gravity/inertia with a curvature in something called space-time. The possibility that light from distant cosmic objects can be understood to grow progressively *younger* as it ages the expanses around it is a chronotopic inversion of the relativity principle. For the negative relativity of relativity to itself is not relative at all but chiasmatic—using the limitations that relativity imposes on the observer to limit the principle itself.

If we can imagine the kind of relativity that exists among the dimensions, such that each dimension that is postulated depends upon the others for its justification, as a kind of *motion*, then *perspective* is a moving picture of itself. Either the perspective holds steady and we ourselves move, imagining that movement as time, or the observer maintains a fixed position and *extension* itself is motion. The objectivity of things, in other words, can be figured in two distinctive ways: as a positive "solidity" coming out of the depth that perspective pictures, or as an antithetical or negative solidity going inward. The art of Escher is remarkable in that it shows each aspect of the objective dilemma to be a perspectival function of the other. It is the visual and in many ways the aesthetic equivalent of gyroscopic action.

The action of the gyroscope is holographic in that it pivots upon, and so pivots, an omnicentrifugal force, one that overdetermines the potential of antithetical, omnicentripetal counterpart. Understood as "forces," each of these is the equal-but-opposite reaction of the other; imagined as "perspectives," each is the negative extensional field of the other. Hence there would be no need, even if we could find them, to look for evidences of a black hole in the cosmos or to use the subagendas of particle physics to rationalize its existence. It is all there in the perspectival art of Escher.

It is tempting to imagine that, upon dying, one recedes into the negative extensional field of the life experience, experiences the holographic vision insinuated in the Barok death feast as the "lesson" of death itself. And it is likewise tempting to understand that motion itself operates perpendicular to our sensing of it, that "the sun, the moon, the clouds, and the stars," as the Daribi told me, "simply *go into the sky* and *come out again*," and that lateral motion is but a "side effect" of this.

But it is most tempting of all to consider the possibility of the mirror-wheel, the device that destabilizes, in fact rides upon, the force or perspective that gyroscopic action holds steady for us, as a deliberately *physical* prospect. "The gyroscope is to the mirror-wheel as the mirror-wheel is to the anti-gyroscope" is easy enough to say, and a bit more difficult to visualize. But unless the principle of it were turned into a deliberate artifact, an ultimate mechanical imitation of what it means to be human, you, the reader, would not believe the text that is now before you, and I, the writer, would not blame you a bit.

For it is even tempting to reconsider what is supposed to be our evolution along these lines. If the means by which *Homo erectus* hurled the hand ax were in any direct way commensurate with the mechanical advantage I have been discussing, if we were preceded by a truly holographic species, the whole facade of our evolution would have to be revised. And the species that invented species would be a sad comedown from its forefathers.

15

Sex in a Mirror

Just how might one *integrate* anthropology's subject, rather than its subject matter, or the sets of concepts, methodologies, and assumptions that promote its possibilities? Can "reality," whatever is meant by that term, assume a proportion within the sense we make of ourselves without remaining a separate issue—a natural, social, cultural, or meaningful reality alone? If that elusive constant, reality, exists only as a metaphor in assumed correspondence with the names, functions, and systems of order through which we would know it, then world-in-the-person and person-in-the-world would lose the identity that makes each of them possible through the other. To put it in another way, if natural phenomena are just as cultural as cultural ones are natural, then the distinction between them is one we impose on ourselves, a "symbolic" denial that becomes apparently real in spite of itself.

Let me return to Wittgenstein for the moment. The logic of statements in his *Tractatus* like 4.011, "A proposition is a picture of reality as we imagine it," is not so much logical as it is opposite to the case that reality makes of it, in that it puts too much emphasis on the ability of human beings to "construct" a sensible world. (Would it make any difference, then, if they only *pretended* to do so, and then congratulated one another, like phenomenologists, on the achievement?) *Reality*, instead, would have to be a picture of the proposition, or in other words, the logic or proposition *no longer matters* in speech or everyday experience because one is then living the sense of thought's accordance with itself as a pseudorelation in its own right. Getting around reality by getting into one's own commonplace version of it. So we have "Every proposition must already have a sense; it cannot be given sense by affirmation" (Wittgenstein, *Tractatus* 4.064) and "Darwin's theory has no more to do with philosophy than any other hypothesis in natural science" (4.1122). Or, one might add, any mathematical proof. A fossil, or a mathematical proof, is a picture of its a priori hieroglyph— a reality encompassing the theory of how it got to be that way in the first place.

It does not matter what reality would have to mean; reality does not "represent" but only presents itself in any way that it may be encountered, used, understood, or believed in. On the other hand, it is the over-familiarity of known and easily manipulable elements—commonplace words and things whose significance we have agreed to agree upon— that generates the sense of knowing one's mind in a topic, and so sustains the paradox of having (e.g., trying) to believe in some things and not others. Time, to take what is probably the perennial favorite mode of subjective integration, relies solely on the comparatives, the "linear" contrasts like past and future or now and then, for the kind of identity-with-itself or integration that gives it a meaning or purpose. But that identity of one temporal phase with another—past in its own future or future in its own past—turns inevitably into a kind of parody of the sequentiality used to make its aphorism comparative in the first place. Better to think of it as a humor, getting the point by not getting it, that prolongs the joke of its own telling. Like the humor of gender, likewise based on comparatives, and likewise indefinitely self-prolonging. Or like the humor of consciousness.

Despite all that has been thought or written about it, consciousness or self-awareness is not profound, mechanical, or even uniquely human. It is very simply the art of surprising oneself, and has no other depth; it is a catlike humor of itself, almost like human sentience. Lynx keeps all the world's secrets to itself and hardly ever lets them out, almost like Wittgenstein. No one has ever heard a lynx laugh, not even, we suspect, the lynx itself; the secret of its humor is the humor of the secret, something of which it is only barely conscious, and pounces upon whenever it can. No surprise, for all that animals are merely human comparatives in this context, misconceived zoologically as the gender half of human twinning is misconceived biologically, or as time is reconstructed out of the comparisons that shatter its subjective integrity. The humor of the secret in this anthropological parable of consciousness can be paraphrased in human terms as I shall paraphrase (very roughly) Sol

Steinberg: "The attempt to explain humor is always part of the humor one is attempting to explain."

Sense closes upon itself in surprise (the "public" face of the secret), humor, reflection, reaction, and sexual climax. There is the tree that cuts the ground as the ground cuts the tree, the ground that is figure to figure as its ground, the double encompassment of motion and extension *(gala* and *kolume)* as they enable one another through mutual underdetermination. The effect, regardless of whether it is attributed as mental, physical, or both, is to bring human faculties into a suspension or subjection, and make the *subject* defined in that way a factor in its own understanding. In that instance, which might be considered the primordial joke of the species and its communication with itself in speech, or the joke of species ("kind") itself, the subject no less than the "faculties" projected from its self-ironic comprehension is no longer simply human, but *any* subject at all. It becomes possible, "holographically," one might say, to *invent,* to say, articulate, or physically accomplish that which could not otherwise be thought or premeditated.

Then it would not simply be vanity or curiosity that brings one to look into a mirror, or even the possibility of getting a look at the "self." One sees a counterimage of one's *looking,* and only incidentally one's appearance, antibody with the poles—sides as well as front and back—reversed. "Reflection" would mean that a contest of wills had been resolved in one's favor, or that the suspension of agencies between the reversed poles were trivial, and one could go forward on one's date or whatever with complete assurance. But since *one does not really look like that at all,* it is clear that something quite different is going on. The being in the mirror has borrowed the action and intention of our "looking," our very perceptual faculty, to see *itself* through our means. What we view is its gaze stabbing back through our own and into our "background." How we may choose to think of that being, what we may call it, and even the rather dicey question of how or whether it might exist at all are beside the point, and the fact that it has borrowed our perception and direction in life. That is the quizzical counterpart of the fact that we make use of "mirror-sex" or perceptual intercourse with that being in order to borrow back our whole sense of objectivity, figure, and outline.

The mirror-interface is the interference patterning of boundary, outline, limit, surface, and therefore of all objectivity, and is the real key to the penetration or transformation of what we consider objective. We live, think, and experience or perceive a world of objects, outlines, and boundaries so definitive that they define us as well. But they must do so from the "outside," the other side of that lateral composite of sided-ness and directed intention that holds the place of "self," and that the mirror-interface turns inside out.

Perceptual intercourse as the basis of our "persuasion," our knowing and feeling of the world, is the gendered mode of laterality, its outward flexure and reflection, and thus the whole basis for my discussion of kinship and supergender in what may seem to be inappropriate terms. At the core of our objectivity is the one in the mirror that has borrowed all of our perceptual strategy in order to glimpse or focus itself. At the core of our self or subjectivity is the one who would borrow it back, live its fugitive existence in the mirror's mirroring of it. We would need the gaze backward into the direction we were coming from as a modeling example, not only to mask our personal appearance and sense of time, but also to control the whole "technological" contretemps with the physical world—and thus, as Jacques Lacan has pointed out, our whole sense of self-esteem as well.

That people with no mirrors used one another for this reflectional check on human facility, invented a world of kin responsibilities upon what we should now call "interpersonal relations," would be the sub-stance of my apocryphal Story of Eve. The whole "reflectional" world that has interposed its interfaces in substitute, texts, painted perspec-tives, the looking glass, and the evolution and perfection of illuminated-screen technologies and their attendant guidance systems transforms that interpersonal sense of existence back into its instrumentive sub-strate. The result is that as a "social" problem kinship exists as a kind of therapy, subterfuge, or recompense, and as an anthropological one a kind of false mechanical rationalization for why anyone should under-take social connection and community in the first place.

Consequence and antecedence are the "facts of life," the obversive conception theory, of mirror-coitus. No one has ever really explained the role of simultaneous orgasm, nor the consequent "chaining" cli-maxes, riding her own reactions, in the female partner, in human con-ception or even "interpersonal relations." Nor could I pretend to un-derstand them or try to explain what they mean. But they do have their analogue in our mirror-sex with the world if only in the double en-compassment that undercuts the distinctiveness of cause and effect, the separate roles they are alleged to take in its conception of things. If antecedence and consequence did not emanate, as explainable counter-parts, from the same synchronic conjunction, they could not work to-gether, or even apart, and would not "work" at all.

All that we know of (causative) agency is known deductively, through the pragmatic afterlife of consequences that must, thereby, be synchronous and coincidental with their own inception, just as the whole past and everything that might be remembered or discovered about it lie in the *future* of the present moment. This means that anything we might want to consider as consequential, even extending beyond our mortal limitations, has already been lived by the time it is anticipated. We live, or experience within, our own pragmatic afterlives, and the universe "evolves" within its own copy of that principle. It cannot "catch up" with its own place in time without, so to speak, extending itself beyond it. So the light that reaches us from distant parts of the universe shows a *younger* version of its evolution, and it is only a perspectival fixation that keeps us from concluding that light grows younger as it travels, turns its example into evidence for an expanding universe. Much as our mechanical or electronic devices and instruments actually operate upon structures designed to simulate cause and effect in their working, so these ostensible natural processes and evolutionary matrices "work" only the imageries upon which we depend for our understanding and observation. They have nothing other than this to do with physical reality. A better, more efficient or sophisticated engine, a more refined computer, would have a more ingenious simulation of antecedence and consequence to work upon; a more elegant or comprehensive model of cosmic or biological evolution would pretend a different, perhaps more "evolved," imagery for its observation and corroboration. But precisely because "better" or "more refined" takes us ever farther in the direction of simulation, counterfeits the arbitrage of cause and consequence more insidiously, the device or imagery comes increasingly to define a niche and a world of its own.

Hence a kind of Zeno-paradox is posed, not only in the relation of perspective and its supportive imageries to the empowerment of their simulative capabilities, but more immediately in that of human invention to our understanding of what it entails. The closer our efforts bring us to the ultimate simplicity of all that simulation portends, the more complex, intransigent, and self-defining the results. (This is the issue of what some have called "complexity theory," and its fractal, or holographic, potential is the substance of "chaos science.") In effect (i.e., deductively, consequentially), Zeno taught the lesson of the holographic worldview backward, the paradox of a perfect ordering of thought as the scale model of all the mistakes made in trying to figure out what it might be. Or what we ourselves might be, for Zeno was closer to the joke of defining human sentience than anyone has been since his times.

So long as that being in the mirror, disposed along entirely different lines than we are, is taken as a mere reflection of what we are and what we know, the objectivity that we borrow back from its purloined perspective will be the *subject* of the double encompassment that deceives us in that way.

The wheel principle, in its many transformations and even the "automation" of its own self-engagement, would not, then, be odd inventions, occurring randomly or in some kind of rational sequence, but mirror artifacts of the mystery that we call "energy." Translations or transpositions, as it were, of the motion-extension interface into the active sequencing of cause and consequence. Could rational thinking and planning themselves be the accident, or at least the mask, of a technology recovered piecemeal through the insights and exigencies of a basically predatory life-form? Would it not make as much sense (or even more, given the centricity of "sense" in the realm of the meaningful) to conclude that a capacity to *invent,* a negative capability inadvertent to reason, desire, or purpose, had simply *chained* itself, as lightning does, across the centuries?

Like the being in the mirror, whatever its true existential status, that borrows one's perception and perspective to see itself? Though one might not even care to know who or what the being might actually be, or how the facility of invention "works," that would mean that a holography of invention in its every conceivable form had distributed itself through all the insights and achievements by which we know our history, our cosmos, and ourselves. Part of its process or disguise in doing so might be that we lose the whole scale of what it portends in acknowledging it, and in consequence of the mirror effect. There are all manner of shapes, complexities, designs, and processes in the pictures we have modeled to make sense of our world, and metaphor has the same indiscernible shape in all of them.

So it would not matter that most of the galaxies we can detect are smaller than bacteria, and most of the bacteria more harmless than interesting, as long as their pictures, in detail or in the aggregate, might justify the magnification necessary to discern them in the first place. Though in that case, keeping the picturing of facts as a necessary constant, we would be using a picture of cosmic structure and process, or an insight into life's subliminal speciation, as an instrument in the study of what magnification means and how it works: magnification of the picture as the picture of magnification.

Space exists, like time or number, as a mirror image of whatever model we might make for it, and has no other reality. The mirror multiplies the model and the model multiplies the mirror. So *number* may be the most original mistake of mathematics, a nonsubjective fantasy of thought's relation to itself through the overdetermination of incidental qualities, just as the wheel images a pragmatic counterpart in its underdetermination of shape's relation to thought. The "proof" of this, if one were needed, is incontrovertible in the pi ratio, linearity to circularity, which forces its own quantification back into an inventory-like recapitulation of numerical digits following the decimal point, as though circularity sought its precise quantification in vain. A wheel rolling back into itself. Instead of proof we get an infinite rephasing of the conundrum itself, a model of what modeling would mean, as punishment. Instead of resolving itself, the ratio slices mental reality in two; the "mind" part obsessed with what can or cannot be done with number, the "body" aspect deriving a whole world of actional possibilities via the wheel and its many avatars. Number copies itself in one direction, the wheel in another. The ancient Finns might have called this "the *vekki* of the wheel," medieval Europeans named it for a kind of torture, "breaking on the wheel," and Barok identified the wheel's *pidik* in it.

For the simple experience of something that goes on and on, or the attempt to grasp it at its far point, is neither an excuse nor a proof for infinity. The mathematician Georg Cantor's definitive sorting of the various orders of infinity, that of possible numbers, that of geometric points (on a line, in a plane, or in a solid), and the infinity of possible curves, does not deal with infinity directly, but concentrates instead on the various means by which it might be counted or computed. In effect Cantor used the intuition of infinity in reverse, to demonstrate actual facts about the human ability to *know from it*. His proofs for the orders of infinitive *marking* as exponential "power sets" are like gear ratios for the mind or imagination that might otherwise outstrip itself in fantasy.

"Real" infinity could only be considered mathematical as the mirror imaging of some finite operations—the "un-quantity" of our quantification of things. Cantor's modeling is an exercise in the ancient and subtle art of *finitization*, thought's knowledge of itself as anthropology, one with which the ancient Egyptians, and through them the Greeks, seem to have been well acquainted, transcending the mistake of quantification itself through the application of known and knowable numerical operations, as in Euclid's famous proof for the infinity of prime numbers. Perhaps the philosopher Hegel had something like that in mind when he contrasted the true infinity of proportional encompassment (like a point made infinitely well) with the "bad," or mathematical, infinity that comes of trying, vainly and incessantly, to transcend the finitary values of our models. We notice gravity too, or motion or consciousness, only when we are out of balance with ourselves.

Anthropology, too, might strive to keep that balance, like the ancient Greeks or the Egyptians, but not the world of finance, with its mirror imaging of value in the future. In the "futures market" of the world the total amount of money, credit, or value on earth at any given time is a quantity that, however incalculable, is pledged upon or borrowed from an infinitive future potential. The more convincingly it is apportioned, metered out, determined upon risk, speculation, interest rate, and probability expectations, the more it appreciates, converges on that potential. The result is very like a Cantorian demonstration; soon we will have the most valuable real estate in the galaxy, but only in our heads.

So why not make a simple *ratio* of the future, train the numbering of finance and the risk of its futures to the minute infinity of pi, and invest in the mirror-wheel instead? Personal mortality is a sure thing, stronger and more reliable than the amortization of capital, and is really the only long-term resource or real estate that we have. The wheel contains its own recapitulation, mirrors its shape in its motion and its motion in its shape. By closing movement upon itself, the wheel principle does for mechanics what Cantor's mathematics did for infinity in setting up the theory of sets, making a consummate advantage of a methodological limitation. As a model of itself, the wheel is intensional to the extensional coordinates of its motion in just the way that the Cantorian power set takes the derivative of extension's infinitely greater compass. There are no external boundaries or limits, no procedural limitations more formidable than the ones encountered *within* the effort made to transcend them.

The mirror version of the wheel, of which automation's imitation of energy is but a shrewd mimicry, would model the inversional power set of motion, strike the definitive chord of movement's resemblance to itself, and then ride with it. Two mirrors set at just the right angle can clone the body's image of itself, or any other image, indefinitely into the forever, and without the procedural uncertainty or biological hazard of DNA (and to no real purpose that I can think of). But what form of biological replenishment, what mass production, technological or otherwise, what broadcasting of the self, computer network, or publication of ideas is not basically reproduction in a mirror? The Nazi state? The Marxian proletariat? The single personality writ large upon the screen, the multitudes of condoms, galaxies, and subatomic particles, the high school reunion or social welfare program? Ethics, ethical relativism, and even environmentalism could only pretend to find an answer.

Infinity is the *opposite* of multiplicity and magnitude, eternity and the past the opposite of the now, and they are not where we think we are headed. If the lateral unity, the twinning inward of the "sides" that makes the body a hinge for its thinking, could be fully displaced, folded outside and around the extension that encloses it, mirror-sex would be real, and the being in the mirror would be wondering whether *you* exist or not. Then anthropologists would have to exercise their rationalizing powers on something other than incest, explain why we do not exist and did not evolve, and why society could not possibly have come into being. For that, too, would be an opposite, the opposite of our clone-wars and historical chronicles, and of the long line of human energy. *Homo non-extensis* is not just our end in death; it is also the species of our end in life.

Understanding the role of "duality" in this, or in twinning, physics, cultural conceptualization, or the bilaterality of the brain, is like acknowledging a schizophrenia one has just avoided in the act of diagnosing it. How does the brain contain or enclose itself in the body, and the very physical essence that sustains it come into existence in the brain? Do the two "neocortical" excrescences of the cerebrum not also play these roles between them, as though mind-in-the-body and body-in-the-mind were engaged in a kind of mental chess of themselves? Each contains the other in thinking as thinking contains the whole corporeal form that thinks it, and the mutual encompassment describes a figure that does not depend upon extension for the sense it would make. But that figure does not, in its turn, describe *it*, its mode of comprehension, or even its evolution. Faced with a difficult problem, such as defining or integrating an all-encompassing unity of things, it would always come up with two of something, and forget that it was only thinking of itself.

Perhaps the only line of reasoning that closes upon the point of this is that of projective geometry, the radical mathematical analysis of perspective. Projective geometry is a mathematical exercise originally intended to reconcile the reality of the *flat* canvas with the sense of depth or spatial extension created in a painting, by demonstrating both as effects of a simple transformation. In the language of projective geometry that transformation generates a "duality," a geometric demonstration of the means by which the unity or focality of perception is "braced" by mutually reinforcing and thus co-equivalent analogues of itself. Their congruence is derived, tested, and proven in theorems that show how the points or intersections-of-lines in each of the disparate figures can be substituted for the lines of the other without affecting the singularity that determines both of them.

Difference and similarity *simulate* each other perfectly in a unity that is at one and the same time both the depth and the absence of depth in the perspective, and in one's acceptance of that perspective as the shape of the world. The significance of this far outweighs the ways in which painting fools the eye, the supposition of a shared, internalized language fools the culture concept, or the notion of "intersubjectivity" has foiled generations of phenomenologists. It is no doubt the fooling strategy of metaphor itself, that works its way into our very thoughts about it, a congruence or demonstrable relation that stands outside of the spatial extension used to make its point. Yet it is right there, before your two eyes, in a painting.

So the chiasmus, the form of double-proportional statement that Lévi-Strauss has elucidated as the Canonic Formula for myth, and even the "elementary structure" of cross-cousin marriage in his earlier work, need not be taken as the form or content of the ethnofeatures they describe, but only exist in a "duality" correspondence with them. To the extent that a veritable galaxy of co-equivalent dualities might be traced out in Lévi-Strauss's work (e.g., that on "dual organizations," or in the "totemic operator" of *The Savage Mind*), they would make their point appositively, as duals of the dualities they represent.

The fact that duality "seconds" itself, twins itself again in any form in which one might know it or model its working, makes an unwitting positivism of this inherent self-mimicry. One would need something like Keats's "negative capability" to catch the intrinsic conundrum, the inside-out copy that extension makes of mind's sentience in the world. Something counterintuitive, very risky, and itself highly contagious, like the trace of metaphor in its own negation, or like Prince Hamlet's viral autoimmunity in acting himself mad.

The negative of a picture is the picture of its own negative form. Ideas of what metaphor may be, or of the significance of imagery and the importance of language in human sentience elicit almost automatically the evidential and emotional "backlash" that confirms them. The afterimage of what an image or an imagery might be is an unprinted photo of itself. We have no emotions, and indeed no "examples," of anything, that are not artificial in this sense, artifacts of the efforts made to bring them to a focus.

Not unlike the wry symmetry of death, pragmatic afterlife as the ultimate joke of itself. "Death would have as much trouble getting over the point of life as life does in getting over the fact of it." Given that the "hereafter" projected in this observation is otherwise indistinguishable from the "heretofore," the summative life experience needed to imagine its own termination, there is an insidious humor, a metaphoric echo effect, in the idea that one might be talking about two separate or separable things. So the conviction of "past lives" lived beforehand or the possibility of "rebirth" into others after the fact would be *consequences* (rather than "causes"), ghost images of one's mistakes in not getting the whole point of it. Like the false dualities that multiply and accumulate inadvertently on both sides of the reflectional interface in the effort to get our twinning right once and for all.

Or like the idea of "event" or "happening" used as a frame to bracket and set off details of something much more extensive than what it can bring to a focus. Or again like the holographic principle spilled out across the human landscape in space and time into many specific motifs or designs for its own recovery as such, all of them easily mistaken for individual "cultures." I once labeled my collection of New Ireland field notes "Melanesian Megalomaniacs, or How the Barok People Came to Be So Few." I was told that "when a Barok person marries an outsider, they generally move somewhere else to avoid the harsh taboos and protocols." Barok people have no real use for their ancestors, so they honor them extravagantly and exaggerate that honor in the interests of a very subtle social place-value system on the expectation, usually vain, that they themselves may eventually come to be so honored.

Like the role of computers in the modern world, or that of afterlife in death, the acute *humor* that sustains the Barok "feasting complex" is treated most obliquely of all in the facts or excuses marshaled to explain it, or those synthesized within its focusing of things. Death, arcane realms of "information," procedure, record keeping, finance, and personal opinion, or the total shaping of object and experience in the Barok world, becomes explainable if not understandable, as though each focus were its own best example. At that point the full humor of the situation has grown too large to be reflected in any other way and, precisely because it is "no joke," becomes a trap for itself.

Can words, too, be used to make a point that is more coherent, more closed upon itself, than the language through which they are articulated? Perhaps we would not have the faculties of speech or thought if this were not the case. "Of all the possible things that could happen in the next moment, or indeed previous to that *as* the present one, *only one of them will.*" Plurality disappears on the event, so that sequential "happening," as well as the "spatial" range of its potential alternatives, is like a posthypnotic suggestion in that it uses its own occurrence to curtail the possibility that things or times could be any different than the one it has. No wonder the idea of it mesmerized me, caught my whole fancy on the warm spring day when it first occurred to me at about the age of ten, standing in line outside of my elementary school. Consequence takes over the very antecedence by which it might be known or recognized, so that even one's realization that this might be the case is part of its process. In the case of a technology or a schooling of the mind that is hypnotized in this way by the point-event of its own invention, it is the key to all of its further applications.

Anton Mesmer's use of electromagnetic "power lines" to cure patients of any imaginable malady was a patent fraud, but now we use the "hype" that Mesmer so successfully engineered on maladies that Mesmer wouldn't even have wanted to imagine. Society's radar of itself, its echolocational surrogate for the physical presence that has come (for that very reason?) to be increasingly resented, and for the definable instances of social reality in form and interaction upon which the whole case for its authority depends. Examined more closely, the mesmerizing potential of those applications looks something like this: every imaginable instance of "waves" traveling invisibly in space is a function ("runs on") of the power lines of self-contained circuitry in the device that sends or receives it. Uncertain as we may be about social reality or what the law really means, we can know for certain that energy fields exist and wavelike transmissions in space-time are real because we ourselves build and control the devices that transmit them and pick them up, and would be totally lost, clueless and echoless, without the reality of that metaphor. Yet, just as the *sense* of "energy" itself depends solely upon the means by which one "kind" of it is transformed into another for its whole recognizance—how it is demonstrated, understood, and manipulated—so the nature and reality of energy fields are determined upon the design and usage of its closed circuitries, its physical and tangible power lines. A society that honed its sense of reality upon this echo-effect would get very lonely about its echoed location in the scheme of things, and want to check whether anyone else out there in the cosmos had been similarly hoodwinked by Dr. Mesmer's device.

If "energy" itself is an echo-effect, a reflection of the ways in which its nature or properties might be defined, contained, or put to use, and the same is true of time, or language, or the very medium of extension itself, then one might as well substitute *hollow* for the *holo-* in holography. The paradox of a culture that is *made out of culture* (as even the most original music is *composed*, made out of other music), from which this inquiry set out, the holographic worldview, takes on a very special significance in this respect. All that one can know about it, in relation to others or to itself, is that one does know about it.

Let me sum up. The sense of physical reality and the physical reality of sense, person, or culture (the one and the many), on one hand, and the circumstantial world, on the other, both imply and integrate one another. There can be no objective certainty about either without the check of the other, and without an objective criterion the whole charade of cultural or naturalistic speculation is like having narcissistic sex with oneself in a mirror. It is a mistake to imagine that the next thing to happen will be a function of the person or the prediction, or that it might happen in as many possible ways as there are persons or predictions (e.g., the "alternate universe" scenario). The idea of *happening* or *event* automatically precludes the reality of it, for it is a reflection of the expectation one has of it, and so a basic reflex of whatever happened to bring one to anticipate or intend it. That is cause and effect. Look into the physicist's bubble chamber, the astronomer's cosmos, the statistician's report, and you will still be looking into a mirror, wondering at your own reflection.

In that way the holography of happening, the multiplex timing and positioning of event in the world, is no different from the happening of holography, the conceptual grasp of the plenitude of things in a single instant. The effect is like the integral paradox of solipsism ("I invent the world, do I not?") that must prove itself wrong to get itself right, and get itself right to prove itself wrong. It is the objective difference between the one and the many, that casts no shadow in either direction, smiling at its private mind in public places and its public mind in private ones.

The general case of holographic world perspective, the cakra of happening, can take many distinctive, variant forms. I have reviewed a number of instances of its mirror-effect in the previous chapters, beginning with gender (chapters 4 to 7), continuing through iconic consumption (chapter 8), the echolocation of the creature world (chapter 9), the techno-sociality of imaginary spaces (chapter 10), the spectral reflexivity of emotion in polyphonic music (chapter 11), and the near-life experiencing of earth in the cosmos and cosmos in the earth (chapter 12). I may seem to have come a long way from the artifice of holographic worldview in New Guinea, the Barok death feast, but in another sense, that of the reinvention (chapter 13) and physical education (chapter 14) of the wheel, I have only reproduced my vision in its mirror, taken the reader through the looking glass.

Losing the autonomy of sense is the price we pay for reflection; meaning divides by itself to invent its invention. Perception twins itself in understanding; understanding twins itself again in the hyperobjectivity of what is actually there, the virtual opposite of what we have learned to call subjectivity. The antitwin of metaphor becomes more real than the referentiality of its telling and of the feeling of what it means. The one in the mirror borrows the action of looking to see itself. The one in the fire steals the spark of kindling to warm itself. The one in the music takes the sound of listening to hear itself think, takes the thrill of performance to feel itself move. The one in the metaphor puts language exactly where it wants us to be.

By using relations and relational schemes like cause and effect, we make an inanimate copy of the body and its participatory social surround. Should we do the opposite, borrow the mirror's objectivity back to animate the inanimate instead, we would arrive at an understanding that is dis-energic, one in which energy and the scheme of its working have changed places with one another.

The use of linearity—lateral space and linear time—to control its opposite in thought and action is a routine, like breathing or the circulation of the blood. The use of the nonlinear to control the linear, like the double action of the heartbeat or the lungs, is in that respect the reflex action of objectivity itself. We echo the humor of the body in anatomizing it, and so humor its echoing of itself, getting the point of it by not getting it exactly so. The wheel that rides the perspective through which it moves, and the perspective that rides the wheel's action, the shadow-echo twins of motion, are twinned with the body as well. For the living subjects for which energy, space, and time are but substitutions encounter the same contretemps between the linear and nonlinear aspects of thought, understanding, and action, the cakra of what it means to be human. The rhythm of our music is the music of our rhythm; history rhymes itself out in the long syllables of time.

What the imitation of distance or extension, on one hand, and that of gravity/inertia, on the other, hold in common is *motion*, the action that converts wheel into gyroscope and gyroscope into wheel. Its counterpart in human embodiment has a wry humor of its own: gender parodies the evolution of a left-handed monkey wench; laterality, the guy who is always "right," suspects the hand of god in this, but I suspect the God of Hand. We make love in the mirror of our emotions; the mirror makes love happen in the world. Turn back to the figure of Kali (see Fig. 7) and try to understand supergender—the way kinship "works"—and you'll get fooled, back to front, exactly as the mirror fools your image.

The theory of human *embodiment* makes a fundamental ass of itself because the *practice* of embodiment starts there. The belly-to-belly metaphor of the human race snuggles us back into the fetal position (see Fig. 5) in the act of love, loses its head in the loins. Incest "prohibits" itself in the very recognition of it, the cognizance or *cognition* that loses its loins in the head. The one in the head steals the act of reproduction to commit its own adultery, the back-to-back metaphor (see Fig. 6) of human perception and lateral facility, the "opposable thumb" of the race.

Transacting the inherent symmetry of extensional and unextended realities is the *opposite* of technological progress, as we might understand political or social well-being as the conquest of the weapon by its more benign and civilized applications. As the ultimate telos or energy-object, the mirror-wheel is not a *nice device* at all; it is the *reconquista* of technology by the weapon.

16

The Single Shape
of Metaphor in All Things

There would always seem to be a tension within the meaningful, straining toward the use or application to be made of it. And likewise there would be a commensurate propensity to mean in any kind of usefulness—that of the body itself or of something made for it or appropriated by it. Meaningfulness is nonuseful and in fact nonsensical when defined or imagined in its own terms, as a thing in itself, just as agency without the purpose of an agent is purely mechanical. As with cause and effect, it is only when these polar extremes are conflated and concretely objectified that agency becomes significant, and significance agentive.

Let me return for the moment to the Barok people's analysis, or rather self-analysis, of the world experience in their mortuary feasting complex. In the line-for-point and point-for-line chiasmus of *kolume/gala,* anything that may count for "world" in one's experiencing of it, all shape, form, substance, and extension, is *kolume,* "containment." Anything that may count for "experiencing" is *gala,* the point of it: the point of the feast is death, and the point of death is the feast. The shape, or form, or substance of that experience is life, but the *way* in which it is experienced is by perpetually *dying out of it,* so that personal death, observed socially in that way, is simply the consummation of the dying-out process that we have learned to call "perception," or "the experiencing of things."

It follows from this that the so-called analysis is not analytic but *synthesizing,* like substituting a fusion for a fission reaction, and its subject not passive but active. Cosmologizing the person by personalizing the world, as though childbirth and interral, feasting and burial—the body of consumption and the consumption of the body—were part of the same elemental movement. Dying out of the circumstances in which we conceive them in order to live; death staged, but only staged, on behalf of the living for the dead.

It might be clear enough that the extensional basis of *kolume,* "world" shaped on the last of its own quietus, and the antiextensional "point" of its experiencing, lasting out, so to speak, the shaping of it, have no real differences from one another, that extension and non-extension depend absolutely upon one another for their comprehension. And thus for any sort of comprehension, under any circumstances whatever; the single shape of metaphor multiplied by all the different applications to different subject matters, and divided by the boundaries that define them. The death feast exhibits all things to all people, and all human potential in all things. Death as consummation is not necessarily simpler, or more complicated, than life itself. Would the non-extensional essence of life's experiencing, that has been with all of us all along and from our very births, realize itself in a nonlife of its own with no afterward? The shape and semblance of extension cuts the same figure in the unextended that nonextension cuts within the sensible shapes and meanings of things. The machine of language is the language of the machine!

It is also *your* life and *your* world that the Barok are talking about, or perhaps not talking, since exotic demonstration makes all the difference in the world to them. On their perspective (big surprise!) they are the absolute center of the world (like the town Namatanai, which translates into Barok as *La Marana,* "The Very Epicenter"), though anthropologists have met with this form of self-acknowledgment among so many peoples that it must really be true for all of them, New York City included. One consequence of that truth is that anthropology has got to be the most absolutely *de-centered* form of knowledge there has ever been. One Sunday in 1983, with nothing else to do, I walked the deserted main street of Namatanai. The sky was overcast and it was hot; the tide was out and there were herons on the mudflats, the copra market was down and the stores either closed or boarded up, and from one of the upper-story windows came wafting the strains of Pachelbel's Canon.

Death shares life's contagion with itself, reproducing endlessly as though the very punctuation of its nonextension were actually a line of music. Every time a mirror looks into a mirror, even at an angle, infinity closes upon itself once again, makes an imaginary "here" of all the possible "theres," and an illusory scale model of time's passage. What would a device that made an active use of this principle actually *do* to our world of convenient rationalizations; what kind of cosmos would it leave us to describe in physical laws, what kind of people would have to describe it that way, and why do I call it a *cakra*?

More to the point, why is it just like a holographic worldview? Just as German is not a language but a hereditary style of making the sentence self-sufficient, so the möbius strip is not a paradox except for a very plain sort of geometry. It is the *surface* of a "hollow," or nonextensional *plane,* and likewise the so-called Klein bottle is the surface of a three-dimensional figure closed upon itself in two, rather than one, of its dimensions. And then, "dimension" itself being the difference between anything so conceived and the extension of the remaining ones, the third or consummate simplification of the series is the figure with no surface at all, encompassing the ambit of dimensional difference itself in its nonextensional reality. Closing off all the avenues to infinity but one, like the archetypal German sentence, like a single death or two mirrors fixed in each other's gaze, or as the wheel does in a single motion.

Why should commonplace experience admit of only *three* dimensional differences from one another, instead of four (Time? Time is three-dimensional too, or where have we *been* all our lives?), or any number that would satisfy the designs of ambitious mathematicians? Why indeed not have as many possible ones as you can connect with your thought, and so justify, if not for commonplace experience itself— our conventional, hypnotic obsession with the wheel, or the wheel times the wheel, as the pragmatic archetype of what we call "energy"?

To make a thing of time (as we do in measuring or reckoning "it") is to use the event of talking or thinking about it as a model for what "happening" itself might be, elicit the duality necessary for its perspective. So the scale modeling of temporal duration as *event* coincides nicely with the kind of backtracking we do to turn feeling or sensation into "emotion," copying ourselves, Hamlet-wise, on ourselves. More than that, it matches exactly with the mathematical analysis of artificial depth, the artist's technique of making dimension real, producing an illusory perspective as the scale model of distance, or extension into a painting.

There is no "perceptual" experiencing of the world, or the self, apart from a scale modeling of this sort. Point-for-line and line-for-point, we become our own projective geometers when we perceive depth in a photograph or in the world around us, imagine ourselves to be the creatures of our emotional self-copying, or understand time itself as the happening of the model we have made for it. Call the point, or non-extension of its figure, *gala,* as the Barok do, and call its lines, or containing parameters, *kolume,* and you will have the secret of what their *Kaba* displays: the lethal shape of the fetus as child-in-the-womb and corpse-in-the-ground at the same time. Call the engenderment, the twinning outward of the human body, one of the twins, and the twinning inward of laterality to form that body the other, and you will have the contingency for our antitwinning, the human infrastructure of the mirror-wheel.

But that is *all* you will have, not the telling of the joke, original or not, but only its scale model in the joke of its telling. Most or all of what we know about the world is not phenomenal, and only barely a function of the languages or pictorial fantasies through which we pretend to know it. We know the pragmatic afterlife of happening upon the dying out of our perception, how we happen to perceive the action of perceiving in perceiving it after the fact. The whole specter of what we consider to be the originality of language takes root in this process and leaves the word behind as a token of happening's happening to itself. When the movie's projected imaging of a wheel's movement catches its progression in successively previous stages of where it should be at, one sees the counterpart version of what motion would have to mean, a picture of the antecedence necessary to confirm the sense of it.

It is always the part of scientific modeling that is nondeliberate, borrowed unquestioningly from the conventional cognition of things, that is identified as "empirical" and accepted as *data*. Raw sensory input has almost nothing to do with it; what we observe and record are only cultural values—we catch "cognition" itself in the cognitive net, the modeling of our modeling procedures. If it follows incontrovertibly from these facts about fact that such things as number, quality, and quantity get to be direct evidence for their own positing, a special instance would be warranted to show exactly how and why this is the case, make the exotic demonstration of "scientific method" to itself. The self-test is implicit, an "implicate structure," in the fractal mathematics of Benoit Mandelbrot, equations that turn ordinary numerical operations into reflexive inversions of unity, make *ratios* of the models of "order" that prediction and its calculation depend upon, and swear in figure-ground reversal as a witness for the prosecution of scientific methodology. For the "facts" of the so-called chaos theory (sometimes seen as evidence for "fractional dimensions") are not direct, but *inverse* functions or expressions (e.g., "predictions") of theory. They are fact *divided by* theory (which is in the *denominator*), and thus by the role that human thought and its modeling plays in the understanding of things—the true image of a false relation, like the wheel's movie of itself.

Just as the origin of language would not be "language" itself, but something said or done in it long after the advent of its "signs," so the biological conception of a person would not come to life until conceived, that is, conceptualized, in the person. Carry the truth of this forward into natural science, and its modeling of events, and even the events of its own modeling, would still be uncertain; carry it forward into anthropology, the human uncertainty about the human, and the time factor might have to be put in the denominator. Scientific *agency* interrogates its own design on the measure of it, and the necessary simultaneity of cause and effect requires an arbitrary division, an intercession in the flow of things, to be agentive at all. Something akin to the pragmatic of automation, our industrial metaphor for agency, times itself historically backward to its first approximation in the escapement mechanism, and simultaneously forward through the ages of scientific discoveries, determines a ratio with itself rather than a rate. Like classical music, which does the work of language backward, teaching itself to the ideas and feelings that words would have to state directly, it *synchronizes* the paradigms of what we like to call a civilization, eliciting what is basically disinformation about temporal duration.

The origin of chess would not be a board game, but a move made on the board long after the sovereignty of its rules was established. Simultaneously with the "development" of automation's process, its evolutionary false consciousness, classical music made a movement of time, grew in a dimension perpendicular to its own historicity. Music, and particularly the severely intentional form of it that we call "classical," is no more purely "aesthetic" or an "art form" than technology and its natural science extensions are utilitarian and strictly task-oriented. And if each defines an otherwise incoherent and unarticulable efficacy of the other (Does meaning have rules? Do rules have meaning?), the more precisely because it could neither express its usage nor use its expression, the two bracket a juncture of opportunity that is not imaginary, and so has no easy cognitive access. The ratio of mind's body to body's mind is too much inside of feeling to be felt, too physical to be mental and too mental to be physical.

A significant work of music is a general-case template for *any* conceptual or emotional issue, but even the most trivial work in physics defines a specificity that music could never match. But it is nothing short of amazing how well their common tradition, that knows the single shape of metaphor in all things so comprehensively in so few of them, keeps the secret of its disciplines in the discipline of their secrets. Music is the dark science of motion, experimenters dressed in black who test the mettle of its past, its inventors, loudly and passionately in large, festive public halls. Physics is the art of stillness, performers dressed in white who compose the inhuman secrets of its future diffidently in small, secluded rooms and bubble chambers. A whole world of cultural values depends professionally on the ambiguity of this knowledge, and on keeping the silent and loud aspects of it—the deadly certain physicist and the certainly dead composer—separate and distinct.

Pragmatically, then, the music that is "classical," confused with the already-achieved character of "art," and the physics that defines the categorization of "science" that would define it are *polarized*. They acknowledge each other's facts and motivations edgewise, as energy is conceptualized edgewise to the work it performs, eclipsed by the very metaphors that define it, and by the engines and working parts that make those metaphors tractable. We pretend the axis, or middle part— the agentive efficacy—of energy in just the same way that the trope or meaningfulness of metaphor is pretended through the words that elicit it.

A strictly pragmatic knowledge of things is useless when it comes to definitions, like the metaphor that would tell us what metaphor is. That the symphony is itself a cosmos (Mahler's insight) and the cosmos musical (Kepler's fantasy) would take more trouble to articulate than to experience. Musicology is dumbfounded when it comes to Johann Christian Bach, prefers the mathematics of his father or the romantic ecstasies of his protégé Mozart. If the relativity of coordinate systems and the wave-and-particle indeterminacy posed such a challenge for physicists, why not reconsider the bogus profiling of energy in these and all other physical considerations? The cause-effect sequencing of its transformations from one "kind" to another, which is neither causal in itself, or very effective.

If we cannot know what energy might be except through the agencies of other energies, or know what a metaphor might say except through other metaphors, we can certainly fake the knowledge, acknowledge the underdetermination of perception as a disingenuous mimicry, a Hamlet-virus of itself. Do we know the *connections* that might be made between the thought and the thing, or among thoughts or things themselves, so well that we miss what thoughts or things themselves might be? Or is it, as the language determinists might argue, that we know the thoughts and things *too* well by marking them, and so only guess at the connections? If each of these alternatives is known only edgewise, through the agency of the other, why then we have made a positive wheel of underdetermination, of the negative capability necessary to know the wheel for certain.

Or the underdetermination of a subject, be it that of language in metaphor, perception in the perceiver, music in its performance, or energy in the physical world, that is necessarily a part of the process it is describing. Even natural evolution, the origins and transformations of life-forms, is a specifically *human* achievement in this respect, and succumbs to its own historical process as the evolution of what evolution is supposed to be. And as the technological device or practical procedure, food production, the processing of work or sensory data, the manufacture of information, or the fantasy of automation, takes over our very thinking about it with such a nice precision, we have no models of anything at all that are not specimens of the very same sort of underdetermination, modelings of the thought processes necessary to their discovery. It would take a very human sort of cleverness to discover the secrets of stellar evolution and galactic structure, the mysteries of dimensionality, number, subatomic particles, or the carbon molecule, for no divinity or superbeing in its right mind would want to make the kinds of mistakes we have to make in getting to them. Or even conceiving of them, for without those mistakes, and without the mistake of thinking itself, there could be no conceivable order whatsoever in the cosmos.

Of all the devices to which human beings have taught themselves, saving perhaps language, the wheel is the most nearly unresolved. It keeps moving in the same trajectory, and carries its automation along with it. And of all of those music, the phonology of a humor that does the work of language backward, is the most nearly resolved. Music is no mistake, but has an originality opposite to that of the joke.

Holography "understands" better than visualization could comprehend itself, makes a better mistake about perception than perception could make of it. The underdetermination of the senses is not resolved through the ways in which the various sensory faculties conflate with or differ from one another, any more than the fact of extension is an artifact of the ways the "dimensions" make the differences that tell themselves apart. Approaching the matter of comprehension "psychologically" in that way is like trying to tell the difference between pain and pleasure in sex, or in love, when what really matters is what they share in common. It is an emotional mistake.

One is apt to make the same mistake about language, in other words, that "language" makes in naming itself that way, modeling reason upon the rationalization of its own procedures. Existence is not a law of nature, but a copyright on the semblance of things, the way they extend themselves in space and in time. Then the world of unextended reality, *res non-extensis,* is not an infraction of that copyright, but a place-value notation for all the claims made on its behalf. It is our patent on reality, more really real than any shape we could contrive for the true semblance of things, or any surprise that consciousness might discover in sneaking up on itself.

Or at least comprehensive enough to tell the difference between natural law and cultural copyright, the implicitly "given" and natural and the explicitly "taken" or cultural known edgewise from one another, like the tree that cuts the ground as the ground cuts the tree in Barok folklore. Then the best possible mistake one could make about the arbitrage of singular motifs used to focus the laterality of engenderment and the engenderment of laterality in New Guinea would be to name them for how they index themselves, as holographic world perspectives. For otherwise the Barok Zeno-biology of *gala* and *kolume,* the Iqwaye tallying of things as the reproduction of people (Mimica), the eternal *adime,* or coming together of extension's forking of its world-space (Sørum, Bedamini) would have to be advanced as the innovative growing edge of a new species of technology, one that civilization had conveniently missed in its shrewdly automated domestication of the wheel. A worldview, especially when understood as a core symbolization particular to some group of people, is not so much a diagnosis as it is a contagion, in that the investigator identifies himself in identifying it, becomes part of a process he is describing for others. And an invention is not property until patented.

So if "holographic worldview in New Guinea," the single shaping of some particular metaphor in all things, would still be a mistake, and its vehicle, the machine that might be made of it, still untested and unproven, attributing its design to the social necessities and economic requirements of a particular population would be a worse one. Holography is not adjective, but substantive, to borrow a distinction from Louis Dumont; it is not experienced by peoples or in cultures, it experiences them.

And it does so comprehensively, with the same demand for illogical consistency—every point in its disclosure threatening a separate line of discourse, a deconstruction of the whole—that would have to be evidenced in a book about it. Like the religion that is written in quicksilver (which of them is not?), undeniable as the word of God because unbelievable as the work of man. The unextended is the perfect subject matter for unbelief, the hollow-graphic matrix or ostensible mother right of its own lines of descent. One could not establish the profile of its genealogy, prove its antiquity in India or the archipelagoes stretching to the eastward because it was there before tectonic plates were invented, and probably invented them as well. As the true shape of our mother earth, the real uncertainty as to whether it is a heavenly body, a planet in its own sky, or the geo-metric baseline for measuring the other ones. The holes in the Net of Indra are jewels that reflect one another so perfectly that *they* cannot tell whether they are one or many. As if to establish a copyright for plurality, the Indians exchange them for real gemstones, as the Melanesians do for pigs.

What grammarians might call its *vehicle,* the rhetorical "device" or basic conceit of the single shape of metaphor in all things, would be a wheel that "caused" its own effectiveness, reflected its own motion so perfectly that it would roll through the unextended as though it were not really there—which, of course, it never is, being always *here* instead. It is the real fiction of a false science rather than a false heuristic of a real one, a more objective mistake about subjectivity than subjectivity could make about it. The cat that spent the better part of its nine lives pretending "no cat" to its prey, and so to itself, surprising its own shadow into consciousness, would come to know the opposite of that technique, elicit a full, physical presence out of nowhere, reappearing again and again as "some cat" in the afterlife it had presently died out of. Like the dreamed image that is more real than the dream that supports it, and like my cat Smokey.

So it was quite possibly the ancient Egyptians who first domesticated the cat, or at least that particular variety, having discovered the felicitous tractability of "some cat" through the mirror-secret of its reproduction. Would they have deliberately *mummified* the creatures to prevent their overpopulation, as an anthropologist might attribute holographic worldview to the subjects of its disclosure to keep from becoming one of *their* subjects, and going native in his own head? Did not those same Egyptians do the same thing, very deliberately, to their world and to themselves, living life to the fullest for the desperate chance of really, really dying, their world along with them, for once and for all? "No cat" delivers "some cat," prevents cat from dying out; "no Egyptian" prevents time.

That the pretense of extension, the dimensional world, is an iconic dummy and quasi-voluntary, that it is a projection—a shadow, an echo, a movie of itself—is not necessarily a philosophical or spiritual discovery. That it can fake emotion or the "inner" subjective person better than language can is not necessarily profound. But if that pretense is edged in the physical world, like the retractable claws of the feline, then perhaps we have gotten the Egyptians, and the "truth" of their concept of *ma'at,* all wrong. If the hard edge, the objectivity of that conception were simply understood as *effectiveness,* or the scale of effectiveness in all things human, then there would always be "some Egyptians" around. Somewhere, or perhaps nowhere, the difference would not matter, and more really real than anyone could possibly have imagined.

That is what the tomb means, and the mummy, the pyramid, objective inscription, the soul of the deceased and the sarcophagus, all the edges and surfaces of the superficial world and the things that matter in it. If the definitive scale of *ma'at* in all things were struck and held, consummated funereally at the flashpoint of death, all of eternity and the shape of extension itself would resonate to its chord, and infinity lose its magnitude. "Higher is the *ka* of Amenemhet than the height of Orion, and it is one with the underworld" is the inscription on the capstone of a pyramid.

Eternity or infinity, the cosmic termini of extension, would serve well enough as a mask for the ways in which it is projected, the way it would have to appear—even the body's natural habit of it—to the eye of the unextended. That extensional edge and surface cuts the same shape in the unextended that *res non-extensis,* its nonnegotiable alter ego, cuts out of it, would be the secret knowledge, the sublime purpose of what we like to call ancient Egyptian spirituality of religion. Its people called themselves "ancient" as well, imitated the long duration of time and the stern outlines of objects, actions, and attitudes that resist it, *made them seem to matter to them* in the most deliberate ways possible. Yet if antitemporality had a prime meridian, it would run straight down the Nile. Come tomb robber or archaeologist, come wind or erosion, they were all safe, and coming generations could mine their gold, set up their trophies again and again without the slightest intuition of their purpose.

They called themselves "The Two Lands," and made their whole polity of divisions. Egypt bisected itself indefinitely, like perception's languaging of itself, to find its unity in losing it, get the mirror view of eternity down pat, the single perspective of life in the unextended. At a certain point in the erasure of these dichotomies there was no difference between pharaoh and divinity and hence, though divinity had enough distinctions of its own, between life and death.

The design was a piece of its own ratio to itself, so no wonder they hated Akhenaten so much, as though he had gotten everything backward, and were trying to invent the symbol once again. For then the all-embracing light and warmth of the aten, its radiant arms tangent to everything, would be another New Age religion. One single icon, the most prodigal of all, is one icon too many.

Infinity is so much like a bat, depending on limits to find its way in the world, that it has the same animation, the same indirect affirmation of itself, as the being in the mirror or the cat's pragmatic afterlife. There is an awareness and a physical presence, but the matter of which of them belongs to you and which to the mirror-being, the cat, or the animal "infinity" is not a riddle but the point that the riddle makes: "What is defined by limits, and necessary to their definition, but has no limitations of its own?"

As the sides of the body's laterality, or those of the world itself interpolated through them, are "sides" only in relation to one another, and as the center of the wheel has no motion, the only limitation that unextended reality could know is that "limit" takes form outside of its compass. The unextended could no more exist apart from the contrast it forms with the extensional means of eliciting it than the dead could exist independently of the living. So the argument of this book is an argument with itself, and to "prove" cakra as the gearwheel of infinity— the engagement of a limit that bears no proof of itself—one would have to borrow the substance of Gödel's syllogism: "Using logic, this hypothesis cannot be proven to be true." Or, of course, be proven to be false, either. It would only prove the coincidence that runs our world.

The unextended could not exist as an infinitesimal geometric point without permeating the whole of extensional reality in that way, as the prime motivation for the third-order simplification of the wheel. Every metaphor—as the identity of marking or naming understood crosswise from itself—every virtue of the human hologram or instance of its pragmatic afterlife, every example of process, operation, or continuity is the elemental trace of a *negative extensional field*—a perfect scale model of all the mistakes made in trying to discover what that field might be.

Nonextension could not wrap around itself, so extension takes its place, and the world of empirical reality and commonplace experience is *magnetized* thereby.

Incest is not the immoral but the immortal shape of the species; it is the remainder or hinder part, "mother right" if you prefer, of the body's passion for the infinite. As well try to comprehend it socially as to take into hand what the species might have been like before the species of the name came into its own. Too much a part of itself to know, or be able to know, the holography of the "other." What might it be like to live "magnetically" instead of socially, through the simplicity of pure attraction and repulsion, procreate the single-celled lineage of oneself upon others who are the same, in a world transfixed like an insect in its own electronic amber? Our "globalization," like much of our anthropology, is an automated model of that world.

It is an artificial mirroring of its wheel, a reflection that looks so much like speed and travel in getting the better of space-time, navigates so well in trading motion for sensing and seeing, that extension's opposite gets the better of *it*. What we have taught ourselves to recognize as "cultures" are accidents of the isolation and relative distancing of human lifestyles, distinctive and distributive foci in discovering the whole-and-part fantasy of that world. To the degree that its distancing is artificially overcome, in fact or in theory, the result is neither a better comparative or general comprehension of what culture itself may be, nor a general amity among its peoples. It is the artificial solution of an artificial problem, a precultural and possibly an anticultural condition: one world *less* than the many we began with.

So there is less a question, all good intentions notwithstanding, of whether something called the "Environment" will survive its peopling, than of whether those peoples will survive their own environing. The anthropologists who go far away to get their insights, get a long distance on themselves, take a long time getting over them, and in a way that those who stay at home to figure themselves out may never understand. Those who busy themselves with problems of origin—the originality of the species in its evolution, the beginnings of the cosmos, the legend of the legend in its legend, are not looking for anything of the sort, and would disbelieve it if they found it. They want to improve origin for its own sake, make it even more original, want the better move on the chessboard, the one that puts the game itself in check.

Accounts of origin, even in science, are never very original in themselves, for they can only reach their beginning in the form of a conclusion. Collapsing space once again in a very speculative fashion, as though a mirror were busy watching itself with no other image to borrow, in a time not really worth the telling. And because opposites attract in a world-space that is bipolar, or automagnetic, one could say the very same thing about accounts of the ultimate end of things, Armageddon or Ragnarok, and not be saying much that is original. Like the obviate mirror, the one that reflects so perfectly whatever appears in front of it that it offers no perspective of its own, and might as well not be there. To talk in riddles and make the riddles talk is the very essence of negative capability, and therefore the negative capability of essence, its nonextensional parameter. The beginning and end of the story— any story—is underdetermined by its content. We live on the obviate planet.

So I should begin my conclusion with no accounts whatsoever of where or how things began, or when they will end up. No hope for me in the world of astronomy; if I should take it up, it would take me down for sure, astronomers being very certain about gravity. It is their best mistake, as holography's obviation of system and systematicity is mine, and perhaps ours. Why should life have evolved, and evolution come to life, in the only double-planet system known, and sun and moon subtend the same angular diameters in our sky, but for the sake of the rare eclipse? The one-of-two and the two-of-one are the *opposite* of chance or coincidence, the form of a-systemic efficacy that happens to coincide with them. And thus coincides so as to happen as well.

Chance is real only in the fact that it always chooses to *mean*, like the true believer in words and numbers, your statistically average averager of things, and never to *be*. It is the most absolutely determinate thing in the world, save that the world *may* not be determinate in that way. So the chance of this particular topic coming up at this point in my discussion is not random, or single, but is married to the possibility that an alternative one might have been chosen. *That means that the reflexivity between the apparent randomness of "event" or "happening" and the choice that is made in noticing it or expecting it runs like a crack through the mirror of mind and all it might disclose.* The natural "event" is a cultural choice, but the cultural model or system is a happening unto itself. The discovery (I would say "invention") of incest and the need for technology would seem to be random aspects of the human condition but for the human hologram, the choice of making an imaginal, retroflexive juncture of our organic heritage—gender's outward twinning and laterality's inward counterpart.

That choice, in the full range of its implications, was the *invention* of chance, which could not have existed beforehand for want of a way to imagine it, and thus to perceive, and to realize, its happening. Dice, to invert Einstein's famous quip, could not play God with the universe. Thus what seem to be accidental features of the astronomy we have imagined for ourselves—that we happen to live in a double-planet system, that its bodies are placed and sized to form the eclipse—would be more significant as the shapers of our expectations than of our existence. And our physics, like our psychology or anthropology, be the science of our obsessions, and we ourselves play "universe" with our dice.

So, for all of its inherent discrepancies, the "cultural" line of argument makes a better mistake about its physical circumstances than the "physical" one could make about it. What Victor Turner called "liminality"—the in-betweenness of the in-between—and defined as the secret shape of human self-reflection (cultural invention), is the best-kept secret of all, so very liminal to its formal representation that it cuts no figure in the extensional world that the unextended does not cut in it. It is always both "there" and "not there" at the same time.

Physics maps only the "distance" factor on the chart of projective geometry, forgets that its canvas is also *flat*. The only possible difference between space and time would be a temporal one, and the only possible similarity would be spatial: the temporal cuts the spatial as the spatial subsumes it. It takes *time* to recognize, deliberate upon, or calculate dimensionality, for the dimensions are only conceivable as their respective differences from one another, and the universe does not have that kind of time. A line in space is a point in time, but time only points in one direction, indexes itself so acutely that the only evidence we could collect for continuity ("continuum") collects the observer instead, through the perspective that is formed in that way. Its relativity is not a model but a model of a model (the Barok "reciprocity of perspectives"), the root paradigm of the holographic mistake.

Physical and cultural relativity eclipse one another in the event of their discoveries and in the discovery of "event," appear in the chance of circumstances to have totally unrelated concepts, like music and physics, because the eclipse is a total one. A comprehensive understanding of technology would imply a coherently instrumental technology of understanding; seeing *past* the past is better than the future, more prescient even than the *now*. A perfect musical precocity resonates the chance of its composition in the composition of its chances, the cakra of Johann

Christian Bach in the shape of energy itself. The perfect melody could not be dreamed, it must be made.

At the moment of totality in a solar eclipse, the sun's corona appears, the light you never saw for too much light, and, a moment later, flashes everywhere at once like a hummingbird, nesting the miniature of its imagery in all the cracks and crevices of the world. The sun reflects the sun without a mirror, makes a hollow-graphic worldview, a bird's-eye universe, of its light. The perfect essence of the wheel is the eclipse of dimensionality itself.

Machines (or languages, or imageries) made more simply than they should be have the added advantage that they simplify the task of using them. So the difficulties, uncertainties, inaccuracies, and needless repetitions in this work are a necessary part of its lesson and its subject; one cannot simplify their complexity without compromising their simplicity.

The most convincing evidence for the existence of a black hole is actually *white*, "the most potent source of energy in the known universe." The singularity itself must be inferred from what is really the opposite sort of evidence, much as we might infer an "inner person" from the evidence of our thoughts and our feelings: the most depressing source of phenomenological disinformation in the human microcosm. All of the light that we have shed on the black hole singularity actually comes *out of* it.

So I would ask you to imagine "thick light" instead, a kind of energy that does not exist, as far as we can tell, anywhere in the known cosmos. Thick light accumulates, by definition and nothing else, on the inside of the imaginal black hole, and is *milked* out by the speculations as to what it might be like. So if this knowledge, or any other, poses a problem for you, do not by any means try to shed ordinary light on it. Simply *pour* thick light on it, and you will not have it as a problem anymore. The problem, instead, will have you.

Glossary of Unfamiliar Concepts

agencies, in explanation: The real or suppositional entities that explanation isolates to do its work, and that are held, if only for heuristic purposes, to be responsible for action.

animal powers: The craft by which a nonhuman species has underdetermined its own evolution; an exotic demonstration of its human knowledge by nonhuman means, often self-paradoxical, like the Sioux observation that moon is Rabbit's reflection in his own eye.

automation: The pragmatic demonstration that a device or process "works by itself"; a contemporary neurosis of the wheel principle.

Bach, Johann Christian: Forget about heaven; that was his dad's province, and he flourished in London. Musical profundity is at best a romantic illusion; the muse of the *youngest* Bach uses music's intimation of motion to accelerate the sense of what joy could have been like had the listener ever been up to it.

brain: We are the species that *brains* itself.

cakra: If there is no "energy" inside of a moving wheel, only a better form of nothing than one could easily imagine or usefully displace, there is no energy either within the living person trying to understand how that nothing may work. The reciprocity of these two negations.

Castaneda, Carlos (Arana):   Whatever their ultimate sources, and however suspect they might be, the twelve books of Castaneda present the only coherent example of a comprehensive pragmatic technique in the extant literature. Otherwise, and with the present work as a possible exception, pragmatics plays an incidental role, as the "hypothetical" fiction necessary to fact.

chance, probability: The art of being about half right, even when one is dead wrong. If we assume that "happening" is always right square on the mark (not necessarily true, but helpful in reckoning chance), then probability measures only the degree of one's ignorance.

chronotope: Mikhail Bakhtin's *physical* (as in "physics") model for the ultimate significance of a literary work; the "thickening" of time that makes a kind of organism of the reader's life experience in coming to terms with such a work.

consciousness: The trick of *surprising* oneself into being; psychological or epistemological mystification is the intellectual way of turning the trick, a sort of academical "boo!" Death is the trick of surprising oneself back *out* of existence, and therefore superconscious.

departures, history as a sequence of: The only way its chronicles could possibly make sense would be as a sequence of departures from what had been, culminating in the final departure from our own reality in the present that would seem to take us back to it.

dimension: **Q:** "How many dimensions does it take to screw in a lightbulb?" **A:** "Three, possibly four, depending on how screwed up you really are, but with a simple twist of the wrist you can get them all in a single motion. And shed some light on the matter."

echo-subject: The objectivity through which *any* form of belief or doubt must be articulated in order to be there at all. Unarticulated thoughts are called "feelings," but by the time we know enough about a feeling to name it, emotion has turned itself around and is now trading in words.

emotion: We have no emotions that are not part of the process of trying to figure out what they themselves might be, so that any conclusiveness about how one might feel is part of a comparative process, like the study of cultures.

exotic demonstration: The need to demonstrate exotically takes its cue from the established fact that no one, not even the anthropologist, could know what anthropology is all about, or what its favorite excuse, "culture," really means.

explanation: After Sir Isaac Newton had sold the world on gravity, or Darwin on natural selection, nobody cared if these ideas explained the facts because they explained themselves so well, and the facts were only sworn in as witnesses.

gender, own: Complete sexual self-possession; what happens when the two "other genders," the female inspiration of manhood and the male inspiration of womanhood, divide one another.

Hamlet, Shakespeare's play of: A virtual archetype of what happens when *any* actor in any situation takes a conscious decision to act out the self, "act oneself mad." The implications are awesome, immeasurable, and probably divine, to be compared with the game of chess or the joke of humor on all occasions.

holographic modeling: A type of representation that uses significant aspects of that which is modeled or represented to reproject the artifice of modeling or representation itself, give a picture of how we "picture facts to ourselves." Hence kinship is not so much based on the proscription of incest as upon its reprojection through legitimate means, and metaphor is language's way of understanding what we mean by it.

holography: The exact equivalence, or comprehensive identity, of part and whole in any human contingency, definitive of the world of subjective extensions, the imaginary spaces of human reason and explanation. "A perfect scale model of all the mistakes to be made in trying to figure it out."

Homo erectus: You know those little silvery creatures, possibly telepathic, that are supposed to run the UFOs? Well, these guys probably roasted them over open fires after having taken them down with their flanged "hand ax" projectiles.

joke, the most original of all: The joke of "the beginning," or the one that came first: **Q:** "Where would those early hominids get the *background* to appreciate the point of its humor?" **A:** "That is what's so *funny* about it." We have been getting the point by not getting it ever since.

language, the fact of: The *fact* of language is not a discovery made by human beings evolving, but one made *about* them, a kind of fossil or sedimentation that is deposited when the *need to remember language as one speaks it* takes over from what one has to say.

language, functions and "signification" of: The attempt to make a better *echo* of human character or presence, of the deep-throat potential of our common, human lowered larynx, as though it were a communication. *Homo erectus* would have *killed* you for less.

language, limitations of: Language is limited by the capability of its resources to make an exotic demonstration of its own agency; we use knowledge to make our metaphors and then use metaphors to make up our knowledge.

mirror-wheel: An imaginal device based on the ultimate simplification of the wheel principle, and concocted by the author as a thought experiment to throw the agencies of automation into relief. If the alleged UFO aliens really had one of these, they wouldn't have to run around the universe showing off.

models, for purposes of understanding: To say that a *miniature* of any kind—map, artistic design, scientific model of a process or structure— replicates the reality it is supposed to represent is to omit the fact that reality has likewise been reduced, and the representation is controlled by its own shadow.

mother right, Das Mutterrecht: The matrix of kin relations as a self-operative pragmatic; how your mother *writes* you, capture by the chess queen in the net of your own DNA. The original anthropological sense of this term as obviated by the more basic fact of containment, so that "matrilineal kinship" is less an originary precedent than a complete *synthesis* of what it means, one that cuts to the quick of "relationship" itself.

negative capability: John Keats's attribution of negative capability—"that is, when a man is capable of being in uncertainties, mysteries, doubts, without any irritable reaching after fact and reason"—to William Shakespeare attributed Keats as well, by that very insight. Something that cats have in abundance, and that dogs would positively kill for.

obviation: The art or technique of using pragmatic error to isolate and define itself as efficient causality, throwing "cultural" assumptions and motivations into high relief.

"pathetic" ethnicity: The dehumanized artifact of postmodern and often feminist self-reflection; culture as the *victim* of its own phenomenological description, its own "interpretation" of itself.

postmodernism: The real killer in death is rigor mortis, the frozen immobility of the body that all too quickly convinces itself it has lost the ability to act, so that its chemical constituency begins a process of autodissection. Death is the body's postmodernism.

pragmatic: The experiential procedure by which objects, which may be words, turn into subjects as one acknowledges the mistakes necessary to incorporate them into one's world.

pragmatic afterlife: "Memory"; the effective persistence of an objective event or mechanical action as "energy" long after its occurrence, as in the re-verberation of language or the music of chance.

psychological symptoms: The classic neuroses, like hysteria and the obsessive-compulsive disorders, occur when the mistakes necessary in the pragmatic incorporation of the subject are projected freely and take on a life of their own. Like teaching *oneself* to cause and effect instead of incorporating them within one's responses.

space: The only kind of time that is still left around, and that really *matters.*

subject: The sub-jected or underdetermined counterpart of agency, hence also the "patient," pathetic, or empathetic phase of the mortal condition, much celebrated in postmodern lore and literature.

subject, active: The point of action, the potential, known to Aristotle, of inverting the patient or pathetic character of the subject; human character.

subject, anthropology of: The human knowledge of what the human condition may be or may be all about, as though a definitive synthesis were possible. The supposition of such a synthesis, as, for instance, this work.

technology, illusional: A perceptual scam, usually, in our case, the use of an illuminated screen in one form or another to simulate the presence of real persons, objects, or events.

technology, ultimate: The ultimate technology would create the illusions of its "working" so perfectly that it could do anything, fabricate the illusion of *res non-extensis,* the unextended. Technology does indeed progress, but it progresses toward its own unmasking.

"working," operation, how things work: The most *useful* (and therefore self-defining) pragmatic error, committed by the insertion of imaginary intervals between causes and effects to the extent that they take on a life of their own, as, for instance, sounds are "segmented" and isolated to foster and sustain the illusion of language.

world-in-the-person/person-in-the-world: The attempt, thus far only conceptual, at a total comprehension of reality, and the coordinate emergence of the human as a completed form of being.

Notes

Chapter 1

1. Victor Zuckerkandl, *Man the Musician,* trans. N. Guterman, Bollingen Series, XLIV-2 (Princeton, N.J.: Princeton University Press, 1973), 65–66.

2. Martin Heidegger, "Metaphysics As History of Being," in *The End of Philosophy,* ed. and trans. Joan Stambaugh (New York: Harper and Row, 1973), 14–15.

3. Friedrich Nietzsche, aphorism no. 224 in *Beyond Good and Evil,* trans. and with an introduction by Marianne Cowan (Chicago: Henry Regnery, 1955), 149.

4. Ibid., 150.

Chapter 2

1. I thank Joel Robbins.

2. Victor W. Turner, *Revelation and Divination in Ndembu Ritual* (Ithaca, N.Y.: Cornell University Press, 1975), 187.

3. I am indebted to Elizabeth Stassinos for this insight.

4. George Lakoff and Mark Johnson, *Metaphors We Live By* (Chicago: University of Chicago Press, 1980).

5. Ludwig Wittgenstein, *Tractatus Logico-Philosophicus,* trans. D. F. Pears and B. F. McGuinness (London: Routledge and Kegan Paul, 1961), 8 (2.1).

6. Ibid., 22 (4.03).

7. Ibid., 63 (6.1231).

Chapter 3

1. Mark Mosko, *Quadripartite Structures: Categories, Relations, and Homologies in Bush Mekeo Culture* (Cambridge: Cambridge University Press, 1985).

2. Dan Jorgensen, "Taro and Arrows: Order, Entropy, and Religion among the Telefolmin" (Ph.D. dissertation, University of British Columbia, 1981). Also F. Barth, *Ritual and Knowledge among the Baktaman of New Guinea* (New Haven, Conn.: Yale University Press, 1975).

3. Roy Wagner, *Asiwinarong: Ethos, Image and Social Power among the Usen Barok of New Ireland* (Princeton, N.J.: Princeton University Press, 1986), 55.

4. I am grateful to Marianne George for the information she brought to the assistance of this analysis, particularly from her interviews with Barok *orong*.

5. Steven M. Albert (personal communication, 1988) reports the perplexity of the Lak people of southern New Ireland at the fact that Barok array *uncooked* pigs atop the *kaba*. This can be understood in terms of the inverse displacement of root and branch: the pigs are "corpses" displayed *above* the ground, but positionally *beneath* the roots of the upended tree, and so dead meat becomes live food.

6. Wagner, *Asiwinarong*, 171.

Chapter 4

1. Jacques Lacan, *Écrits: A Selection*, trans. A. Sheridan (New York: 1977, Norton, 1977), chap. 1.

2. Gregory Bateson, *Mind and Nature: A Necessary Unity* (New York: Bantam, 1980), 92–94.

3. Marcel Mauss, *The Gift*, trans. I. Cunnison (Glencoe, Ill.: Free Press, 1954).

4. Louis Dumont, *Homo Hierarchicus*, trans. M. Sainsbury (Chicago: University of Chicago Press, 1970).

Chapter 5

1. This is depicted as plate 262, together with notes by a missionary, Rev. R. H. Rickard, in Noel Gash and June Whittaker, *A Pictorial History of New Guinea* (Milton, Queensland: Jacaranda Press, 1975), 128.

2. Western jokes were new to the Barok at the time of my fieldwork, and I seemed never to get the point in their telling of them. But I became highly popular in Namatanai for my *tokpisin* version of a very obscene Greek joke.

3. Bruce Josephson (Ph.D. dissertation, University of Virginia, 1992).

4. Clifford Geertz, "Deep Play: Notes on the Balinese Cockfight," in *The Interpretation of Cultures* (New York: Basic Books, 1973), 141. For many writers and reviewers Geertz's work has served as a benchmark of "cuteness" in self-reflective writing, as though he had gone ahead and done the thing that no one else had dared to do, written a thoroughly humorous ethnography of the Balinese, made a permanent bad joke of the Moroccans. Perhaps the pique is understandable on the part of those whose seriousness in policing "scientific" standards has outstripped their imaginative resources.

Chapter 6

1. Warren Shapiro, "Semi-moiety Organization and Mother-in-Law Bestowal in Northeastern Arnhem-Land," *Man* 4 (1969): 629–40.

2. Roy Wagner, "Analogic Kinship: A Daribi Example," *American Ethnologist* 4 (1977): 623–42.

3. Wagner, *Asiwinarong*, 92–98.

4. Marilyn Strathern, *The Gender of the Gift* (Berkeley and Los Angeles: University of California Press, 1988), 240–46.

5. This citation is developed from my notes on an oral presentation by Peter Lovell at the annual meetings of the Association of Social Anthropologists in Oceania, New Harmony, Indiana, 1983.

6. Claude Lévi-Strauss, *Structural Anthropology*, trans. C. Jacobson and B. G. Schoepf (New York: Basic Books, 1963), 37–51.

7. Strathern, *The Gender of the Gift*, 131ff.

8. Jadran Mimica, *Intimations of Infinity: The Cultural Meanings of the Iqwaye Counting System and Number* (Oxford: Berg, 1988).

Chapter 7

1. Donald B. Redford, *Akhenaten: The Heretic King* (Princeton, N.J.: Princeton University Press, 1984), 193.

2. Ibid., 178.

Chapter 8

1. Charles S. Peirce, *Collected Papers*, ed. C. Hartshorne and F. Weiss (Cambridge, Mass.: Harvard University Press, 1932).

2. Marcel Mauss, *The Gift*, trans. I. Cunnison (Glencoe, Ill.: Free Press, 1954), 8–9. See also Marshall Sahlins, "The Spirit of the Gift," in *Stone Age Economics* (Chicago, Aldine, 1972).

3. Stephen A. Tyler, *The Unspeakable* (Madison: University of Wisconsin Press, 1987). The eye-con is diagrammed on page xiii.

4. Sidney Mintz, personal communication, September 1997.

5. Stanley Walens, *Feasting with Cannibals* (Princeton, N.J.: Princeton University Press, 1981), 10.

6. John R. Farella, *The Main Stalk* (Tucson: University of Arizona Press, 1984).

7. Rainer Maria Rilke, *Sämtliche Werke*, vol. 1 (Wiesbaden, Insel Verlag, 1955), 505. The text here translates the German lines "Sein Blick ist vom Vorübergehn der Stäbe/so müd geworden dass er nichts mehr hält" and "Nur manchmal schiebt der Vorhang der Pupille/sich lautlos auf—Dann geht ein Bild hinein / geht durch der Glieder angespannte Stille/und hört im Herzen auf zu sein."

8. Ibid., 753. The lines, from the fourth sonnet of the second part of the "Sonnets to Orpheus," are, in the original, "Sie nährten es mit keinem Korn/nur immer mit der Möglichkeit, es sei."

Chapter 9

1. Joel Robbins, personal communication, 1996.
2. David McKnight, "Men, Women, and Other Animals: Taboo and Purification among the Wik-mungkan," in *The Interpretation of Symbolism*, ed. Roy Willis (New York: Wiley, 1975), 92.
3. Ibid., 91.
4. Ibid.
5. Ibid., 94.
6. Ibid., 95.
7. G. M. Allen, *Bats* (Cambridge, Mass.: Harvard University Press, 1940), 224–29.
8. McKnight, "Men, Women, and Other Animals," 92.
9. Roy Wagner, *Lethal Speech: Daribi Myth as Symbolic Obviation* (Ithaca, N.Y.: Cornell University Press, 1978), 73–75.
10. *Larousse Encyclopedia of Animal Life*, 1967, 495.
11. Allen, *Bats*, 225.
12. Kathleen Barlow and David Lipset, "Transformation of Male and Female in Murik Outrigger Canoes," *American Ethnologist* 24 (1997): 4–36.
13. Barry Holstun Lopez, *Of Wolves and Men* (New York: Scribner's, 1978), 4.
14. Joseph Epes Brown, *Animals of the Soul: Sacred Animals of the Oglala Sioux* (Rockport, Maine: Element, 1992).
15. Ibid., 1.
16. Ibid., 82.
17. Ibid., 47.
18. Ibid., 87.
19. Eva Hunt, *The Transformation of the Hummingbird: Cultural Roots of a Zinacantecan Mythical Form* (Ithaca, N.Y.: Cornell University Press, 1976).

Chapter 10

1. James F. Weiner, *The Lost Drum: The Myth of Sexuality in Papua New Guinea and Beyond* (Madison: University of Wisconsin Press, 1995). See the discussion of Freud's "deferred action" as it relates to Weiner's use of "retroactive implication" (174ff.).

Chapter 11

1. Heinrich Schenker, *Neue Musikalische Theorien und Fantasien* (Vienna, 1906), 35.
2. Zuckerkandl, *Man the Musician*, p. 190f.
3. Billai Laba, "Oral Traditions about Early Trade with Indonesians in Southwest Papua New Guinea," in *Plumes from Paradise*, ed. Pamela Swadling (Queensland: Papua New Guinea National Museum / Robert Brown & Associates, 1996), 301.

4. Steven Feld, "Sound as a Symbolic System: The Kaluli Drum," in *Explorations in Ethnomusicology in Honor of David P. McAlester,* ed. Charlotte Frisbie, Detroit Monographs in Musicology, no. 9 (Detroit: 1986), 87.

5. Steven Feld, "Aesthetics as Iconicity of Style, or 'Lift Up over Sounding,' Getting into the Kaluli Groove," *Yearbook of Traditional Music* (1988), 78.

6. Feld, "Sound as a Symbolic System," 86.

7. Edward L. Schieffelin, *The Sorrow of the Lonely and the Burning of the Dancers* (New York: St. Martin's, 1976), 94–116.

8. The Bachs were like that, always going for the hair. Sebastian Bach, Christian's father, once tried to suffocate a musical adversary with his own wig.

Chapter 12

1. Lucien Dällenbach, *The Mirror in the Text,* trans. J. Whitely and E. Hughes (Chicago: University of Chicago Press, 1989).

2. Mikhail M. Bakhtin, *The Dialogic Imagination,* ed. M. Holquist, trans. C. Emerson and M. Holquist (Austin: University of Texas Press, 1981), 84.

3. See the last six lines of his "Ode on Melancholy" for a superb example.

4. Wagner, *Lethal Speech.*

5. Paul Ricoeur, "Metaphor and the Main Problem of Hermeneutics," *New Literary History* (1974): 106.

Chapter 13

1. Josiah Royce, *The World and the Individual,* 2:139, cited in Jorge Luis Borges, "A New Refutation of Time," in *Labyrinths,* ed. D. A. Yates and J. E. Irby (New York: New Directions, 1964), 224f.

Chapter 14

1. Heinz Gärtner, *John Christian Bach: Mozart's Friend and Mentor,* trans. R. G. Pauly (Portland, Ore.: Amadeus Press, 1994), 257.

2. Ibid., 253.

3. Ibid., 250.

Index

Abel, Karl Friedrich, 218
Adam, omitted, 73
adult embryo, 54–56, *ill.* 55
Akhenaten, Pharaoh, 106–111, 246
Albert, Steven M., 258*n*5
Allen, G. M., 260*n*7
anaphor, 53
animality, 129–131, 138*f.;* and social
    thought, 147, 251
anthropology: alternative options for, 183;
    and automation, 247; needing "no ex-
    ternal enemy," xxi; as positive quotient,
    155; a real, xvii; of the subject, xvii*f.,* 18,
    21, 51, 54; subject of, 221; subjective
    possibilities of, 29; *your,* xiii
Antitwins, the human, 49, 51, 58, 76, 175*f.,*
    211, 234
Aristotle, 201
automation, 176; cosmic, 197*f.,* 201, 204*f.,*
    209, 217, 226, 240, 247, 251, 253; second
    or multiple-wheel power, 195

Bach, Johann Christian, xiv, 11, 158*f.,* 163,
    165, 171*f.,* 180, 197, 217*f.,* 241, 249*f.*
Bach, J. S., 158–160, 163
Bach lineage, 169
Bachofen, J. J., 77
Bakhtin, Mikhail, 178, 198, 252
Barlow, Kathleen, 260*n*12
Barok people, xiii, 22, 27–30, 31–47, 49*f.,*
    53, 61, 67–70; eye-imagery of, 118*f.,*

123*f.,* 179, 186*f.,* 211, 220, 227, 231, 234,
    236–239, 243, 248*f.;* marriage among,
    85–88, 97–100, 114, 117; procreation
    theory of, 73*f.*
Barth, Fredrik, xvii
Bateson, Gregory, 53*f.*
Beethoven, Ludwig van, 110, 159–162,
    168–170
Bella Coola people, 139
Bergson, Henri, 196
Best, Elsdon, 115
Biyenge people, 78
Black Elk, 140
black hole, 15*f.;* and Hamlet, 104*f.,* 177*f.,*
    186, 220, 250
Boas, Franz, 77, 123, 198
Bohm, David, 19, 171
Borges, Jorge Luis, 205
Bossuet, Jacques-Bénigne, xxi
brain: as confused with mind, 184; as illu-
    sory "thinking" organ, 21; monotreme,
    131*f.;* as organic transplant, 145; as self-
    enclosing in thought, 229, 251; split, 49
Brown, Joseph Epes, 140
Bruckner, Anton, 118, 155
Bush Mekeo people, 52

cakra, xv; of happening, 233, 238, 246,
    248, 251; musical, 159, 167, 169; music as,
    197; sublation of, 199, 214; and wheel,
    194*f.*

Compositor:	G&S Typesetters, Inc.
Text:	10/13 Galliard
Display:	Galliard
Printer & Binder:	Thomson-Shore, Inc.